THE VINEYARDS OF BRITAIN

CELLAR DOOR ADVENTURES WITH THE BEST OF BRITAIN'S WINES

ED DALLIMORE

T0272496

FAIRLIGHT BOOKS

COPYRIGHT

First published by Fairlight Books 2022

Fairlight Books
Summertown Pavilion, 18–24 Middle Way, Oxford, OX2 7LG

A CIP catalogue record for this book is available from the British Library

1 2 3 4 5 6 7 8 9 10

ISBN 978-1-914148-11-8

www.fairlightbooks.com

Printed and bound in Great Britain

Designed by Fairlight Books

FSC

CONTENTS

Walk this way, my friends… Carlton Towers Walled Garden Vineyard in East Yorks

INTRODUCTION

Oh, here's to other meetings,
And merry greetings then;
And here's to those we've drunk with
But never can again.
—Stephen Decatur

I genuinely remember my first beer, but not my first wine. That's because the latter has always been around: at the dinner table; in the bottle-shaped brick holes beneath the stairs; at Sunday lunch with family and friends. Wine is always with us, at birthdays or weddings, celebrating new jobs or achievements, commiserating losses, or as a toast to absent friends. Or because it's a Friday… or a Tuesday.

I was first properly aware of wine on a broader level when I was about ten. Dad worked in brewing and Mum loved – and still loves – drinking wine, so it's very much in my blood. One day Mum and I went off to a well-known national warehouse-merchant and loaded up the boot. One bottle was smashed on return, and not in a good way. Mum has been a social worker for over fifty years and counting, so I like to think she has a pretty good grip on perspective, but as the tears emerged in her eyes it slowly dawned on me that wine must be really special. Turns out I was right.

Wine is at least 8000 years old, and it connects almost every society in history. Best of all, not only has every single version of it been made with enjoyment in mind, you and I might have completely different opinions on the same wine – and, in terms of how it tastes to us, we're both right.

I've spent pretty much all my career thinking, talking or writing about wine, and if I'm not doing that, I'm drinking and sharing it. In London, December 2010, I was so amazed by a seven-year-old Hunter Valley Semillon I moved to Australia and worked for the winery that made it. This ultimate desire to discover at source the vineyards, history and people behind the wine has only ever increased. It's the same passion that brought me back home to England at the end of 2020.

Never before have I been as excited about wine as I am now; for what the future holds for our industry here. For so many years those of us who've worked in the industry have poured thousands of professional hours into championing the amazing wines that belong to other countries. Now, given the strength in depth and versatility of what Britain's vineyards, grape-growers and winemakers are producing, some of our wines are competing with the best of all, and celebrating them just feels so good.

With over 800 vineyards now planted in Britain, total production in 2018 exceeded fifteen million bottles.[i] Thanks to these incredible sites, an industry of hugely talented people and a sharp focus on premium quality, Britain is now one of the world's most exciting modern wine regions.

From grapes grown in British vineyards consisting of just a few vines, to those that stretch over a few hundred acres, these grapes are made into wine in probably the most eclectic range of wineries in the entire world: from the stables of a seventeenth-century country house, to the basement of a former windmill in Cambridge, or beneath railway arches in Bethnal Green.

At the start of April 2021 I hit the road to discover as many of the most interesting producers of wine in Britain as I could. This is their story; the story of the wines they make, the places they grow the grapes and the reasons behind it all. I hope I make a good travelling partner, and that at least a few of the tales inspire you to taste the wines for yourself. It's so very much worth it.

A vineyard tour worth being on at Woodchurch in Kent

A HISTORY OF WINE IN BRITAIN

In all likelihood, the Romans planted Britain's first vineyards. Since then, wine has survived shipwrecks, thwarted the Third Reich and overcome louse-inflicted devastation of the world's vineyards. But our attraction to wine as humans is likely to date back a little further...

Among the vineyards of Groot Constantia in Cape Town, drunk baboons have been known to storm the vineyards and gorge on Sauvignon Blanc grapes. Attracted by the ripening fruit, and aware that by crushing them sets in motion a process which seemingly makes them tastier,

the baboons would fall asleep in the vineyards following a session of partially fermented fruit.

Robert Dudley's 'drunken monkey' hypothesis dates back about ten million years, and suggests that the origin of human attraction to alcohol stems from our primate ancestors, and that it might even play a role in evolution.[ii] With the ability to detoxify what is ultimately as a poison, humans can consume alcohol in fruit for use as an energy source. At the same time as when our ancestors were gorillas, chimps and bonobos, the enzyme our bodies used to detoxify alcohol underwent a single

Pinot Noir and Chardonnay at Artelium in East Sussex

mutation that left it forty times more efficient. Tempted down from the treetops by the sweet scent of alcohol emanating from fermented fruit on the forest floor, the primate's ability to smell out and metabolise the alcohol aided their evolution to life on the ground. As a result, Dudley's theory says that we as humans are addicted to the scent of alcohol because we're genetically coded to be so.

Shards of clay jars unearthed in modern-day Georgia, Europe, and carbon-dated to around 6000BC, are believed to be the oldest-known evidence of wine actively made from grapes. Excellent examples of these 'Qvevri' vessels were discovered in Pompeii, following the settlement's hasty abandonment in 79AD. Later spelt with a 'Q', reflecting their shape, modern-day Georgian winemaking has led to an increasingly popular revival of their use in – quite literally – underground winemaking. At Tillingham winery near Rye there are fourteen modern Qvevri in use today, buried underneath a traditional Kentish oast house.

Together with worshipping their god of wine, Bacchus, the Romans planted many vineyards across Europe and dug the original chalk cellars underneath Champagne, the foundations for what would become the world's most famous wine region.

In 278AD, third-century Emperor Probus gave the Britons, Gauls and Spaniards permission to cultivate vineyards and produce wine. It's thought there were third-century vineyards up to 11 hectares in size in modern-day Northamptonshire, and others in Cambridgeshire and Buckinghamshire.[iii] The majority of the Romans' considerable consumption, however, was in wine they transported from the warmer climes of France and Italy.

According to the Domesday Book, completed in 1086, there were forty-two vineyards planted in Britain at the time, quoting Gloucestershire as the most heavily planted county. The following 900 years didn't exactly reflect a huge increase in planting or production. Given that the latter half of this period is known as the 'Little Ice Age', this is not altogether surprising. But in 1875, at the renovated Castell Coch just north of Cardiff, Gamay and Millie Blanche vines were planted by Andrew Pettigrew, at the direction of the Third Marques of Bute. Eventually, up to 10 acres were planted, resulting in a production of 12,000 bottles from the bumper crop of 1893. The site lasted forty-five vintages before being pulled out in the 1920s.

Pre-1700s, anything other than still wine produced in Champagne was considered faulty. The English physician Christopher Merrett became the first to write of Champagne as a sparkling wine, and the fact its process was similar to that of cider production in his home county of Gloucestershire. It's likely the wine's fermenting yeast became dormant in the cooler months following harvest, but when bottled on arrival in England, fermentation between yeast and residual sugar restarted when the temperature increased in spring. Crucially, these bottles were produced with coal-fired glass – much stronger than their French wood-fired equivalent – and were able to withhold the resulting CO_2's pressure, capturing the fizz. Merrett noted the wine's popularity among the courts of London and, to hit demand, merchants realised that adding 'all kinds of sugar and molasses' to most wine would have the same effect. He presented his paper about the 'wine that drinks brisk and sparkling' to the Royal Society in 1662. Six years later, the so-called 'inventor' of Champagne, Dom Pérignon, arrived in that region for the first time.

Napoleon III's wine-ranking system, the Bordeaux Classification of 1855, is a market metric still influential today. The supply of Bordelais wine to Britain was by then so great, it was known by the Olde English term, Claret, probably due to colour but also possibly linked to the white grape 'Clairette', grown in Bordeaux at the time.

In the twentieth century wine regions were ravaged through two world wars, and British vineyards of the day were uprooted in favour of produce which was more befitting to the war effort. Economic depression during the 1930s also didn't improve the chances of early twentieth-century wine production in Britain, with not one single commercial bottle of wine being released between the two world wars – but the biggest destructor of vineyards in history is a tiny North American louse called phylloxera.

Discovered in Kew Gardens in 1827, having first crossed the Atlantic in steamboats that enabled the crossing to be quick enough for it to survive the journey, the louse would go on to decimate vineyards throughout Europe and across the world throughout the nineteenth and twentieth centuries. With such an economical, as well as viticultural, threat at hand, the French government offered a huge 320,000 francs incentive to anyone who could find a cure. With the louse piercing a hole in the vines' roots in order to lay its eggs, the answer came in grafting resistant indigenous American root stock onto a superior fruit-producing European vine. Leo Laliman and Gaston Bazille are credited with this innovation, and it is still implemented throughout modern vineyards today. However, deeming it a prevention rather than a cure, the French government refused to pay them the reward.

Tucked away in Devon, Swanaford Estate vineyard

Old basket press at Eglantine Vineyard in Nottinghamshire

Pathfinders, pioneers and the shift to professionalism

Despite the post-Second World War boom, total production in 1964 in Britain was recorded at just 1500 bottles.[iv] Quite a jump, then, over the following half-century, for it to be producing more than fifteen million bottles in 2018. Much of the early resurgence is due to the pioneering work of the wonderfully named Ray Barrington Brock. In 1946, at his own expense, he established the Oxted Institute for scientific research into grape varieties, planting over 600 varieties over the following twenty-five years in the process. He also built a winery, in which he experimented with different winemaking methods and yeast cultures. Many of the early plantings around Britain were of vines that came from his nursery.

Through the twentieth century the vast majority of the British industry was an amateur pastime of hobbyists and enthusiasts. So, with some notable exceptions, the results weren't great.

During that time joyfully ripening, disease-resistant grape varietals from Germany were often favoured with a view that some crop was better than no crop. It's not that we couldn't have ripened seemingly more desirable grapes in the sixties and seventies. We didn't, because for the most part, they weren't planted. Those that were, struggled, due to a lack of warmth, proper tending or inadequate site selection. The warming climate makes it more likely that we're able to ripen these and other varietals more regularly, but the biggest reason we're now producing world-class wines is overwhelmingly due to a huge shift in professionalism: investment in technology; equipment; infrastructure and highly skilled people. The beginnings of this modern era were inspired by a series of trailblazers – like Brock – who saw an opportunity few others believed in, and steadfastly followed their incredible foresight.

In Britain, it could be argued that the modern wine era began in 1952 at Hambledon Vineyard in Hampshire, planted by the person with perhaps the most quintessentially British name of all time: Major-General Sir Arthur Guy Salisbury-Jones. 'Sir Guy' fought in both world wars and was later posted to the British Embassy in Paris, as military attaché. Back home at Hambledon in 1952 he sought advice from France, visited Burgundy and specifically chose varietals – mainly Seyval Blanc – and vine-rootstock according to the chalk soil and its similarity to that of Champagne. He would later go on to plant Chardonnay, Pinot Noir and Pinot Meunier – 'traditional method' Champagne's three most prevalent grapes – work with Embassy favourite, Champagne House Pol Roger, and even export his wine to the US.

Americans Sandy and Stuart Moss were of the opinion that with the same grapes, techniques and high-end equipment, quality sparkling wine to rival Champagne could be produced here. They were right. Their first sparkling wine at Nyetimber, in West Sussex, made from the Chardonnay grape in 1992 and released in 1996, won the Trophy for Best English Wine in 1997. With their second wine, made from all three of the aforementioned grapes, they cleaned up on the world stage, bringing home to West Sussex the Trophy for Best Sparkling Wine in the World at the International Wine and Spirit Competition in 1998. They are generally regarded as the first to plant those three grapes exclusively for what WineGB call 'classic-method' sparkling wine. But five years before Nyetimber's vines were in the ground, Piers Greenwood, with fruit from his New Hall vineyard in Essex, produced Britain's first bottle-fermented sparkling wine from Pinot

Noir and Chardonnay in 1983. The Greenwood's vineyard was planted – as a commercial enterprise – in 1969 by his parents, who by 1976 had the winery capacity to crop 30 tonnes of grapes. Their first vintage, however, 1971, was made by Shelia Greenwood in the kitchen sink.

The same year that the Greenwoods planted, Joyce Barnes heard a Radio 4 programme about vine growing and was inspired to plant Kent's first modern-day vineyard at Biddenden with her husband Richard. Today, both New Hall and Biddenden are thriving, and are still owned and operated by the same respective families.

In 2004 Champagne House Duval Leroy was in talks to buy land in Kent – probably motivated by record temperatures of the 2003 summer in France and the slow dawn of realisation that increasing warmth was becoming a greater challenge in Champagne. These plans didn't materialise, but a decade later both Champagne Taittinger and Pommery planted in southern England, adding huge gravitas to an increasingly popular place to establish vineyards.

Along with Nyetimber, Sussex-based winemakers Ridgeview and Chapel Down have championed premium sparkling wine production since the late nineties. Both buy in the majority of their grapes from contracted growers – just as the major Champagne labels do – sourcing fruit with contrasting characteristics and providing a greater choice in the poorer years, while allowing them to focus on the making and the marketing.

At a location originally called Spots Farm, Stephen Skelton planted the first vines at what would become Chapel Down in 1977, making the wine there, too. Approaching fifty years in the industry, he continues to advise growers as a vineyard consultant and his is probably the one name that has come up more than any other during my tours of the vineyards of Britain. Planting the right grapes in the right sites and working the vines to maximise ripening potential, as well as proper analysis and understanding, is a reflection of where we are today, and much of it is thanks to the learnings of those who went before.

In a country that is hugely passionate about wine, full of incredible topography and geology, with increasing ripening potential and a history of fantastic fruit growers of multicultural heritage, it is no huge surprise that we're now making wine to rival the very best in the world. From those early successes on the international stage that Nyetimber enjoyed, to world-class awards from the most respected competitions that continue to come our way. Exports grow every year, and between 2020 and 2021, an estimated three million vines were planted. The majority of these were of the three major sparkling wine varietals – Chardonnay, Pinot Noir and Pinot Meunier, in the most popular place to plant: the South East. But pockets of great sites and exciting varieties exist throughout England and Wales, and the professionalism and talent of those planting, harvesting and producing are contributing to a hugely varied industry of both still and sparkling wine that is going from strength to strength, increasingly supported by incredible infrastructure. As it does so, it garners more column inches, more conversation, bigger networks and greater sharing of experience, which all leads to better wine, more awards and more vines in the ground.

In 2020, 50% of wine sales in Britain was direct from our wine producers' cellar doors. This represents an incredible connection between maker and drinker in an industry that is otherwise dominated by supermarkets and volume production. People bring these great sites and their great wines to life, and now we have the opportunity to see where the magic happens first-hand, and take those stories with us, and share them with others.

Ferment in progress at Danbury Ridge in Essex

Roebuck Estates Blanc de Noirs in magnum

Sunrise over Velfrey Vineyard in Pembrokeshire

Britain's site, soils and sub-regions

The single biggest factor in successfully ripening grapes for wine production is that big burning ball of inferno in the sky. Without exposure to enough growing-season hours of sun, grapes won't ripen, and there's not much you can do about it. Different grapes ripen at different times, in different sites, requiring varying degrees of warmth to do so. How vine roots react to the soil they're planted in is of vital importance to the fruit it produces, therefore something that you can affect is where you plant your vines and the varieties you choose. Fortunately, we're blessed with amazingly unique sites, soils and sun traps in Britain, all of which contribute to some incredible fruit in their own unique ways.

There's much made of the chalk soil underneath parts of Champagne, the same band of which stretches underneath the channel, rising up to form the white cliffs of Dover and carrying on underneath the South Downs and into wider parts of the South of England. Part of the story not often told is that it's most prominent in Hampshire – accounting for more than two thirds of the major soil type across the county's land area. Certainly not confined to the South East, it also sits beneath the Yorkshire Wolds, Dorset and the Chiltern Hills; 'Chilt', being the Saxon word for chalk.

Holding moisture but allowing the excess to drain, retaining acidity and allowing root exploration makes chalk a great soil for growing grapes for wine, especially sparkling varieties. Chalk-based Chardonnay has the potential to produce a stunning salinity and freshness, but it offers so much more – and is usually one part of a final blend – from vines planted in different soil types in the same vineyard or across multiple sites. When this chalk was a seabed millions of years ago, flint formed in the burrows of ocean-floor dwelling organisms. Used as tools and weapons by Neanderthals, flint presence in chalk now helps the ripening process by storing and radiating heat back up into the vine. Sandy soils – of which there's also a lot of in Britain, in the South East particularly – also provide heat retention and drainage.

With ample water vines will happily put all their efforts into growing – rather than producing fruit. Clay – and its vast water retention propensity – has usually been seen as inferior for vine growing, often with an accompanying cliché that 'vines don't like having cold wet feet'. This much is true, but the ripest fruit in all of Britain is coming from Essex's Crouch Valley – which is full of clay. As is the Rother Valley in East Sussex – where great ripening for both still and sparkling is achieved. This is probably due to how dry these eastern parts of the country are, and as clay dries, shrinks and cracks, those vines' roots surge through. Crucially, those clay soils rich in smectite can swell, too, effectively restricting further water penetration and holding moisture above and away from the vines' roots. Both Crouch and Rother valleys benefit from higher-than-average warmth and the latter, especially, from lots of woodland that offers natural windbreaks.

As well as benefitting drainage and sun exposure our many, well-protected, south-facing slopes help generate airflow; cooling vines to promote slow ripening, creating delicate flavours and also pushing off potentially devastating frost pockets. Most of the cold and wet comes into Britain from south-westerlies so undulation helps protect little pockets of land from the adverse effects of these.

Vine-laden rolling hills at Three Choirs

The climate crisis: how the wine industry is changing

According to the National Academy of Sciences in the US, if the predicted temperature rise of 2 degrees Celsius this century takes place, more than half of the world's vine-growing regions will be rendered unviable, with Spain, Italy and Australia being the worst affected – the average harvest in the Barossa Valley now starts a month earlier than it did twenty years ago.[v]

In the northern hemisphere, this general increase in temperature pushes greater ripening potential further north. It makes planting a vineyard a more viable option commercially, enables us to ripen more 'fashionable' grape varieties more regularly and also provides greater potential for still wines – an ever-increasing bracket in Britain.

At the current rate, geologist Dr Richard Selley says it's likely that much of southern England will be too hot for wine grapes within the next sixty years.[vi] Chardonnay and Pinot Noir will be ripening north of the border in Stranraer. Stranraer!

Parts of England and Wales sit about one degree Celsius lower than the average equivalent temperature in Champagne and the Loire valley, but fifty years ago, the temperature there was more than one degree colder than it is now.

However, it's not quite as simple as this, because weather patterns in every direction are becoming more dramatic. 2021 had the coldest and wettest April and May on record, so bud burst – the onset of new season fruit – was delayed as a result. Which means growing needs to be extended at the other end of the season, bringing colder and potentially wet weather into play at the most crucial time. Heavy rainfall at flowering – usually around mid-June – can severely affect fruit potential too, as can most dramatic events just prior to, or during, harvest.

Generally, winters are becoming milder, which leads to earlier bud burst, but spring frosts get more severe, regular and later – as late as mid-May in 2020. Spring frost can destroy this new season fruit, and with it, wipe out an entire year's crop. Wales had twenty-eight consecutive spring frosts in 2021; though most will have missed bud burst during an unusually late season and there are frost preventions, most are extremely expensive, labour intensive and, incidentally, not particularly environmentally friendly.

Spring frosts are maybe not as wholly devastating as bush fires or earthquakes, but if there's no crop, there's no wine. Producing a crop of grapes is a once-a-year opportunity; at this marginal end of the climate, in these times especially, it's often on a knife-edge, and not always as romantic as it might first appear.

New Year snow among Woodchester Valley's vines

Tommy Grimshaw, head winemaker at Langham Estate in Dorset

An opportunity for Britain

Legislation dominates much of European winemaking, mainly due to fears of over-production and a resulting drop in overall quality. Tradition, too, makes change and experimentation much harder, as vineyards and wineries are usually passed down through – often paternal – generations. Flexibility and freedom outside of Europe has led to greater variation and contrasting styles, but chasing volume and dollars has led to some seriously damaged reputations. In Britain we sit somewhere between the two, which isn't the worst place to be. Furthermore, British winemakers can build a repertoire of worldwide experience, seeing how high-tech wineries in Napa, California operate, or what centuries of tradition are saying in France's Beaujolais region. Back home, they can marry the best of both as they see fit, honing their own style, and sharing it with an ever-growing network.

Despite gradual decline, we're still bringing in the best part of thirty million bottles of Champagne into Britain every year – the UK is its biggest export market. We're a nation that has loved this style of wine since before it was made intentionally, and now we're making wines as good as the best of them – that should be celebrated for what they are rather than in comparison to. Looking to what Champagne has done as a region and as a brand in its own right over the last couple of centuries, our approach can be inspired by some of these incredible wines – essentially made in the same way, but with our own fingerprint and reflective of our unique sites and seasons. We can also hit a pretty tasty and totally accepted price point. Accepted it should be, too, for the quality of sparkling wine we're producing, which generally represents sensational value.

Remi Krug once said if you order Cristal in a restaurant, you sit with the label facing outwards so everyone can see what you're drinking. If you order Krug, the label faces in, because it's only relevant that you know what's in your glass. This concept is even more suited to amazing Grower Champagnes like Larmandier-Bernier or André Jacquart – who grow their own grapes and produce in smaller quantities than the major labels whose products have, in part, become more about marketing than making. The majority of our sparkling producers are positioned along this Grower model of producing wines that are hugely expressive and rich in personality – and we're so much better for it. Small-scale, handmade wines must focus on premium quality because there's no viable model to do anything else. Their marketing is then taken care of by how good the wines are, rather than owning the rights to a specific label colour or by buying your way onto wine lists.

But Champagne needs its big labels as we need our big brands – marketing investment in whatever wine or producer it may be benefits the entire category – and the more people drinking wine from Britain the better.

Generally, you need more sun hours and greater ripeness for still wines than you do for sparkling, so on the back of the stand-out 2018 vintage, many producers diversified in this direction, and in general we're producing more still wine as a result. We drink more of it than sparkling, and it adds variation, so producers become more accessible and attractive.

Producing wine in Britain is of course not without its challenges. The biggest barrier – in mindset at least (especially in terms of still wine)

– is cost. Which is at times odd, given most still wines are cheaper than most sparkling, for the same amount of liquid. The average cost of every wine sold in the UK is just over £6, thanks to the huge volume of large-scale production imports – and the emissions to go with them.

Wine made in Britain is more expensive, for three main reasons: scale, climate and quality. But of your six-and-a-bit pounds of Pinot Grigio – almost half of this is tax. Which, plus the actual bottle itself, the label, closure, marketing, logistics and profit, doesn't leave a whole lot for the actual juice inside. Duty stays the same – for domestic producers as well as foreign – whatever the cost of the wine, so you're proportionally better off as the price of wine increases, as there's greater investment in the actual wine as it does so.

This marginal climate of ours also in part dictates style – ideal for sparkling bases and many still whites. There are at least two examples of Merlot planted in Britain – but don't expect to see any rich, voluptuous reds from these, Cabernet Sauvignon or Malbec

Vintage 2021 in full swing at Sandridge Barton

anytime soon. These varieties need lots of sun and warmth to ripen – the kind that Bordeaux or Mendoza might be experiencing almost too much of. Ironically, we've probably the best climate in the world to make light, chilled reds – a great and hugely underrated category – but possibly not the best climate to drink them in!

Our cellar door culture, where you can visit, taste and buy wine directly from the vineyard or winery, is thriving, and has so much potential to increase further. Aside from meeting the people who make the wines and enjoying them at source, days out eating and drinking are just such good fun – and if you're not a fan – I can only imagine you've been given this book by someone who doesn't like you that much.

Britain is a place with a centuries-old market for wine. It has approximately thirty-three million wine drinkers and a huge network of vastly talented sellers, sommeliers and marketeers, running amazing restaurants, bars and pubs. We've collectively spent so long championing the wines of others, with no major domestic industry to shout about, but times have changed.

Good times

MY PHILOSOPHY

It's a tough call to name my absolute favourite thing about wine. The sheer magnitude of variation, from regions and people all over the world, is almost beyond comprehension. Wine is a living blend of art and science, a challenge of merging the two in expression of both people and place.

Wine can be a continuous journey of discovery built on subjectivity and personal preference – individual opinion is so important, no matter who you are or what your level of interest or experience is. Wine is synonymous with fun, celebration, relaxation and good times, and along with those things, one of my favourite things about it is that you need absolutely zero prior knowledge to be able to enjoy it.

Partially due to the huge number of ever-changing options, sometimes there's a perception of snobbery derived from the fact that wine has been a symbol of sophistication and class since Roman times – and there really doesn't have to be… though sometimes we don't make it easy for ourselves. I've read tasting notes about wines that verge on the ridiculous, albeit amusingly, and have no idea what relevance they have or what they mean to people who are either new to wine or confused by it. I think those of us in the industry should talk about wine with words that actually mean something, in a way that makes it accessible to everyone.

Wine can be superbly technical. It's made following very simple principles but involves huge complexities in its process, and a thorough understanding of winemaking from incredibly talented people. There's a need for descriptives – if the wine isn't in a glass in front of you, or if we're exhaustively assessing its potential professionally. There's science behind why wines taste as they do, too – as a result of the soils in which they were grown, the season they did, the way they're made and the vessels used to make them. Certain grape varieties are related to particular fruits, and often taste similar. What's most important is what wine means to you. Whether it tastes of tinned pineapple syrup or dried unicorn's tears is to a certain extent important, but it's still subjective, and ultimately, wine is all about the enjoyment of the person drinking it.

The aim of this book is to provide an accessible and comprehensive overview of what's going on across this land of great wine, but I'm just pointing you in the direction of what I think is worth tasting. The rest is up to you. While scores out of 100 and awards can be useful as a yardstick, they're not really my thing. Trophies at the best shows are certainly to be respected, but personal preference is paramount.

Nothing can be as relevant, therefore, as tasting it and making up your own mind. Taste as much as possible, never generalising about producers, regions and especially grape varieties – saying you don't like Chardonnay is a bit like saying you don't like sandwiches. Or only listening to Ed Sheeran and deciding you don't like music. If you think you don't like it, keep tasting, because chances are you just haven't had a good version of it… yet. By picking up a few useful nuggets of information along the way – most importantly about what you like or why you do – can only lead to greater enjoyment and the ultimate realisation that if desired, you can never stop learning about wine, and never stop enjoying it.

The things that make the most difference are usually the simplest, too. Some decent glassware – not necessarily expensive – and giving wine some airtime where required, makes a huge difference, and is best learnt through doing. Though you might look a bit of a plonker taking your own glasses to your favourite BYO restaurant, it's definitely worth doing if you've got some good booze on you. In a land so suited to producing such high-quality sparkling wine, the best thing you can do is take the 'Champagne flutes' to the charity shop. A flute might keep a few extra bubbles a few minutes longer – but restricts air getting in, and in turn such a great variety of flavours coming out – so you'll have a much better time in a more open, 'white wine'-shaped glass for quality sparkling wine.

In general, I think we've developed such a disconnect with local produce and, like meat consumption, it's generally better for everyone if we do it less often, to a higher standard, rather than all the time with average products. There is, however, an increasing demand for produce of provenance, from local sources who are actively working to reduce environmental impact. This approach is perfectly aligned with our wine producers, and supporting them supports this philosophy.

The majority of wine consumed in Britain is shipped in from thousands of miles under blankets of preservatives, having been produced in large volumes to hit economies of scale. Supporting local production creates fewer food miles, and on a smaller scale, more premium production requires much fewer synthetic chemicals. Given our unique sites, too, and hugely talented people, organic production is widely implemented to produce best-quality fruit. Our climate is far too marginal to be mass producing so we must focus on quality, which is where the opportunity lies.

The single best place to learn about wine is at source, with the people who grow the vines and make the wine. Doing so puts so much back into rural communities, champions a small-scale, premium industry and best of all – owing to the quality and variety – means you'll have a much

better time drinking your way through what you come away with. With a lack of an available European workforce, the 2021 harvest was almost exclusively carried out by local communities. It's amazing to see people come together among the vines, or travel out of cities to contribute to harvest; it's a nostalgic throwback to farming of old. We're an essentially young industry, full of people who have either come to wine as a second career or are experimenting and embarking on a career producing wine that will be passed down through the generations. As a result, this is an industry full of humility, and essentially people like you or I, who just love drinking wine, and want to invite you in and get rid of an, at times, perceived barrier to the subject. The best way to do so is through tasting and making your own mind up, and our cellar doors are full of people who will happily pour these samples for you. There's no required knowledge or status here, it's turn up and drink, and see what you think! By doing so you're supporting generally small-scale producers who are genuinely passionate about looking after the land on which they grow; people who toil year-round to get one shot at a season's crop, and making wine reflective of it.

Cellar door is also a great place to share wine with like-minded people. At Gusbourne in Kent, I met Ellie and Adam. Ellie's dad backpacked around Europe in the eighties, stopping in Bordeaux to do some grape-picking at Château Margaux. Despite a lack of water – instead being hydrated with red wine from a barrel on a cart – he was able to take a few bottles home with him. Thirty-five years later the family were having fish and chips in the garden and Ellie's mum went in to get 'another bottle of red'. They thought it tasted pretty good – and it turned out to be his last bottle of 1980s Margaux. Though it was consumed entirely by chance, his view was that this was exactly where it should have been drunk and is the most important place for the best wine – whatever that means to you – shared with special people in your life. Maybe not the single best match for fish and chips, but the epitome of a great approach to wine, so here's to you, and everyone like you, Ellie's dad.

At this marginal end of the climate, making wine is ever more challenging and becoming increasingly so. As much as I loved that first beer and have enjoyed every one consumed since, this is not the same – you can't just churn out another batch in two weeks' time – you get one crack a year and how that season unfolds is largely out of your hands. So, to the winemakers, grape-growers, pickers, processors, cellar door staff, drivers, chefs, tasting and tour hosts and everyone in between, who, like all farmers, toil all year round: you have my eternal gratitude, respect and thanks.

Meunier in the press during the vintage of 2021

The Thames Valley And Chilterns

FAIRMILE HENLEY-ON-THAMES

Harrow & Hope
@HARROWHOPE

Marlow Winery, Pump Lane North, Marlow, SL7 3RD
https://harrowandhope.com

What: Tastings, cellar door sales and tours
Recommended wines: The lot

'It's reight gud', says the sign above the bar in the tasting room at Harrow & Hope. A bit of Yorkshire in Marlow, at the purveyors of what is possibly England's most sleek range of sparkling wines. Crafted by Henry Laithwaite, they are inspired by the Grower Champagnes and made with skills honed in Australia and Bordeaux, imbued with probably the truest sense of a life in wine that you could come across.

Son of Barbara and Tony Laithwaite, Henry was in the Grand Cru vineyards of France before he was out of nappies, accompanying his parents on their buying trips sourcing wines for what is probably Britain's most successful wine merchant, Laithwaites. Following that he has harvested in the Ardèche in France and made wine in McLaren Vale, South Australia. Under the family merchants' Bordeaux label, Château Verniotte, his career in site-expressive reds continued, as did his passion for the work in the vineyard, often arriving in Bordeaux a few weeks before harvest and feeling as though he was missing out on a huge part of the process.

The competition between the Grand Marque – or major label – Champagne houses and the resulting challenge of wine marketing rather than winemaking, combined

Henry Laithwaite hard at work on the bottling line

Tanks, barrels and bottles of superb sparkling

Henry inside the winery at Harrow & Hope

with their sourcing of fruit from a multitude of different sites to hit volume, didn't exactly culminate in attracting Henry to sparkling wine. That was until he was inspired by the lesser-known Grower Champagnes. This smaller scale and fewer sites approach aligned perfectly with his desire to make wines that are ultimately a reflection of place.

Moving back home with a young family in mind, the hunt was on for the perfect site to do so. His partner Kaye's hometown of Sheffield was always likely to be second to the unique, rolling hills of flint and chalk in the Thames Valley Chilterns. The retreating Thames, which flowed through this site half a million years ago, left a steep-sloped topsoil of flint and gravel in orange clay over chalk. As a lover of the ocean who grew up not far from here, I can tell you it's about as far away from the sea as you can get in Britain. But this brings warmer summer days and cooler nights, providing great ripening potential while, crucially for quality sparkling wine, maintaining acidity.

In 2010 about 80% of the vineyard was planted to Pinot Noir and Chardonnay with the balance of what is now 6.5 hectares planted to Meunier. The old tractor shed was turned into a tasting room, with the impressive winery just a few yards away. As much as I like old tractors, it's great that the shed now has a bar, because a visit to Harrow & Hope without a tasting is like going to an Ottolenghi restaurant and just looking at the kitchen.

I'm not sure there's a more precise range in all of Britain than here; it's a struggle to think of a more concise portfolio in any of my wine travels or tastings of an individual producer, anywhere, ever. There are four stunning wines, all sparkling. The non-vintage, a blend of the three grapes according to the planting percentages, a single vintage, 100% Chardonnay

Blanc de Blancs, an ethereal Blanc de Noirs also from one harvest, and a vintage rosé.

It is incredible to see the depth and structure throughout the range, especially from relatively young vines. Signature characteristics are aided by up to 20% barrel-ageing for the non-vintage, which accentuates its wonderful texture and weight in the wines' numbered series of releases. All elements across each wine are so brilliantly in sync with one another, from reserve wine addition, barrel maturation, to thirty-six months lees ageing – forty for the Blanc de Noirs – to dosage, acidity and best of all, supreme fruit. It's as much a credit to the curator as it is truly a reflection of this magical site – one that James McLean, the vineyard manager at Wiston Estate, rates as the country's best.

For me, the rosé embodies all that wine should. It's a rosé drinker's rosé, a sparkling fan's rosé, a wine lover's rosé – it's as much a wine for good times in the garden with your mates as it is for drinking in a Michelin-starred restaurant with your partner. It's easy-going and fruit-forward but full of complexity and interest. It's a wine for everyone, which is what wine should be.

Of the four, the Blanc de Noirs is the wine to lie down and watch develop, if you can. It's drinking well enough already to pick up back-to-back trophies for Britain's best at the WineGB Awards in 2020 and 2021.

Having rescued vineyard dog Alfonse from the streets of Bergerac, Henry, Kaye and family established Harrow & Hope in the belief that the flint-laden slopes above Marlow would one day yield a sparkling wine to rival the world's greatest. Well, that day is not only here, it has been realised several times, and as soon as there's another release that day will come all over again. It's better than reight gud.

WINDING WOOD
@WINDINGWOODVINEYARD

Orpenham Farm, Winding Wood, Hungerford, West Berkshire, RG17 9RJ
http://www.windingwoodvineyard.co.uk

What: Cellar door sales and tastings by appointment
Recommended wines: Classic Cuvée, Demi-Sec

Down the single-track lanes in between the hedgerows just outside Hungerford, you might stumble across the beautiful Orpenham Farm. This is quintessential English countryside, and on arrival it feels like you could be situated at some time during last hundred years, except for one major exception. Orpenham Farm is now the home of Winding Wood wines where a driveway dissects two premium plots of vines – as if transported directly from Burgundy: on the right, Pinot Noir; to the left, Chardonnay.

I've been lucky to meet many lovely people through my travels in the wine industry, and Christopher Cooke is right up there with the best of them. A former publisher who grazed sheep on this perfect patch of England, he decided in 2013 it might be more interesting to plant vines and make wine instead. A premonition I would strongly agree with.

Christopher's is only one of two vineyards in Britain to employ a wire heating system throughout, protecting new budding fruit from potentially crop-destroying frost. When the thermostat reaches a pre-set temperature, it automatically heats the air around the vines to a cosy 20 degrees. More economical to run and considerably more relaxing to operate than getting up to light

Christopher Cooke at Winding Wood

fires at 3am every cold April or May morning.

Though potentially more challenging, working with the ever-changing environment has inspired them to organic conversion, striving for both the best fruit possible and the healthiest use of the land. Daniel Ham makes the wines at his Offbeat winery in Wiltshire. Formerly of Langham Estate in Dorset and partly motivated by Daniel, Christopher will make a leap of faith in attempts to make Winding Wood a fully biodynamic vineyard. These are exciting times, and Christopher's passion and humility in putting his trust in Daniel and moving forward together is a really very tasty recipe for success.

The quality-first approach is equally evident in the vines and the resulting sleek range produced from their fruit. There are just two wines, both made with the same classic method, a slightly Chardonnay-dominant blend that sees three years' ageing in bottle on their yeast 'lees': Classic Cuvée and Demi-Sec – the latter meaning half dry, suggesting a dosage of between 33 and 50 grams of sugar per litre, according to Champagne production laws.

The Classic Cuvée is vintage-dependent, but generally bottled around 2 grams per litre, whereas the Demi might see up to 40. Both are great examples in variation and, though ultimately they are the same wine, one addition made to the latter results in a completely different taste. Demi-Secs are so underrated, and provide versatile food-matching potential – fantastic with fruit-tarts traditionally, or as entrée companions to butter-sauce scallops or burrata.

It's easy to imagine more vines in the adjacent sun-drenched slopes, so the further potential for rosés and Blanc de Noirs is proving quite tempting. But for now, with already 3000 vines over two plots, hand-tending is more manageable and the transition to bio-dynamics will be slightly more straightforward.

As average annual production goes, 3000 bottles

Working wine dog Ludo

is relatively minimal, but it's of premium quality – most of which is pre-sold before vintage release. Winding Wood are also offering a very limited membership scheme, providing exclusive access to dinners, events and tastings in the stunning vine-side eighteenth-century timber barn.

Robert's dogs Bolly and Tatty, named after favourite Champagne houses, are the forebears to current wine dog, working cocker Ludo, who seems as happy and content as Christopher. It's easy to see why, his naming perhaps broke with the tradition, but you can't name your dog after your own vineyard now, can you?

Daws Hill

@DAWSHILLVINEYARD

Town End Road, Radnage, High Wycombe, HP14 4DY
https://dawshillvineyard.co.uk

What: Vineyard and winery tours, events, cellar door sales
Recommended wines: Sparkling White, Sparkling Rosé

When you first meet someone and they're really quite hungover, I always think it's a pretty reassuring sign: they're one of us. Still, it was just after 3pm on a Tuesday when I met Holly. The Tuesday after the Monday that pubs reopened in England following months of lockdown in 2021.

'Were you booked in for the lunch or evening session?' I asked. 'Both,' was her reply. Brilliant.

Driving down the network of tracks that lead to Daws Hill Vineyard, I was particularly struck by the steep slopes on either side. I wonder how long it will be until all these south-facing chalk slopes are predominantly vine-heavy.

There is a stunning tree-lined, gradually increasing incline to the top of the vineyard, home to five rows of Pinot Noir followed by Pinot Noir Précoce. Chardonnay is planted in the adjoining paddock. Bollinger have a vineyard called La Côte aux Enfants – the Children's Hillside – that was considered too steep for the backs of fully grown adults to pick fruit on, so they employed kids instead. Youthful exuberance would come in very handy picking the fruit from the steepest part of the Daws Hill vineyard, but that slope is a great benefit, maximising sun exposure and greater

Rack full of great booze

Rosé sampling in the former stables-turned-winery

ripening potential. Air flows down slopes, cooling fruit during summer and reducing disease and the threat from spring frosts. Air frost still descended in 2020, however, costing Daws Hill 90% of that season's crop.

Returning home from Ibiza, Holly pretty much learnt winemaking from scratch, taking over the winery from her father in 2016. Henry, winemaker at Harrow & Hope, has helped out too – Holly's father helped Henry plant his now celebrated vineyard, so the support goes both ways. There's even some Cabernet Sauvignon and Merlot in the ground, though given this is Bucks rather than Bordeaux, they're yet to yield anything resembling ripe fruit.

Everything is done on-site, by hand, from picking the two-paddock plots' grapes to classic-method bottle-fermentation in the converted stable's winery. Riddling racks hold the ageing wines from previous vintages and disgorging, corking and labelling is all done here, too, just a metre or so from the tanks that, fortunately from a tasting point of view, come with a tap at the bottom.

There's a stunning synergy throughout the range, full of bright and precise fruit. The core range are a blend of Chardonnay and Pinot Noir, all aged for a minimum of four years before release, which is a year longer than is required for vintage Champagne. A tasty point of difference is in the sparkling Auxerrois, which at just 10% volume and with an uplift of residual sugar, is fresh and easy, and makes an awesome little breakfast wine. Or maybe a great option as a hungover palate refresher before today's pub booking. It is Tuesday, after all.

ALDER RIDGE VINEYARD
@ALDERRIDGE

Cobbs farm, Bath Road, Hungerford, West Berkshire, RG17 0SP
https://www.alderridge.co.uk

What: Cellar door sales, tasting, shop, café and tours
Recommended wines: Blanc de Noirs, Classic Cuvée, Special Cuvée

Tom and the team at Alder Ridge planted Pinot Noir and Chardonnay on this flint-topped band of chalk just outside Hungerford in 2011. It raised some eyebrows when fruit picked only two years later became their first release. I say 'only', because wine knowledge taught in the boardrooms of large merchants says you must wait at least three years from planting before any worthy crop can be produced. That very wine won best Blanc de Noirs at The Champagne and Sparkling Wine World Championships in 2017.

Moving to more regenerative methods in terms of land use was partly the motivation of dialling back the soft fruit side of the farm. With 8 acres currently under vine, on a 60-acre property that is pretty much the same soil mix throughout, there's huge potential for an increase in production, but volume is certainly not the goal.

Even at 120 metres above sea level, spring frost – as late as mid-May in 2020 – is a major threat to new season fruit and hastened the installation of a frost-prevention system. Water can be drawn off the on-site reservoir and sprayed over the vines when necessary, covering their buds with a protective film that stops that potentially crop-destroying frost from settling.

Quality fruit, of course, is only half the battle when it comes to producing brilliant wine. Made

Tom pouring the good stuff

by champion winemaker Emma Rice, it's in the winery at Hattingley where the premium philosophy is really exemplified. It's a minimum seven years' bottle ageing for the top two wines, and generally a low 2 or 3 grams per litre dosage, keeping the focus on pristine fruit. This extended lees-time softens natural acidity, adds roundness and amazing complexity through the interaction between wine, yeast and good old time. It is an incredibly long process, economically speaking, but the desire at Alder Ridge is for the wines to be released as the best possible showcase of fruit and the season in which it grew.

The portfolio of the three premium sparkling wines all drink amazingly young and fresh for their age. The Blanc de Noirs carries a richness you would expect, being 100% Pinot Noir – another good reason for that extended ageing.

Classic Cuvée is exactly that in make-up, ever so slightly dominant in Chardonnay over Pinot Noir. Marrying that crunchy rich Pinot with riper and creamy Chardonnay brings an additional super-long finish.

The latest addition to the range is the Special Cuvée, which adds Pinot Meunier and Pinot Noir Précoce to Pinot Noir and a balance of around 50% Chardonnay. Still six years on-lees for this entry-level non-vintage wine, it's the most accessible of the three, benefitting from a more fruit-forward style. As entry-level, drink-tonight options go, this is about as premium as it gets, which is in keeping with every other facet of Alder Ridge.

There's enough wine tucked away from a couple of later vintages that could be released now, but, as Tom says, it's getting better with time – so what's the rush?

The vineyard at Alder Ridge, with the new water-spraying frost-repellent system

All Angels

Church Farm, Enborne, Newbury, West Berkshire, RG20 0HD
https://www.allangels.com

What: Cellar door sales, tours and tastings, invitation lunches and dinners
Recommended wines: Sparkling Rosé, Classic Cuvée

More has happened in the vineyards of Britain over the last decade than the last 1000 years combined. This means, though, that we have a relatively young wine industry that is surrounded by centuries of fascinating history. Planted next to the twelfth-century parish church of St Michael and All Angels, Mark Darley's Enborne vineyard is about as fine an example of this contrast as I've seen. Dog Company, 101st American Airborne Division were stationed here prior to the D-Day landings, and this site was also home to a Roundhead encampment during the first battle of Newbury in 1643. On a clear day you can see five counties from Combe Gibbet, south-west of the vineyard – a spot chosen so that the fate of those hanging there would act as a very visible deterrent.

The gently sloping, south-facing sandy loam site is an excellent base for the 2010 plantings. The early ripening Rondo was a good choice at 220 metres above sea level, but such has been the temperature increase that early bud bursting of new season fruit leaves it ever more susceptible to spring frosts. It's blended with Pinot Gris to produce a vibrant sparkling rosé that's deep in colour, with the Gris bringing a lifted brightness of ripe fruit.

Classic Cuvée, Mark's go-to wine, is an appropriately traditional blend of Pinot Noir,

The 'Church Block' vineyard beside the twelfth-century parish church of St Michael and All Angels

Spring sunshine on the vines at Enborne Vineyard

Chardonnay and Meunier, with just a touch of Pinot Gris. Three years on lees accentuates the rich, creamy style, though not at all masking the elegant English garden fruit shining through. With a healthy chunk seeing extended lees ageing for late release, All Angels are premium producers only going in one – extremely tasty – direction.

Tucked away behind the main house and tasting room sits the very special 'Church Block'. Barely an acre in size and planted exclusively to Chardonnay, almost as an extension to the church grounds, the adjacent vineyard will provide All Angels's first Prestige Cuvée. From only the best vintages, and with a minimum 10 years' lees-ageing, this Blanc de Blancs might yield 500 bottles annually. We probably won't see the first edition until the early 2030s, but when I eventually taste it, I'll remember walking into that small vineyard for the first time

and being as excited about wine as any time prior.

Just when you think it's getting a bit serious, All Angels 340, referencing the number of bottles produced, adds some left-field variation. Mark says the Sparkling Rondo is a bit of fun, winemaker Emma Rice calls it alcoholic Ribena. Maybe not for everyone, but what wine is? Big, bright, blackcurrant fruit, it just sort of sits on the palate like a Bloody Mary – so much so it almost reminds me of hangovers and great nights out – and I think that's why I like it.

I can't imagine many other producers creating something like the 340, and similarly I can think of few other regions that could curate the kind of quality as the Classic Cuvée, or rosé, and where else can combine this kind of history? The future is as bright here as anywhere else, and as for the Church Block Blanc de Blancs, I'll see you in 2032 for the pre-release tasting.

Chafor Wine Estate
@CHAFORWINE

High Hedges Vineyard, Preston Bissett Road, Gawcott, Buckinghamshire, MK18 4HT
https://www.chafor.co.uk

What: Cellar door sales, tours, tastings and bar
Recommended wines: Elegance, Chardonnay, Classic Cuvée, Sparkling Rosé

In 2009, Tim Chafor followed a gut instinct that said there was a massive opportunity for making wine in this part of Buckinghamshire, and so left a family farm and IT background and set up a vineyard in Gawcott.

Chafor Estate sits on what you would call a mega-mix of soil type: Jurassic limestone, flint, pebble – part-marble, part-sand, with nuggets of chalk all bundled together on top of more chalk. In among all that there's a great mix of heat retention and free draining potential, yet there's moisture retained when required, and, as a result of this combination, there is an opportunity to create wines unique to this very place.

Tim is running four businesses here: grape growing, winemaking, sales and events – the vineyard bar caters for a couple hundred punters to come and enjoy drinking the vineyard's produce right next to the vines that grew it, as well as offering private tours and tastings.

With classic-method sparkling wine in mind, in the ground initially went Pinot Noir, Meunier and Chardonnay. Then 2018 came along and the fruit ripened so well that still versions of the first and last of these were possible.

Madeleine Angevine and Pinot Gris make up two further still white varietals, blended

Vine grower and winemaker Tim Chafor

together to the tune of about 80/20 under the self-explanatory 'Elegance' label. Chafor's signature in the still department is fundamentally their Bacchus, which is planted across two sites, both very much in the aromatic spectrum – the only real problem is in getting your hands on some.

Winemaking has been done on-site since 2015, allowing Tim ownership of process and the creative freedom to experiment with small batch releases. It's a smart portfolio as a result. About 50% of their riper vintage Chardonnay matures in oak, creating a slightly bigger, richer style compared to most. With the other half of the wine ageing in steel tanks, you still get the clean, crisp acidity, but it's married with mouth-filling ripeness and fatter Chardy good times.

The versatility of both the range and Tim as a winemaker shine through strongly in the sparkling instalments, both of which are made in the classic method, packed with the kind of complexity you would expect from wines produced this way. The rosé is pretty much an equal blend of Pinot Noir and Meunier that sees two years on lees and is developing into a great mix of soft red fruit and toasty richness. The white Vintage Cuvée has about 40% Chardonnay to its predominantly Pinot Noir make-up, and a further twelve months on lees. It's another classic, delicate with a touch of creaminess to go with the ripe apples and stone-fruit – a wine that is drinking so well at a relatively young and fresh age that it suggests plenty of ageing potential.

There's a lot to unpick in each of the wines here, and a visit to the vineyard's picnic tables would not be doing it justice if you didn't try the entire range. You might have to be quick to get there in time for the latest release of their Bacchus, but when you do, it's worth making sure someone else is driving.

Chafor Wine Estate, home of Buckinghamshire's best Bacchus

Fairmile, Henley-on-Thames

Fairmile, Henley-on-Thames, Oxfordshire, RG9 2LA
https://www.fairmilevineyard.co.uk

What: Tastings by appointment, cellar door sales on open days advertised on website
Recommended wines: Rosé, Classic Cuvée

More than a few vineyards in this book take a bit of finding, tucked away down winding country lanes, away from main thoroughfares and obvious waypoints. Fairmile is not one of them. On the long straight road of the same name leading into Henley-on-Thames, steep slopes climb away from the road on both sides. It's one of the few British vineyards that sits within a town boundary. All of a sudden on the south-facing slope, 12,000 vines rise above you, and if you can't see them, you probably shouldn't be driving.

After a long search for their perfect home and a suitable site to realise their vineyard dream, Anthea and Jan Mirkowski acquired Melbury House and the adjoining 14 acres that came with it. Theirs was the first purchase the property agents handled that was subject to a vine-positive soil analysis, and I'm pretty sure it won't be the last.

Aesthetics aside, this place was certainly worth waiting for. The flint-topped, chalk soil of the Chiltern foothills sits beneath the slope that climbs at such a gradient that the vines are exposed to almost a third more sunlight than those on the flat surface at the crucial flavour-developing end of the ripening season. Frost pockets tend to roll down these slopes and air movement along the Stonor valley helps keep humidity at bay, reducing the risk of disease and slowing the ripening process and desirable

Golden patch of vines at Fairmile Vineyard

Vine-laden slopes of the Stonor Valley

for the development of delicate, complex flavours.

As an enthusiast, Jan used to make wine in his airing cupboard. Establishing a slightly larger scale of operation in 2013, he employed a German vine-planting team with a GPS-guided kit hooked up to thirteen satellites, ensuring accuracy of planting to 15mm at the rate of 1000 vines an hour. From the outset it was all about premium sparkling wine and, at just 150 miles north of Champagne, no prizes for guessing this means the three grapes of choice are Chardonnay, Pinot Noir and Pinot Meunier. There are only two wines in the current range, the Classic Cuvée and the rosé, both classic method and aged on lees for a minimum of three years. The wines themselves are as succinct as the approach. Jan and Anthea are onto a seriously good thing here, and it's great to see them maximise quality rather than quantity.

There's no mistaking the Classic Cuvée for a classic-method drinkers-drink; three years' ageing on lees is enough to provide a hint of toasty texture, yet it manages to keeps the pristine fruit at the fore. The rosé too is traditionally pale in colour; fresh, summer fruit-forward and with just a touch of richness holding it all together well. Both drink vibrant, young and zingy but are not at all in the 'must cellar' bracket, though I'd love to revisit them a couple of years down the track. Speaking of which, there's an intriguing Blanc de Blancs currently seeing some extended lees ageing, which is tucked away down at Hambledon winery where the Fairmile range is made. This will be a limited, late-disgorge release. The purity of their Chardonnay will make it a must-try for all but their one complainant to date, who said he wasn't a fan of the wines because they were 'too tasty'.

If you too aren't a fan of premium, tasty sparkling wine, then I would steer clear of Fairmile, otherwise get down to Henley-on-Thames, get along to Fairmile, and get stuck into some of what Jan and Anthea have to offer.

Autumn stroll with the team at Fairmile

Autumn in South Oxfordshire

BRIGHTWELL VINEYARD
@BRIGHTWELL.VINEYARD

Rush Court, Shillingford Road, Wallingford, OX10 8LJ
https://www.brightwellvineyard.co.uk

Recommended wines: Oxford Gold, Sauvignon Blanc, Pinot Noir, Oxford 'Regatta' Dornfelder

Originally planted in 1987 just 8 miles south of Oxford, the vineyard at Brightwell had run into a state of disrepair by the time Bob and Carol Nielsen bought the adjoining property almost thirteen years later.

Bob wanted the house, but the former owner wanted rid of the vines. The vineyard was saved from the bulldozer in part due to Osama Bin Laden – not one normally referred to in viticultural circles. RAF pilot Bob was about to go and fly commercial airliners from Heathrow, but 9/11 changed all of that, and when civilian pilot jobs disappeared overnight, it seemed there was nothing to lose from one trial harvest.

The result was, in Bob's words, a mess. But a small amount of Dornfelder convinced him there was some potential from a vineyard that in another year, may have been thrown on the bonfire.

Growing up in Wellington, Bob remembers the New Zealand industry in the sixties and seventies was dominated by imports as the country was considered too cold to make wine domestically, which sounds somewhat familiar. At a seminar in 2001 he was told by an Australian winemaker not to 'bother even trying to make

Old vines at Brightwell Vineyard

red wine in England, because it's impossible'. Bob replied, 'That's because you're an Aussie, mate.' So, thanks also to a bit of cross-Tasman rivalry, the future of Brightwell was secured.

Sitting in the Thames valley, about as far away from the sea as you can possibly get in the UK, makes Brightwell one of the warmest and driest parts of the country. Glacial shifts deposited a mega-mix of gravel, chalk, clay, loam and sandy grassland across the site, but it's the additional sunlight that's valued highest.

With Bob clear from an economical and quality point of view that off-site winemaking was not a sustainable approach, in went the winery and on went the experiments. The hottest and best vintage to date at Brightwell, in 2003, helped kick-start things. And with multiple 2000-litre tanks the same juice can be fermented with different yeasts, rather than the same one-size-fits-all approach.

There are two different wines from the German by origin: high-yielding Huxelrebe grape variety 'Oxford Flint' is picked slightly early, when still pale and fresh, is light and crisp as a result. Weeks later and only in the warmer years comes 'Oxford Gold': a ripe, expressive and tropical fruit-driven wine that to taste blind you would barely even place in the same country, let alone the same row of vines. This was the result of part-experiment, part-accident, when a full winery left some Huxelrebe hanging on to the vines, so picking was pushed back. The resulting wine worked so well they kept making it.

Pinot Noir and Chardonnay were both planted with sparkling wine in mind, but with increasing competition and consistency on this front, Brightwell's Pinot Noir is now exclusively for still red production. Part barrel-aged for two years before release, it's the wine Bob is most proud of, his clearest expression of winemaking fingerprint. Well-rounded, rich and rustic, the wine's red fruit sits brilliantly with its earthy and smoky secondary development.

Despite not wanting to compete with what's becoming a large market of quality English sparkling, part of me thinks this really is Bob's way of having a bit of a laugh at those winemakers who, not even two decades ago, said English red wine couldn't be done. As that Aussie winemaker might say, 'Good on ya, mate.'

Brightwell Vineyard, 8 miles south of Oxford

STANLAKE PARK WINE ESTATE
@STANLAKEPARK

Waltham Road, Twyford, Berkshire, RG10 0BN
https://www.stanlakepark.com

What: Cellar door sales, shop, bar, tastings, tours and events
Recommended wines: Stanlake Brut, Madeleine, Kings Fumé, Rosé, Reserve, Pinot Noir

'Good wine, good life', says the sign a few yards ahead of the fifteenth-century, 120-acre Stanlake Park Wine Estate, just outside Twyford. Charles II apparently stayed here prior to the occasional meeting with his long-term mistress, Nell Gwyn, at local pub The Dog and Badger. Classic Charles.

The Grade II-listed stables now house the winery and barrel room, and if there's a more beautiful winery in all of Britain, I'm very much looking forward to seeing it. Jon Leighton originally saw the opportunity for vines in the estate grounds and today there are 10 acres planted. He began in 1979 with Britain's first Gewürztraminer vines, an incredible choice and the only example I'm aware of in Britain. By 1987 he and Australian Andrew Hood made their 'Siegerwürzertraminer', a blend of Siegerrebe, Würzer and Gewürtz with a name so catchy I'm amazed it hasn't caught on. They're gnarly old trunks, those Gewürtz vines these days, and so short in number that their produce is blended with Madeleine and Schönburger and bottled as Stanlake's 'Hinton Grove' white.

The walled garden in which the vines sit both protects and adds greater ripening degrees and is as impressive as the winery – it's like stepping into Renaissance France, and easy to forget you're a short distance from towns

Old Pinot Noir vines at Stanlake Park

The winery at Stanlake Park

made famous by local legend David Brent.

In 1988 another Aussie – John Worontschak, now at Denbies and Litmus – transformed the winemaking at what was then called Thames Valley Vineyards. His high-quality, professional approach was years ahead of its time, and his departure was a notable loss to the winemaking department. Today, winemaker Nico Centonze has again galvanised the operation, as has his partner Natalia Pezzone for the cellar door experience. Hailing from Southern Italy, Nico studied winemaking in Florence and Turin, has made wine in Argentina, the family estate in Puglia, and, following a 2013 spell with Nyetimber, returned to England with Natalia to take the roles at Stanlake.

From twenty-five varietals, they're down to just over ten, producing a contrasting range: three sparkling wines, five whites, a rosé and two reds – and 70,000 bottles a year, half of which are under contract for local growers. With all the kit to do everything on-site – even label inspiration is taken from the estate's gardens and wildflowers – and with a capacity of 200,000 bottles, there's scope to increase production on either front.

Pinot Noir is the Mariafeld clone: originally Swiss, producing healthy yields that provide bright, dark fruit and perfumed juice that's only bottled in the best years. Their Dornfelder is the best I've seen, with a few years' bottle age, which is a hallmark. It's showing lots of secondary, tertiary flavours, a proper fireside-with-cheese type of red.

Nico's philosophy is that wine is made to be drunk and enjoyed, one glass after the other. Stanlake hosts weddings and up to four tours a day, and also provides a wine bar and shop, with picnic tables and lawns lining historic buildings – a great place to test that philosophy.

Heritage Brut is a great option for Prosecco fans after something a bit more serious, though the best seller is the Pinot Noir 'Rosé Superior' sparkling. At two years on lees, it marries the 'strawberries and cream' style with that classic toasty richness, but all in easy-going balance.

Madeleine Angevine offers a slightly riper, fruit-

Gnarly old Gewürtz vines

driven option, but the wine I'll meet you in the Dog and Badger for is the full-bodied, butterscotch bad boy – labelled King's Fumé – which is an equal split of Chardonnay and Ortega, both possessing the great fruit weight needed to stand up to two years in French barriques. The rosé is light in colour and screams summer outdoor drinking, but with a personality that belies its short one to two hours skin contact time.

It's ever interesting that an Italian and Argentinian winemaking and hosting duo prefer Twyford to Torino, but wander a little deeper into the estate at Stanlake Park and it's pretty easy to see why. A long history and a great future. Good wine, good life.

Wyfold Vineyard

Oxfordshire
https://www.wyfoldvineyard.com

What: Not open to the public
Recommended wines: Brut Reserve, Rosé

Owning and working a vineyard is a dream for a lot of people. It was also a dream for Barbara Laithwaite, but after fifty years in the wine industry, it came with a caveat that the vineyard in question absolutely had to be focused solely on producing the very best wine possible.

The Laithwaites' family business began with a white van and a railway arch HQ, rented from British Rail for £20 a month, in 1967. Bringing back their favourite wines from France seemed a good idea to writer Hugh Johnson, with whom they established the Sunday Times Wine Club. It went pretty well, and the Laithwaites' mail-order business now includes a 1000-tonne capacity winery in the Barossa Valley, their own Bordeaux Château and a strong presence in the US, Australia and New Zealand, all together shifting the best part of five million cases of wine a year… if that counts as going pretty well.

Barbara is still driven to hand-tend her 9000 vines over 2 hectares of south Oxfordshire vineyard. In 2003 the perfect location was sought: a due south-facing slope of gravel on chalk. Owned by a friend who shared the vineyard dream, it was given the thumbs up by pioneer Mike Roberts at Ridgeview, who made the first vintages from Wyfold at his Sussex winery.

Twenty years ago, the industry was overwhelmingly enthusiastic, but almost exclusively amateur. Barbara joined the local vineyard association meetings as the only commercial grower and has seen a huge shift in professionalism.

There were only three varieties likely to be planted at Wyfold, and Barbara likens them all – Chardonnay, Pinot Noir and Pinot Meunier, in no particular order – to her three sons: winemaker Henry (Harrow & Hope), brewer Will (Loose Cannon – the brewery that is) and Tom, who is taking over as head of the Laithwaites business. Chardonnay has been strong from the outset: 'A good grower, a good child, doing what it's supposed to!' It represents 50% of the vineyard but always yields more than its share. Pinot Meunier took a while to get established but once it was it did very well, albeit with a tendency to be a bit all over the place, often misbehaving and doing what it likes. Often referred to as the talented yet temperamental child – developing much later than the others but capable of absolute brilliance – is Pinot Noir, planted to a third of the site.

Two parcels of Phylloxera-free vines remain planted on their original, un-grafted rootstock in Champagne: Chaudes Terres and Clos

St-Jacques in Aÿ, both planted to Pinot Noir, producing a wine under Bollinger's Vieilles Vignes Françaises label. The current release is about fifteen years old, and you could feasibly be drinking a bottle of it this weekend, but you'll be about £650 worse off. Again, thanks to Hugh Johnson, who got his hands on some and shared cuttings with Dermot Sugrue and Barbara for her Wyfold vineyard from which she could produce perhaps twelve bottles – or six magnums. I'm not sure they'll ever be a 'Vieilles Vignes Angleterre' however, as much as I'd like to see the reaction in France – and taste the wine of course.

Henry makes the wine at his Harrow & Hope winery, which is a nice thing to do for your mum, though Barbara expects nonstop gold medals from now on, of course. Having had the fortune to taste both wines, she's not the only one.

Wyfold Brut is serious melt-in-the-mouth elegance – forty-eight months on lees with additional time on cork ahead of release, the naturally rich acidity softens wonderfully, lingering oh so long. There's a flinty minerality to the wine that is drinking so young and vivacious despite its seven-plus years in bottle. The rosé equally so – just hinting at a gamey richness but not at all losing its premium red-fruit style.

'No tours, no weddings, just wine' is the approach at Wyfold, but it's also so much more than 'just' wine. Wine so good that, let alone choosing my favourite wine from this entire trip, I can't even decide on my favourite from this one family. The 2014s were labelled to celebrate the family's fifty years in the wine industry; I'm very much looking forward to tasting my way through the next fifty.

Barbara Laithwaite at Wyfold Vineyard

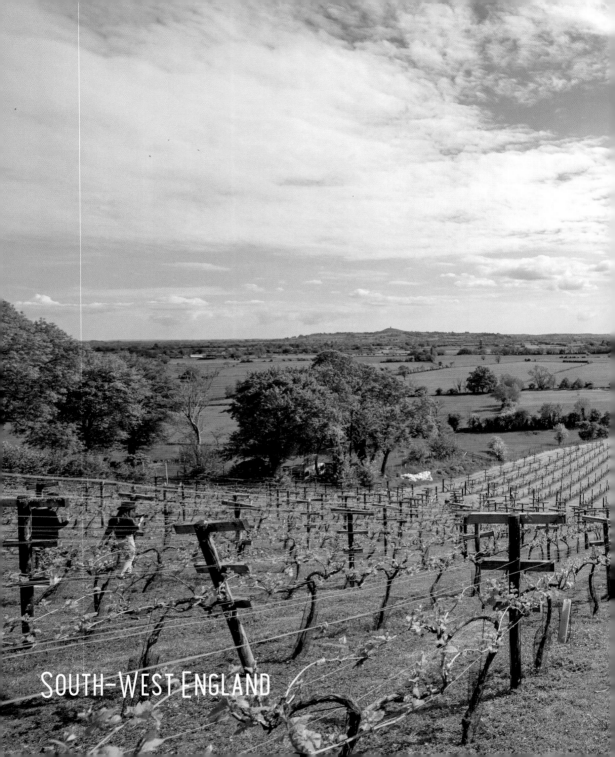

SOUTH-WEST ENGLAND

FENNY CASTLE VINEYARD

Wraxall Vineyard
@WRAXALLVINEYARD

Wraxall Road, Shepton Mallet, Somerset, BA4 6RQ
https://wraxallvineyard.co.uk

What: Vineyard, tasting room and cellar door stays scheduled for summer 2022
Recommended wines: Somerset Sparkling White, Somerset Sparkling Rosé

At the Barber family cheesery in the village of Ditcheat you'll find the biggest library of mother cultures of cheese in the world, and the oldest continuous production of cheddar. Not a bad place to be, and David and Lexa's Wraxall vineyard has a pretty tasty spot in itself. Sloping due south, you can see about as far across the Somerset Levels as your eyes will let you.

Originally planted in 1974, the 2-acre vineyard ran into disrepair until the current stewardship took over in 2019. Following careers running businesses in London, they realised soon after that they were now running a few more: as grape growers, winemakers, a sales and marketing outfit, plus a cellar door tasting room and wine tourism operation soon followed.

There isn't a single facet of the venture that hasn't been considered and meticulously planned for, from soil profiling to in-vineyard weather stations. This is no romanticised long-term retirement project, it's a change in style and size of professional occupation. Despite no reports of site frost damage to date, probably due to the frost rolling down the ongoing slope that continues beyond the last

Lexa and David, custodians of Wraxall Vineyard

As far as the eye can see across the Somerset Levels

row of vines, no chances will be taken here. So, if the weather station alarms dictate, rows of bougie (paraffin wax) candles will be lit in the early hours of cold April and May mornings.

The original Madeleine vines were replaced several years before David and Lexa arrived, as much as we all wished at least one old row had been left. Some old Pinot Noir vines needed replacing, too, but the core of the vineyard still has well-established vines, with Chardonnay still to be planted above and to the side of the current plot, alongside the extant Burgundian clone Pinot Noir, as well as Bacchus and Seyval Blanc.

The site has until now been managed according to what the 1990s said was the best way, which was simply not sustainable, from either a business or soil health point of view.

There's a huge amount of history here, not least in cheese and wine, but also in evidence that suggests the Romans were the original viticulturists of the local area. Huge profits are not the motivation, more so a desire to take heritage and build upon it to become well-known for producing great wines that are enjoyed by many, and leave the site in a much better place than how it was found.

These delights are combined with Frome's famous sausage rolls, artisan chocolates made in Bruton and Hembridge's award-winning chutneys and jams, and you can picnic from the top of a vineyard with local produce. The first wines under Lexa and David's custodianship were made in 2021, and by the time they're released, a glass-fronted tasting room that slices into the hillside should be open, too.

SMITH & EVANS

@SMITHANDEVANSSOMERSET

. . . .

Higher Plot Farm, Aller Road, Langport, TA10 0QL
https://www.smithandevans.co.uk

What: Vineyard tours and tastings, vineyard accommodation
Recommended wines: 'Higher Plot' Sparkling, 'Trilogy One' Multi-Vintage, 'Natural Ferment' White

Wine merchant Guy and film editor Laura (Smith & Evans, respectively) finally found the Higher Plot vineyard after an almost five-year search for their perfect location. At a time when good ol' west-country cider was seen as equal in quality to the finest wines, terraces were built into the hillside orchard which, 300 years later, now benefits ripening grapes, too. The best walk here is undertaken by heading straight up to the top of the orchard and turning around, gazing out over miles and miles of the Somerset Levels.

Most vineyards tend to be beautiful, but this 1-hectare plot is especially stunning. It's not just aesthetics, though – the calcareous limestone soil in which Pinot Meunier and the Burgundian clone Pinot Noir and Chardonnay vines are planted, combined with the additional sun exposure the slope allows, make this one of the warmest and best ripening sites in all of Somerset, if not the entire South West. The latter is where the prevailing weather comes from, breaking over the Exmoor flats and depositing its rain over much of Cornwall and Devon, instead of over the vineyard. That makes Higher Plot potentially as dry and as warm as the best parts of the South East. Guy estimated that over a ten-year period since

Vineyard manager Bert

planting, there would be at least three complete 'wipe out years', though he's only suffered that fate once so far, in 2012. The other vintages have seen near perfect ripeness – at times lower yields, but exceptional in quality and intensity.

Every vineyard needs a good dog, and although my visit to Higher Plot was early on in my travels, Bert the rescue Lab-Pointer cross is going to take some serious beating for my very own Wine Dog of the Year award. Be careful when you're leaving the vineyard – you might find yourself halfway home, only to check the rear-view mirror to see Bert sitting on your back seat. Chances are he hopped in when you were loading up the boot with some of the Smith & Evans portfolio.

Of all the sparkling wines produced here to date, Guy is most proud of the 2015. Aged on lees over four years, it combines a racy, crisp acidity with a well-rounded richness, and with 15% reserve wines dating back to 2010 it's a complex offering that's only going to improve further with time in bottle. Going up at least a rung or two in terms of rich mouth feel is their Trilogy One sparkling; a multi-vintage blend of the reserve wines around a decade in age. Bottled with no added sulphur and at 0 grams of sugar, too, this is the sort of wine that you want to sit down and pair with some lobster or crab meat, and indulge yourself.

There's also a still white, blended from skin-less Pinot Noir and Chardonnay, and fermented with naturally present yeast. It's bright and fresh, and has great depth and signature texture.

Also residing here is a nature reserve, but the vineyard is worth a trip for the view alone. Plus, Bert.

Looks good this way

OATLEY
@OATLEYVINEYARD

Cannington, Bridgwater, Somerset, TA5 2NL
https://www.oatleyvineyard.co.uk

What: Vineyard tours, tastings, cellar door sales and picnic area in the vines
Recommended wines: Kernling Pet-Nat, Barrel-Aged Madeleine

Jane and Iain Awty moved to this perfect parcel of Somerset in 1985. Packed up the car in West Hampstead with everything they needed, and wanted to start a vineyard: three small children, a Collie, two cats, two rabbits and a tortoise, along with a wine knowledge developed mostly from drinking the stuff. Fast forward a quarter of a century, and they've been winning awards for their brilliant wines for almost as long.

The two originally bought a 1951 Ferguson T20 tractor for £350, eventually selling it almost three decades later to an enthusiast for the depreciation-beating sum of exactly the same amount. They enrolled their children in the local school, picked up part-time jobs and planted a couple of acres of Madeleine Angevine and the lesser-seen Kernling. A mutation of Kerner, itself a crossing of the notoriously late-ripening Riesling, the variety thrives in the rich, red sandy loam soil, at only about 30 metres above sea level. This is a well-sheltered, drier, warmer spot that is therefore more conducive to ripening than most.

Even still, in 1985 adequately ripening fruit was still a struggle. Jane and Iain's adaptability and ability to embrace these glorious original vines, in a forward-thinking style, has come almost full circle, and is a very admirable approach. Madeleine is a light yet super bright, aromatic grape and one of their two versions

Jane and her most loyal supporters

Home among the vines

that matures in a couple of Fraîcheur oak barrels. Specifically developed by specialist Cognac Cooper, Seguin Moreau, to enhance lighter white varietals, the barrels have acacia oak heads which add a further creamy richness, still allowing the fruit to shine.

The 'Leonora's Kernling' adds a great alternative to the range; it's a fragrant, rose garden-scented wine, with a precise acid line and great food matching potential. The Pet-Nat version for me is almost symbolic – a merging of the Great British Vineyard scene of yesteryear and the exciting future we find ourselves approaching grown by true custodians of traditional English viticulture in their thirty-five-year-old vineyard, and made as a minimal intervention natural sparkling wine that I am convinced we will only see more of.

Pet-Nat itself, short for Pétillant Naturel, meaning naturally sparkling, is in itself the oldest method of making sparkling wine, pre-dating the Champagne method. Yet it's so on trend, irrespective of history or image. Oatley Vineyard's is utterly sublime: classically fresh, vibrant and accessible, loads of lime zest, and crunchy green apples – it's super-easy, yet there's so much to unpick. At such outstanding value, you would struggle to find a box it doesn't tick.

In the adjoining paddock next to the main vineyard son Ned is in the process of planting brand-new Pinot Noir vines. These new plantings are all Champagne and Burgundy clones. I doubt there'll be a classic-method sparkling wine from Oatley, with no Chardonnay planned, and it doesn't strike me as their style, either. A still Pinot may be the most commercial of the range in years to come, but I'm sure there'll be some slightly left-field numbers, too. The really tasty, exciting kind I'm very much looking forward to seeing.

ALDWICK ESTATE

@ALDWICKESTATE

....

Aldwick Court Farm, Redhill, Bristol, BS40 5AL
https://www.aldwickestate.co.uk

What: Events, bar and restaurant, tastings, tours, cellar door sales and stays
Recommended wines: Sparkling Seyval, Mary's Rosé, The Flying Pig

A Google Maps review of North Somerset's River Yeo insightfully records the river as 'wet'. For as long as rivers are wet, the village of Blagdon will be beautiful. Equally attractive and tucked away within a wander of the river is the fifth-generation farm at Aldwick Estate. Primarily used as an impressive wedding and events venue, the farm's first 2000 vines were planted in 2008 by Chris Watts, to Seyval, Pinot Noir Précoce and Bacchus.

Tragically Chris left us in 2011, a year in which fruit from his Seyval vines saw the inside of a bottle for the first time. Initially planted due to a love of wine and also to complement the wedding venue, the vineyard was taken charge of by Chris's sister Sandy, and it became both a fitting tribute to him and something that could be looked after and passed down through the generations. During this time, family friend Elizabeth asked what she could do to help and Sandy replied, 'Come up to the vineyard, and bring the secateurs.' Elizabeth continued to help tend the vines at Aldwick until her retirement in 2020. The most fitting thing of all was that the entirety of the first 350 bottles were consumed in tribute to Chris at his memorial.

The clay-topped limestone hillside overlooking the Homefield plot saw a larger planting of 9000 vines in 2010, with Pinot

Dramatic skies over Blagdon

58

Noir, Regent and Solaris, plus more Seyval and Bacchus put into the ground. It's a family affair at Aldwick; Sandy's brother in-law and proud Cheshireman Howard leads the tours, talking warmly of 'Our Chris'. It's a similar close-knit approach at harvest when the extended family grows to include teams of pickers, who also join for a harvest supper the following May.

A good chunk of the 20,000 bottles produced are consumed at around sixty weddings annually. 'Jubilate', meaning joyful, is a good name for a wedding sparkling and Seyval is a great grape for it too – light and zingy, and very easy to drink another glass of. Exactly the sort of sparkling that best suits a celebration. A well-curated range, made by Steve Brooksbank, has this consistency throughout. 'Mary's Rosé' is pale and very easy-going, driven by tropical flavours that are held in check with a crisp, dry and refreshing structure.

With Chris originally a pig farmer, the locals were slightly taken aback upon seeing the planting of grapes – red especially. So much so that they told Chris there was more chance of his pigs flying than of him being able to make red wine in England. 'The Flying Pig', a predominantly Regent-based Pinot Noir blend, looks fantastic, and is brilliant to have slightly chilled on a warm Somerset afternoon.

Aldwick's logo epitomises the vineyard's ascent: a heraldic pig with elevated wings. Chris, I'm sure, would be very proud to see the elevation of his vines and the wines they produce in the place that's so lovingly looked after by his family now, and most probably for many generations to come.

The main plot at Aldwick Estate, Blagdon

Fenny Castle Vineyard

@FENNYCASTLEVINEYARD

Panniers Farm, Castle Lane, Worth, Wells, Somerset, BA5 1NL
https://www.fennycastlevineyard.co.uk

What: Vineyard tours, cellar door sales
Recommended wines: Blanc de Noirs, Barrel-Aged Ortega

Londoner-turned-west country-winemaker seems a fairly well-trodden path these days. James Cumming was studying, and initially set up his printing business in town, which he then moved to what is now the winery at Fenny Castle vineyard. The reason this building is now producing wine, however, is largely thanks to his partner Gill, who instantly recognised the adjoining few acres as a great place for a vineyard.

She was right, and it's a unique spot, too. It houses a slope about as steep as it gets before you're in need of employing both hands to help you scramble up it. This is a vineyard of two halves – Pinot Noir at the top, where the incline increases to maximise sun exposure, and the naturally earlier-ripening Ortega down below, beyond which the views stretch all the way to Glastonbury Tor. There's a small plot of Bacchus beside the chooks, opposite the winery too. The band of celestine rock beneath is so unique it's actually a triple-designated point of scientific interest. The mineral usually occurs in sedimentary rock soil in very small quantities, notably in its pale blue crystal form in Madagascar. Just south of Wells, underneath Fenny Castle vineyard, however,

From the summit of Fenny Castle's vineyard to Glastonbury Tor in the distance

One of Britain's smaller wineries

it stands as a wonderful source of minerals for the vine roots, retaining heat and improving drainage, both aiding the ripening process.

James took two years out and spent them studying winemaking at Plumpton agricultural college, planting 2000 vines in 2011 and '12. Clearing the land adjoining the now vineyard, they discovered an early twentieth-century orchard, which is currently under restoration. It seems like it was meant to be, as the couple have three other orchards that grow the apples for their 20,000 annual bottles of cider – a smart and tasty diversification to put funds back into the famously expensive sparkling wine production.

The picnic benches in the gully beneath both the winery and Bacchus vines, just a short stroll across the paddock from the main vineyard, is a great spot to hear about the vineyard's story, philosophy and, of course, to taste the wines. The Blanc de Noirs is testament to James's skills. Aged for forty-two months on lees, this is a hefty investment in both time and cost, but it does not mask the pure flavours of summer fruits, red cherries and crunchy red apples that are at the fore of the resulting wine. A creamy texture underpins the palate; it's a beautifully made sparkling and it's super moreish, as sparkling should be – perfect on a sunny day in the Wells countryside.

As well as a delicate, pure Pinot Noir rosé and fresh and easy-going Bacchus, there's a pair of classy Ortegas that perfectly showcase the varietal's versatility. The tank-fermented version is approachable, fresh and fragrant, and orange peel and rich stone-fruit-driven – so classic of such an enticing varietal, whereas the barrel-fermented one adds a bit of additional weight, texture and richness. Fenny Castle, from just a couple of acres of vines and as probably one of the smaller wineries in Britain, punches well above its weight in range and quality. A beautiful spot, with equally great wines to go with it.

Shiny stickers equals great booze… is not always accurate, though on this occasion it rings true

A grape flower cluster known as the inflorescence

LIMEBURN HILL

@LIMEBURNHILL

···

Westfield Farm, Limeburn Hill, Chew Magna, Bristol, BS40 8QW
https://limeburnhillvineyard.co.uk

What: Tours, tastings and events by appointment
Recommended wines: 'Samhain' Pet-Nat Red, 'Lammas' Pet-Nat Rosé, 'Beltain' Pet-Nat Amber

Perched high on the slopes above the Chew Valley is Limeburn Hill, the South West's original biodynamic vineyard. A lecturer in Landscape Architecture, Robin hand-planted the 2-acre site with partner Georgina, with 1800 vines in 2015 and a further 1200 in 2020 and 2021.

The south-facing slopes capture maximum sun exposure, aiding drainage downhill and also protecting against frost, which heads in the same direction. They're also close enough to benefit from wind rolling in from the River Severn. At the core of their philosophy to viticulture is Robin's dedication to following the principles of biodynamic agriculture. Therefore, the site is considered as a living organism in its entirety; overall land health is promoted through an interconnected network and self-sufficient eco-system. Robin is probably the leading voice on this approach in Britain, and he has been developing an exhaustive course to be delivered through the Biodynamic Agricultural College.

A series of biodynamic preparations or 'teas', prepared from plants such as nettles and yarrow, are applied to the vines in place of sulphur, to reduce the threat from mildew, a fungal disease the plants have evolved a resistance to. Cow manure feeds the soil and vine roots, nourishing

Limeburn Hill Biodynamic Vineyard

the vines as naturally and as healthily as possible, by enriching life in the soil and improving plant growth. A slow fermentation in a cow's horn buried underground develops a manure that is rich with micro-organisms which, when diluted with water and sprayed in large droplets on the soil, increases mycorrhizal fungi, helping plant roots absorb nutrients and attracting earthworm activity, in turn improving soil structure.

This year, Robin and Georgina made their own preparation using manure from a neighbouring organic farmer. Ultimately, the aim is to produce the best quality fruit that is the truest and most natural reflection of its place of origin. Grass is cut twice a year for three main reasons: it's easily the most dominant plant and therefore reduces opportunity for biodiversity; mulching the cuttings back into the ground puts nitrogen back into the soil; shorter grass reduces the risk of ground frost. Using a scythe also reduces impact and soil compaction.

Greater biodiversity improves soil health, promoting the uptake of nutrients and minerals by vine roots. With more bee life in the vineyard, the natural yeast strains that develop on grape skins and all around are transported throughout the vineyard, enabling natural fermentation and eradicating the need for commercial yeast, in turn making the final wine a greater reflection of place.

In the fourth year of conversion, disease was greatly reduced, and the overall eco-system had adjusted sufficiently to be producing some seriously good fruit. When I visited Robin in May, every other vineyard I had been to was at least three weeks behind on the back of an unseasonably cold two months. This is in theory a cooler part of the country, at good altitude, with constant airflow. Yet Limeburn is flourishing; it abounds with wildlife, the land is as healthy as anywhere I've been and fruit onset is ahead of everywhere else.

The wines are made just over the hill (the idea of going to such great lengths in the vineyard for the grapes to then be transported for several hours to a biodynamic contract winery in Kent or Sussex, as you might imagine, did not particularly appeal).

The only problem with the wines themselves is that they're too popular – in such great demand that you have to move seriously quickly to get your hands on some, usually released in July following harvest. It's so worth keeping an eye on the website calendar page for the range of workshops and tours – this place is about as special as they come.

The Chew Valley from the top of Limeburn Hill Vineyard

Robin and his biodynamic vines

Huxbear winery & Vineyard
@HUXBEAR_VINEYARD

Chudleigh, Newton Abbot, TQ13 0EH
https://www.huxbear.co.uk

What: Tours and tastings by appointment
Recommended wines: Artio Bacchus, Classic Sparkling, Orange

Contrary to popular belief, the best-made plans are those instigated amid drunken evenings with friends. One night, several wines in, Ben and Lucy Hulland's declaration that they would one day have a vineyard was the catalyst that saw Ben embark on a winemaking course at Plumpton college.

During his three years in Sussex Ben had spells with acclaimed producers Ridgeview and Nyetimber, when he set out to learn, and taste, as much as he possibly could. Following a dissertation on site selection, and accompanied by three-legged Show Cocker Spaniel Toby, 2007 saw the couple acquire the 14-or-so acres near Chudleigh in Devon's Teign Valley, where they planted the first of today's 16,500 vines.

On the former site of Huxbear Estate, the label takes its inspiration from Ursa Major, the Great Bear constellation that can be seen in the night sky high above the vineyard. Off-grid and powered largely through renewables, the on-site winery and tasting barn is the perfect place to produce and showcase a stunning range of wines from their Pinot Noir, Meunier, Chardonnay, Bacchus, Siegerrebe and Schönburger vines.

The range is as smart and succinct as the labels on the bottles. 'Artio' Bacchus is picked in two batches – one crisper, well-structured

Lucy in the tasting barn at Huxbear

Huxbear beers, barrels and bottles of great booze

and zesty that is blended with a riper, more floral style, an approach which aids balance, complexity and interest, all true to the easy-drinking character Bacchus is known for.

There are two wines made with a blend of the same grapes, Siegerrebe and Schönburger, that are a great example of winemaking versatility and nous. The 'Corbinian', named after a seventh-century bear-taming saint, is a perfect match for a spicy dish, with refreshing elderflower, peach and just a hint of spice. The unfiltered orange wine version takes the rounded texture of the skin-contact style, but at five weeks on a quarter of the skins, it is in no way overpowering or at all fruit-masking, it merely adds another element while still allowing the natural brightness of the grapes to shine through.

It's a philosophy that's reflected in production of their 'Classic Sparkling'. Extended lees ageing can, at times, exacerbate the dominant yeasty, biscuity flavours and risk overpowering the delicate fruit. At twenty-seven months on lees, the three traditional-grape blend lets the leading fruit flavours of citrus, red apple and redcurrants shine through, underpinned by a richness from the Pinot Noir and a body of those creamy yeasty flavours playing the supporting role, all superbly balanced.

I love the couple's sheer enthusiasm for wine, and the beautiful expressions of grape and site, but above all, the production of wines they just love to drink. There are a few American oak barrels that some premium Chardonnay has been ageing in, and this will head down an exciting path when the release is ready. American oak is usually brighter and creamier than French, so it will require a delicate handling approach to continue the fruit-first philosophy, but I am sure that it is in very safe hands.

LYME BAY WINERY

@LYMEBAYWINERY

Shute, Axminster, Devon, EX13 7PW
https://lymebaywinery.co.uk

What: Cellar door sales and tastings
Recommended wines: Classic Cuvée, Chardonnay, Bacchus Block

Established in 1993 as the Lyme Bay Cider Co., and true to their history, 'LBW Drinks', are producing a range of still and sparkling wine under the Lyme Bay Winery brand, as well as fruit wine, mead, cider and spirits. The winery was founded by Nigel Howard, though it wasn't until 2009 they had vines of their own in the ground, planting a total of 26,000 at Watchcombe and Southcote.

A passion to drive the still wine revolution led Liam Idzikowski, a Langham winemaker, to move to Lyme Bay in time for the first still wine vintage in 2014. Sourcing fruit from all over the country, notably Kent and Essex, enables LBW to craft a range of wines with riper fruit from potentially warmer, drier parts. Liam was so impressed with the Crouch Valley especially, he's since moved on to head up the winemaking at the super premium Danbury Ridge – but not before helping put Lyme Bay on the map.

Managing Director James Lambert took over head winemaking duties, having been with Nigel at LBW since 2006. They're currently sourcing the ripest of their Pinot Noir and Chardonnay from Missing Gate and Martin's Lane vineyards in the Essex Crouch Valley. The signature vintage Classic Cuvée is more than three quarters Pinot Noir to Chardonnay, a third barrel-fermented

The shop at Lyme Bay

and on lees for two years with partial malolactic fermentation. This all helps soften acidity and lets the ripe, rich and structured Pinot Noir shine. They're also making an entry-level version, from 90% Seyval that's super fresh and easy. Zesty and crisp, but above all it's got that classic English orchard style the varietal is synonymous with.

The premium range, however, is built on a long-term project with Pinot Noir and Chardonnay. Only produced in the very best years, with the best fruit, the first of these wines were made in 2020 when the Crouch Valley reported a batch of Pinot Noir with a potential alcohol of 14.7% – a record for Britain.

100% Martin's Lane Chardonnay was fermented with a mix of wild and Burgundian yeast strains and aged in a mixture of French oak and steel – the ripe and richness is impressively fruit weight driven, with supporting buttery texture from the eleven months' lees-stirring in barrel.

The range is ever-increasing in size, as it seems to be with Essex grapes, but across their portfolio there's some pretty serious wine being produced – and plenty of cider, gin and mead too.

© Hannah Newbery

Calancombe Estate

@CALANCOMBEWINES

....

Modbury, South Devon, PL21 0TU
https://www.calancombe-estate.com

What: Cellar door sales, tours and tastings
Recommended wines: Blanc de Noirs, White Pinot, Bacchus

Motivated by a desire to travel, winemaker Olly Shaw was on his way into the Devon-based Royal Marines until deciding making wine, not war, was a much preferable route to travelling the world.

Following studies at Plumpton, and with winemaking stints in Beaujolais and New Zealand's Hawkes Bay, as well as Lyme Bay and Denbies in England, Olly moved back home to Devon and was put in touch with Caroline and Lance Whitehead, thanks to Duncan at Sharpham. He's ably assisted in the vineyard by Sunny Walker, in between North Devon surf trips, and Mike Andrews, a neighbouring high-quality beef farmer.

Halfway between Dartmouth and Plymouth, the estate itself dates back to the sixteenth century, and is one of the most striking vineyards I've ever seen. The winery and farmhouse sit in the valley by Shilstone brook; the land rises dramatically on three sides around it, to well over 100 metres of vertical gain in the space of a few fields. Twenty-three acres of the south-facing slopes were planted in the three years from 2013, to Pinot Noir, Bacchus, Pinot Gris, Madeleine, Chardonnay and Ortega.

Pinot Noir is the hero varietal, with almost 8000 vines in the ground, a quarter of which are the early-ripening Précoce. As well as planting cider apple trees and blackcurrants,

Tucked away in a hidden valley in South Devon, the estate at Calancombe

the Whiteheads also installed a winery, cider-making facility and even a very special copper distillation pot that Lance uses to make premium gin, under his Dartmouth English Gin brand.

Olly's already established a wealth of experience in his winemaking travels, and it shows in the quality of his wines. With twelve hours' maceration on skins for the Pinot rosé that is sourced exclusively from the single plot of Burgundian clones, it sits nicely between the easy-drinking and slightly richer and textural channel. The Bacchus, too, is fresh and floral, but not overly aromatic or too punchy. My pick is the white Pinot Noir, a style that's starting to pick up a bit of a following, and suits slightly cooler regions or seasons when the ripeness is not quite sufficient to make a red. Flavoursome and stone-fruit driven, it is however supported by a hint of richness from some old French oak ageing. There's so much personality to this style when well-handled, as it is at Calancombe.

The Blanc de Noirs is also exclusively sourced from the premium plot of 5800 Pinot Noir vines. With two years on lees and just 3 grams of sugar dosage, it keeps fresh in acidity but with an intriguing touch of richness.

Calancombe are still relatively young in their journey but there's a lot to look out for in the years to come. Despite their contrasting career experience, Caroline and Lance's mutually valuable skill in spotting people with talent has let them put their faith in Olly, and given him the canvas to craft some seriously good wines, with all the kit a young winemaker could wish for.

Winemaker Olly

Alder Vineyard

@ALDERVINEYARD

Lewdown, Okehampton, Devon, EX20 4PJ
https://aldervineyard.uk

What: Cellar door sales, tours, tastings, kitchen and bar
Recommended wines: Madeleine, Rondo Rosé

The Hodgetts family have been custodians of this rolling piece of Devon for several generations, though they've always done things a bit differently. They hadn't actually farmed the land since the sixties, when the current grandparents converted some sheds on the farm into the home of their surf brand, Alder Sportswear. Planting Rondo and Madeleine in 2010, largely motivated by combining their love of the outdoors and the stunning part of Dartmoor they call home with the kind of wine they like to drink.

They timed it well. Having previously sold their grapes, 2014 brought great ripening, good yields and, with the wine made at Polgoon in Cornwall, they decided to put their own label on it and sell a few bottles from a small shop on-site.

On the back of this promising start, they planted more vines and made more wine, showing people around the vineyard at the same time. Becoming increasingly involved with the vines and with wine in general meant third-generation Tom was inspired to take his passion to the next level, enrolling on a winemaking course at Plumpton.

In 2020 they installed a new building on-site, split lengthways down the middle. The back half is dedicated to a very sleek winery that is compact but in no way lacking the kind of kit you expect

Leaves about to fall at Alder

from a premium offering. The issue with sending the grapes off to be made into wine is in part down to the scheduling constraints, but Tom felt there was a lack of involvement in the wider process which for them de-valued the local product feel. In the front half of the building is the new shop, kitchen and bar, with a tasting terrace that looks down over the vines and into the valley below. This is one of the best views going when it comes to vine-side drinking, and, while you might need your binos and a fair chunk of patience to spot them, the wetlands below are home to a colony of beavers.

As well as establishing the vineyards of Devon website, the shop also supports other local produce. There are two wines currently – single-varietal Madeleine and a Rondo rosé – both of which are super approachable but bright, ripe, very easy-going styles. Tom thought the area under vine to Bacchus nationally was a good reason to do something different on the white front. But with more vines going in and plenty of additional land at their disposal, combined with the space and equipment to experiment with new styles, it's worth getting down there to see what they're up to.

Sandridge Barton – the home of Sharpham Wine

@SHARPHAM_WINE

Lower Well Farm, Waddeton Road, Stoke Gabriel, South Devon, TQ9 6RL
https://sandridgebarton.com

What: Cellar door sales, tours, tasting and café
Recommended wines: Pinot Noir, Bacchus Stop Ferment, Sparkling Blanc, Dart Valley Reserve

Celebrating forty years in 2021, the vines at Sharpham sit among 200 acres of wider estate. Before joining as winemaker in 1992, Duncan Schwab worked as a surveyor in London. Having grown up in Lebanon's Bekaa valley, where legendary producers like Chateau Musar provided a rich wine history from an early age, he helped his dad plant 3 acres in the South West, including Madeleine and poly-tunnel Chardonnay. Discovering Sharpham were on a similar path of discovery, he never went back to surveying, and has been on the banks of the River Dart ever since.

With few other producers around, initially Sharpham had a trial site of up to fifteen varietals – as Duncan says, 'You can't just ask Uncle Jack how he got on with his Pinot Noir back in 1924 – you have to put them in the ground and see what happens yourself.'

Duncan spent most winters travelling the world and its wine regions, making wine everywhere he could along the way, from Perth to Peru and back again. Building up such an array of winemaking experience across different cultures and countries, and having the opportunity to hone an individual style moulded from the best bits of everywhere else, is one of the major advantages for emerging British winemakers today. Duncan

was perhaps twenty years ahead of his time.

In 2008 Sharpham were approached by the owner of Sandridge Barton Estate on the eastern riverbank, who wanted some help with planting vines on the basis that Sharpham might take the grapes. When Duncan saw the land, he realised it was an absolute no-brainer. Rich with limestone, as are some of the world's great vineyard regions, together they planted 8 acres of Burgundian clone Pinot Noir at the Stony Field vineyard, and a further 16 acres on the wider estate.

Stony Field will provide the best Pinot Noir as a result – a further 10 acres went in ten years after the first which, combined with the original 8 acres at Sharpham, leaves them with a total of 44. An ultra-modern, 120,000 bottle capacity winery was built over this side in 2020, with a visitor centre and café following in 2022.

Solar-powered, with rain and waste-water harvesting, the two-level winery is adjacent to where the majority of fruit is coming from, so it makes perfect sense to relocate and re-brand to the Sandridge Barton name. Tommy Grimshaw from Langham started his career under Duncan and today there's a team of young winemakers working with him, tapping into much experience. Charlie manages a couple of vintages a year,

Sandridge Barton Estate, the home of Sharpham wine, on the east bank of the River Dart

with travels to the southern hemisphere, and has that glint in his eye akin to all the best creatives. The kind of guy who likes to pair Barolo with bacon and eggs – look out for him in the future.

When Duncan started with Sharpham, they might have been able to crop a decent yield in three or four years out of ten. There are now perhaps three or four years a decade where they don't get a decent crop. This is still very marginal climate viticulture, but the odds, at least, are slightly more in their favour. There are a couple of versions of the rewarding Madeleine 'Dart Valley Reserve' that show off the stone-fruit ripeness and concentration the grape so gallantly throws, while the 'Estate Selection' is slightly leaner, more floral and a touch zestier.

'Stop Ferment Bacchus' is another outstanding example of versatility in both grape and making. Regular tasting allows the balance of natural grape

sweetness and zingy acidity to be just right before the tank is cooled and the fermentation is, well, stopped. The result is a bright, fresh, off-dry belter of a pairing for spice, or a deckchair in the sun.

A combination of fruit from well-established, several-clone, Pinot Noir vines, part whole-bunch ferments with stalks and six months in second-fill oak barrels gives a depth and structure which puts the Sandridge Pinot Noir in my top five examples from this entire trip. Bright and youthful, it opens up so well with some serious airtime, becoming rich and earthy, and suggesting a few years tucked away would do no harm at all.

There are a lot of experiments going on, as there always have been – a blend of the traditional and the modern – which is an approach as embodied in the people here as it is the vineyards and winery, and they marry this blend absolutely perfectly.

Pebblebed Vineyards

@PEBBLEBEDVINEYARDS

Marianne Pool Farm, Clyst St George, Exeter, EX3 0NZ
https://www.dartsfarm.co.uk

What: Cellar door sales, tours and tastings
Recommended wines: Sparkling White, Sparkling Rosé, Still White

Pebblebed started as a community project in 1999 when eleven local families, under the direction of Geoff Bowen, came together to plant the first half acre of vines just to the south-east of Exeter.

Realising their developing love of viticulture, Geoff and his wife Anna, with considerable help from the community and local farmers, grew the site to more than 20 acres of vineyards across three separate Clyst St George plots, producing up to 50,000 bottles a year.

It is now part of the Darts Farm group, the focal point of which is the cellar and shop just outside the old port town of Topsham. This is awesome produce shopping as it should be – you can quite easily lose a few quid in these sorts of places but you'll come away with seriously well-harvested local food and (now) wine, and about as much cheese as you can carry. It's also a thriving community hub, with other local wines on sale in the cellar bar – a great place for regular tastings.

Given their history, Pebblebed very much encourages visitors and volunteer support in the hopes they will enjoy discovering its vineyards and the wine the grapes go into. The harvest of 2021 was carried out

Plenty of local booze on sale at Darts Farm

The barrel wall at Darts Farm

with the help of nearly 500 volunteers, with winemaking activities following, including a constant flow of liquid lunches throughout.

A blend of good ripening and disease resistance was desired in the initial plantings of Seyval, Madeleine, Phoenix, Rondo, Regent, Solaris and Pinot Noir. The first wines from the community vineyard were made in 2002, and named 'Dodo Tree', after a tree on the skyline of the vineyard that resembled the extinct bird. From 2010 the wines have been made on-site by winemaker Alex Mills, who remains at the helm under the Darts' stewardship.

Sparkling White is a blend of Seyval and Rondo; freshness and fragrancy are provided in different ways from both – elderflower and orchard fruit from the former and a bright summer complexion from the latter. All that is

then softened, and a touch of richness is added by two years on lees. The rosé version adds some still Rondo back to the same blend so it results in being a bit brighter in red fruit, but is equally easy and refreshing. The still white adds Madeleine and Phoenix to a third part of Seyval, and is a great showcase of ripeness in tropical fruit. A Rondo, Regent and Pinot Noir blend sees twelve months in French oak for added depth in the red offering, but the house blend – Seyval and Rondo – is reverted to for a customary fruit-forward still rosé.

What started as a great community initiative now represents over two decades of history and vines in the ground, and seems as if its best days are yet to come.

SWANAFORD ESTATE
@SWANAFORD

Swanaford Road, Bridford, Exeter, EX6 7HG
https://www.swanaford.com

What: Cellar door sales, tours, tastings and cottage stays
Recommended wines: Sparkling Rosé, Classic Cuvée, Kingfisher Bacchus

Following a move to the South West from London, Ben and Caroline Goulden found their perfect spot in Devon's Teign Valley. They didn't know it at the time, but this two-paddock plot of well-protected, south-east-facing land is about as suited to vines as anywhere around here. They ultimately planted in 2013 with the help of a team of Germans and their laser-guided kit.

Almost a decade after planting, both vines and growers alike are establishing themselves in this part of South East Devon, with a seriously concise offering in both wines and visitor experience. In 2017 a bespoke tasting barn was built at Swanaford, complete with pizza oven and picnic tables backing onto the vines.

There's an awesome offering here, from sit-down feasts to wellness weekends, and the 50-acre site is also home to three great holiday cottages, listed on Airbnb under Branfield, Rose and West Park Cottages.

But it all comes back to the wine, and the range is led by sparkling, and the three main Champagne varieties accordingly. Almost half of the site is planted to Chardonnay which does incredibly well here, yielding good amounts of ripe bunches that benefit from the natural sun trap.

Classic Cuvée is a predominantly Chardonnay

Ben Goulden in the tasting barn at Swanaford

blend, therefore, with a third Pinot Noir adding a touch of depth and structure, but it's fresh and fruit-forward primarily, added to by a touch of bright Meunier. Zesty and floral, with some secondary richness from a couple of years' lees ageing. It has great balance and a very clean, uplifting finish. Both the classic and the sparkling rosé hit the sweet spot, so to speak, for classic-method sparkling – both are dry, crisp and fresh, and super approachable in fruit that is added to in the complexity department by a touch of yeasty richness, but very much fruit-supporting, rather than masking. The rosé is all refined summer red fruit from both Pinots, with a super-fine Chardonnay elegance and zing to its finish; both are easy-going but super interesting, seriously well-made sparkling wines.

The stills, too – Kingfisher Bacchus and Estate white – have been really well thought out, produced first and foremost as good wines, from easy-going, aromatic varietals that make them very popular styles, but still expressive of their unique location. The Bacchus is exuberant and bright – going down the tropical fruit path – and great with some spice or enjoyed from one of the picnic tables in the sun. Estate white is a blend of Siegerrebe and Schönburger, and true to the former's Gewürtz parentage, slightly exotic and passion fruit-driven but still super easy and fruity at its fore.

There are a range of collaborations in the pipeline: the plan is to unite with local 'food heroes', and maybe add a few more wines to the range. But whatever your reason to visit – of which there are more than a few – make sure you find your way to the bar in the tasting barn.

The cottages at Swanaford

Camel Valley
@CAMELVALLEYVINEYARD

Nanstallon, Bodmin, Cornwall, PL30 5LG
https://www.camelvalley.com

What: Cellar door sales, tours and tastings
Recommended wines: Cornwall Brut, Sparkling Rosé

Former RAF pilot Bob Lindo and his wife Annie planted the first 8000 Camel Valley vines in 1989, having bought the farm in the heart of the Cornish countryside several years earlier. Seeking a change from service life and searching for the perfect place to bring up their young family, they initially farmed sheep and cattle on the sun-drenched slopes above the river Camel, wondering if vines might enjoy such an aspect.

Bob went off to do a vintage in Germany, and read extensively on the subject of vine and wine (all this was before the YouTube generation of learning, and though Plumpton had begun offering a course in viticulture and winemaking the year before, it was a far cry from what it is today). The available infrastructure and shared winemaking knowledge that we benefit from now was equally sparse, so Bob and Annie built their winery and equipped it as well as they could afford to.

Thirty years ago, with no real market demand or wider backing, this dedication is especially impressive. Annie says the early years were a real struggle; everything was done by hand, and they practically lived in the vineyard – when harvest came it was just them and a few friends picking, and Bob would stay up all night crushing grapes. But ultimately, like anything with longevity, they

Planted in 1989, Camel Valley vineyard

Still or sparkling flights on the tasting terrace, or both

absolutely loved what they were doing so together with winning a national medal for their first ever wine, they knew they were doing something right.

A new, modern English winery became the first built from EU funds in 2005, taking the capacity to 200,000 litres annually. From 2002, Sam Lindo returned to Cornwall, eventually taking over head winemaking duties, ever supported by Bob. Having spent time with Kim Crawford in New Zealand, he installed a cooling system for fermentations at Camel Valley and under his guidance, they became Britain's first winery to use Stelvin screw caps.

In removing Triomphe and replacing it with Pinot Noir, Bacchus and Dornfelder, the majority of the fruit harvested is sourced from warmer, less exposed parts of the country. From the outset, and still true to tradition, their sparkling range focuses on a fresh, fruit-forward style, rather than investing in long lees ageing which could potentially mask the delicate fruit quality.

The smart approach, in terms of attractive offering on the wine side of things, is more than matched in venue – the tasting terrace backs out onto a fantastic view over the vines on the slopes below and the rolling hills opposite. From there you can tuck into a flight of either stills or sparklings – or both. As producers since the 1980s, it's no surprise to see Seyval feature, but so great to see it championed – especially in aged form. The 'Annie's Anniversary' 100% Seyval is a tribute to Annie and her one million vines single-handedly pruned – at four years old it's baked and flavoursome, and acts as a nice point of difference to both the wider range and Seyval in its usual, super-fresh form.

The signature, vintage 'Cornwall Brut' has been served in Rick Stein's restaurants, Nathan Outlaw's two Michelin-starred restaurants and in First-Class British Airways bars. It is slightly Seyval to Chardonnay dominant, super fresh, zingy and vibrant fruit-centric, perfectly supported, but not outplayed by its toasty richness.

Tasty terrace views at Camel Valley

It's a similar approach for the Pinot Noir sparkling rosé, made solely from the free run juice, the balance of which is pressed off for still. It's bright and floral fruit-forward, very delicate and long – a classic, elegant and light, pale-coloured pink.

Of the still wines, Bacchus Dry and Atlantic Dry are zesty and floral – the latter sees equal part Chardonnay added to its Bacchus for a touch of extra body and stone-fruit. This is crowd-pleasing kit, and you have an equally enticing spot to enjoy it in. An iconic label in an amazing part of the world, with a great history; I'm looking forward to their next three decades and counting.

Polgoon Vineyard and Orchard

@POLGOON_VINEYARD

Rosehill, Penzance, TR20 8TE
https://www.polgoon.com

What: Cellar door sales, tours and tastings
Recommended wines: Seyval Sparkling, Pinot Noir Sparkling Rosé

John and Kim Coulson bought the run-down flower farm that is now Polgoon vineyard in 2002. Scaling down their careers as fish merchants in Newlyn, and thanks to advice from Camel Valley's Bob Lindo, they planted in 2004 ahead of their first harvest two years later. Lindo's sound advice was not all positive: the reality of the south-west is that this is the direction the weather comes from, and, Scilly Isles aside, they're right on the cusp of it.

They do, however, benefit from some natural protection – the vines sit in a tree-lined dip in the land. Initial plantings were of Rondo, Pinot Noir Précoce, Seyval Blanc and Ortega and, when harvested, Sam Lindo took the grapes up to Camel Valley and made the wines from the first vintage in 2006. The following year's crop was all but lost, heavily affected by the heavy rainfall, but this set in motion two major events in the history of Polgoon.

The yield harvested was so low that John didn't bother sending it to Sam at Camel Valley for commercial production, thinking instead he'd have a crack at winemaking himself. Secondly, the realities of grape growing at the marginal end of a marginal climate inspired the Coulsons to invest in a backup crop of cider apple trees, the product from which have since become a major feature and funder of the wider business.

Equally tricky vintages and a steep learning curve followed in 2008, but in 2009, the weather gods began to smile on Polgoon, and they've barely looked back. Now with a holiday cottage, shop and regular tours, and no lack of tourists (in 2021, especially), the Coulsons are still making a range of single varietal wines, ciders and juices.

The Rondo is impressively dark fruit-driven, rich and rounded, yet classically approachable. Rondo and Seyval work so well together as a rosé, the latter providing all the easy-going, refreshing orchard fruit that's added to with a touch of complexity and red fruit from the former. Which is true of the white too: Ortega in place of Rondo, adding a touch of fruit weight and body – added to with a bit of oak, via blocks in the tank for a week or so.

All three are great summer wines, and just as good for the dinner table as they are for one of the region's signature beach days.

St Michael's Mount, Marazion, on the drive into Polgoon

Knightor Winery
@KNIGHTOR_WINERY

. . . .

Trethurgy, Cornwall, PL26 8YQ
https://www.knightor.com

What: Cellar door sales, tours, tastings, restaurant and bar
Recommended wines: Portscatho Bacchus, Barrel-Aged Bacchus, Barrel-Aged Pinot Noir

Just down the road from the Eden Project and the legendary St Austell Brewery, Knightor is a boutique winery, kitchen and events venue, nestled just above the bay. Any visit is at very least worth combining with a pint of 'Proper Job', the home of which is just a ten-minute drive from the winery (though this is not a day you want to be driving).

Adrian Derx originally planted at Seaton in South East Cornwall, and Portscatho on the Roseland Peninsular, as well as sourcing fruit from other local growers, ahead of the first vintage in 2011. Winemaker David Brocklehurst had an allotment as a thirteen-year-old, growing fruit and veg, flowers and 'random seeds' he had collected. He took a cutting of a vine, planted and soon had over sixty grapevines producing more than 100 kilos of fruit. While still at school, he was offered a job at Nutbourne in West Sussex and has never looked back.

Following experience making wine in the Loire Valley's Chinon, where they would pick the grapes when the walnuts fell, because they always have, he's now been at Knightor for a decade.

In an old cow shed, a small amount of the 2019 Bacchus crop was fermented in old French oak, with the intention of blending it with some of the same varietal in tank. However, these

Ten years and counting at Knightor: winemaker David Brocklehurst

three barrels naturally stopped fermenting, leaving behind considerable residual sugar, so as a result were bottled in a limited release. David and Knightor aren't afraid of sugar, and it's great to see – in a climate naturally producing grapes with higher acidity, sugar can balance, soften and uplift fruit. This off-dry – rather than sweet – wine is a great example: slightly creamy, the bright florals cut through attractive oak richness and, at just 8% in volume, it's shaping up to be a very tasty morning.

As well as conventionally tank-fermented, dry and zesty version of their Bacchus, there's an even smaller release – just 150 bottles – of the fascinating 'Portscatho'. Fully fermented in old French oak, where the juice sat for ten further months, the resulting wine was bottled without fining or filtration, and with hand-written 'labels' direct to bottle, along with a note from the winemaker. This is exactly the opportunity for small-scale producers not relying on contract-making facilities, they can do exactly what they want – or what certain vintages allow or dictate – without having to worry about minimum volumes or the schedules of others, and best of all with the freedom to experiment.

There's a Gewürtz-esque blend of Siegerrebe, Schönburger and Müller-Thurgau, labelled 'Trevannion', that shows exotic spice and a hint of lychee, and a great mix throughout the portfolio of blended reds, whites and rosés alongside signature, single-varietal Pinot Noirs and Chardonnay. Don't miss the sparkling offering either: at three years on lees for the non-vintage – which even takes fruit from their half-row of Riesling – and five years minimum bottle age time for the vintage offering.

From the granite barns and 4 acres of Cornish hedgerows, pasture and orchard, feasts and celebrations are hosted featuring local produce and great booze on all fronts. Knightor have got the visitor experience nailed here. Extensive tours and tastings are available at the winery, but you can still turn up to the shop – one side of which is the bottle-labelling line – and taste some wines: a shortcut to the good stuff. You might also bump into weddings, brass bands and the Knightor winery Dachshund called Sausage.

You tend to see a greater number of wines in the ranges of producers like Knightor, which are harder to keep up with in terms of availability, but lots more fun to investigate, and always another reason to return.

So much to appreciate… winery weddings and loading up the boot

Trevibban Mill Vineyards and Orchards
@TREVIBBANMILL_VINEYARD

. . . .

Dark Lane, Padstow, PL27 7SE
https://www.trevibbanmill.com

What: Cellar door sales, tours, tastings, bar and stays
Recommended wines: Blanc de Blancs, Blancs de Noir, Chardonnay Pet-Nat, Skin-Contact Orion

If Knightor have St Austell Brewery, Trevibban Mill have The Seafood Restaurant at Padstow, where it all began for Rick Stein back in 1975. Tucked away down a campion-lined Cornish lane, Trevibban Mill is a family-run working vineyard, winery, cider producer and events venue just 3 miles from the harbour town. Historically home to a miller, the land is now a base for vines, apple trees and native English Southdown sheep, the latter of which sit proudly on Trevibban's labels.

When Engin and Liz Mumcuoglu arrived here in 2007, the initial plan was to restore the mill. But when they met the local farmer who was selling the surrounding last two plots of land, the vision went in a slightly different direction. Engin was on long-term leave and 'pretty bored' at the time, and saw a great opportunity to put the land back into productive use, establishing the vineyard to produce high-quality sparkling and still wine on the North Cornish Coast. Everything from wine and cider making to bottling, disgorging and labelling are done here, which, much like southern neighbours Knightor, gives them the freedom to experiment with small batch blends.

Planting took place in 2008, which saw 1700 apple, sweet chestnut and other fruit trees also added. The gently sloping site is a great home to 7 acres of vines, and nestled right at

South African cellar door-inspired tasting lodge at Trevibban Mill

A very relaxing afternoon tasting in store at Trevibban Mill near Padstow

the heart of them is one of our best cellar doors.

In 2014 work started on the building which now houses the winery, cellars, bar and restaurant. Inspired by the cellar doors of South Africa, the safari lodge-style building looks like it's been here a lot longer than it has, with the terrace looking out over an outdoor fire pit, wildflower meadows and herb garden. There is a great offering in the ever-changing, laid-back tasting flights, where currently for £15 you can taste seven wines (and usually a cider also thrown in), that were all made in the winery below.

The 'grand walking tour' includes a light lunch and indulging in seven wines at a tasting, which is a good way to spend the best part of four hours, or you can just tuck in at the bar along with a range of mixed plates. From the outset, Liz and Engin have employed professional winemakers to best showcase the fruit, and right at the top end too – currently Salvatore Leone is curating the Trevibban range alongside his role making some of Britain's best wines at Oxney Estate.

The Blanc de Blancs – made from an equal split of Chardonnay and Seyval and aged for four years on lees – is a fantastic showcase of rich and rounded Chardonnay meeting bright and expressive Seyval. There's a minimal dosage Blanc de Noirs and 'Black Ewe' exclusively Seyval sparkling that is bone-dry and super refreshing.

Though it belongs in a market dominated by sparkling and a region by Camel Valley, still wine will always be at the heart of the Trevibban range, which is extensive, but not at all suffering from a dilution in quality as a result.

The 100% Chardonnay Pet-Nat and Skin-Contact Orion are good examples of where experimental hearts may lie, and these are well-founded desires if the rate at which both traditionally sell out is a good indication of how well received the results are. The latter is on skins for a week, which extracts some great texture, flavour concentration and a touch of tannin, but is still so true to varietal – rounded, rich and herbaceous. There's also some rarely

The tasting terrace at Trevibban Mill

seen oak contact for Reichensteiner and Seyval under their 'Merope' label, which together with a blend of Bacchus shows some attractive tropical, white peach and melon fruit, perfect for a sunny day on the terrace.

Of the reds, the 'Black Ewe' Pinot Noir Précoce is attractively darker and richer than you might expect from this classically light and bright variety, and the 'Black Ram' takes this up a further notch. An equal blend of Dornfelder and Rondo, bramble fruit and cassis sit at its core of richness and depth. One of the few English reds that would stand up to a decent steak or – if not too offensive to the subject of the wine's label – roast lamb.

LANGHAM WINE ESTATE

@LANGHAMWINERY

....

Crawthorne, Dorchester, Dorset, DT2 7NG
https://langhamwine.co.uk

What: Cellar door tastings and sales, barn events, vineyard café
Recommended wines: Corallin NV, Culver NV, Pinot Meunier Sparling NV, Rosé NV,
Chardonnay, Col Fondo

So often on this trip I've been asked which producer is my 'favourite'. I normally say something along the lines of 'That's like trying to choose your favourite child… if you had 150 kids.' But most important things considered – wine, people, place and approach – it would be difficult to look past Langham as a top contender. The International Wine & Spirit Competition awarded them world's best sparkling wine producer in 2020, but they're so much more than that.

The Langham family have farmed the land around Melcombe Manor House since 1980. John planted a few vines in his garden, which inspired his son Justin to plant on a commercial scale, choosing the best 30 acres of the site to do so. South-facing atop ten chalk strata, it is well sheltered and benefits from the North Atlantic drift, and is far enough east to avoid the worst of the south-westerlies. It's only 15 miles north of Weymouth and the nearby seaside towns that receive almost 1900 hours of sun annually, which is about 40% more than the UK average.

More than 100,000 vines of predominantly Champagne clone Pinot Noir, Chardonnay and Meunier provide so much variation in flavour profile across different blocks of vines, and all give winemaker Tommy Grimshaw plenty to play with. There's much vintage variation at this marginal end of the climate, but that's attractive too. As Tommy says, it would be boring if every year was guaranteed to be a good one and you made the same stuff the whole time.

One of Britain's youngest winemakers, Tommy tells me he got into the industry after messing up his A levels and needing a job, which he then landed at his local winery, Sharpham, in Devon. In 2019 he moved up to Langham under head winemaker Daniel Ham, and when Daniel left to set up his own project, all of a sudden Tommy was in the hot seat. But you make your own luck, and with him at the helm, Langham are producing some of the best wines in the country, all down to a great site, a fastidious approach and a team of great people.

From this multitude of specific micro-site parcels of high-quality fruit, it's all about creating a broad range of styles, through layers, depth and complexity of flavour and character. A lot of wine producers try to keep oxygen away from the winemaking process, but it's actively encouraged here, partly employing hyper oxygenation which makes the juice more tolerant of it in the long run. Oxidation

Picking 2021 fruit at Langham Estate

also develops flavour and additional variation from different batches. Some Chardonnay fruit might see some time on solids for a touch more extraction, others might actually be slightly more reductive, and there might be some savoury components – every clone from every grape, from every part of the vineyard developing a slightly different character to the next. From one four-hour press cycle there are possibly nine different parcels of juice, of which some might go into oak, of different sizes, ages and origin, some into steel tank and some into concrete vat.

Oak now accounts for about 50% of vessel use at Langham, from old Bordeaux and Burgundies to a single acacia barrel, and a 2000-litre foudre (a large German vat). Across the multiple variations, around ninety-five different batches of base wines are produced from a single season.

These are blended with a small percentage of reserve juice from prior vintages into a core range of just three wines with meticulous precision.

The Chardonnay in tank is zingy and crunchier than that in barrel, which is generally more rounded, or fuller, in texture. Just outside the winery there are seven 4000-litre underground concrete vats that are used as a solera-style fractional blending of reserve wines. This sits right on the knife-edge of being oxidised, with some drawn off each year for blending in the makeup of the non-vintage range – adding nutty, savoury and saline layers of complexion. Its contribution is just one part of the reserve wine additions, which might be up to 30% in total, though more recently it's more likely half of that. The concrete vats are then freshened up with wine from the current

2021 was a vintage largely picked by local communities. Here's
Jerry enjoying his day prior to winning Movember

vintage to maintain that delicate balance, and let the juice within continually evolve.

It's a very hands-off approach, which in itself is quite a skill – just letting the various fruit profiles develop and blending different percentages accordingly. The core range is led by the 'Corallian' and 'Culver' Classic Cuvées – both names of the chalk strata beneath the vineyard. Corallian is predominantly Chardonnay-driven, Culver led by Pinot Noir. At an outstanding price point you get two completely different styles of wine. Best of all, at the cellar door you can taste both and decide which one you prefer, and 'both' is a more than acceptable answer.

Corallian is slightly softer, Chardonnay-elegant, fresh and orchard fruit-driven upfront and the slightly more linear of the two, bottled at a touch lower pressure than big brand sparkling, and with hugely attractive developing stone-fruit roundness. Culver is more red fruit dominant and floral, with slightly richer, riper stone-fruit – both have such fine acidity and a touch of salinity that rounds out the wines seamlessly.

Completing the non-vintage trio is the rosé, which is usually around 50% Pinot Noir and the other half split between Meunier and Chardonnay, to a varying degree depending on season. Langham's is the best example I've seen of marrying both fruit-forward, easy-drinking and a richer, more complex style of rosé in one wine. It's really approachable upfront – fresh and appealing, but there's just so much to unpick too, with its incredible depth, structure and richness. Ever evolving and interesting, it's a very serious wine given the right situation, but just as good paired with a picnic in the park.

The 2018 vintage was ripe enough for Langham to experiment with some still wines; the wild ferment Jura-style Chardonnay has evolved into a savoury, fleshy and slightly smoky number that just gets better and better.

The touch of oxidation is so attractive and reminiscent of the Alpine region's style of precise fruit and texture, and its high-calibre wines, which have developed a cult following.

One of the most special moments on this entire journey was tasting Langham's 'Judy', a 2000-litre foudre vat of outstanding Chardonnay from the most desirable of the few prior vintages, blended solera-style since 2017. It was tasted still and easily good enough to be bottled and sold as such, but the vision is for it to be England's best Blanc de Blancs. It might see some slightly extended lees ageing – the aim across the range here is for this to provide a further complexity in flavour character. Bottling will be scarce and low in number, but however small, there will always be a proportion of that initial 2017 vintage in there – even if, as intended, Judy outlives all of us.

Both current and back-vintage release Blanc de Blancs add extra strings to a very strong bow, as does the sparkling 100% Meunier, in showcasing how incredibly expressive, flavoursome and brilliant this varietal can be in single varietal form. There's a still rosé and still red on the way too, even some Col Fondo that's exclusive to keg for restaurants. Tommy wanted to make a Saignée style rosé called 'Saignée West', which really needs to happen.

Aside from the incredible depth, complexity and sheer quality in probably Britain's best-value classic-method wines, what I like most of all about Langham is the people behind it: Tommy, Andy and Becky in the winery and building on the great work done by Olly Whitfield in the vineyard, plus the legend that is Fiona at the cellar door. From barn events and pizza oven catering to vineyard picnics and good old-fashioned tastings, there's much fun to be had, most of all it seems by those who work there, which reflects so evidently in the entire offering. If there is one producer this book inspires you to visit, or one range of wines to taste, let it be Langham.

English Oak Vineyard

@ENGLISHOAKVINEYARD

Flowers Drove, Lytchett Matravers, Poole, Dorset, BH16 6BX
https://www.englishoakvineyard.co.uk

What: Cellar door tasting and sales, weddings, corporate hire
Recommended wines: Chinkapin Rosé, San Gabriel Blanc de Blancs, Wainscot Blanc de Noirs

As a local vineyard to Rick Stein's Sandbanks restaurant, it's no surprise to see English Oak at the top of a pretty impressive wine list. What is now the vineyard was, however, fields of cattle, ponies and turnips back in 2006. But top-end sparkling wine is far tastier than a field full of turnips, as the saying goes, so Sarah and Andrew planted 16 acres to predominantly Pinot Noir and Chardonnay, along with 20% Pinot Meunier.

An eighteenth-century barn has become a brand-new tasting room and theatre-style visitor centre, backing directly onto the vineyard – the centre piece of which is a beautiful 350-year-old English oak tree.

Sarah, originally a horticulturist and Andrew, from a hotel and catering management background and most recently also computer sales, met when their respective career changes collided. Fairly confident their combined experience covered the growing and the selling parts of the wine process, as an indication of the quality they were striving for, they sought Dermot Sugure to do the making.

Not trying to hit volume, they're producing high-quality, classic-method sparkling wine, with low carbon output, that sells locally.

Early signs of life

It's a total philosophy encompassing the entire operation, based on a boutique scale of production, despite the hugely vintage-varied crop output, which was as low as 7 tonnes in 2012 and 2016, compared to a huge 87.5 tonnes – from the same vineyard – in 2018.

Focusing on personal relationships across a local customer base is the key to both their success and their reduction of 'wine miles'. Hosting staff from partner restaurants at the vineyard for wine training and food matching sessions, for example, in the solar energy-powered tasting room, drives this philosophy. As does Andrew himself doing the wine deliveries in an electric van.

On by the glass in popular restaurants is a good route to shifting some (recycled cardboard) boxes of great wine, but it's also brilliant exposure. It's a good example of most in the domestic scene who see carbon reduction as a total commitment rather than something that just happens in the vineyard or is used as a marketing tool. Whatever the offering at English Oak, be it tasting room sales, corporate away-days or weddings, everything goes back into wine, the primary focus, in itself based on quality fruit production.

Each vintage wine is named after a species of oak tree and crafted to express their own natural style and the year from which the grapes were picked. The 'Englemann Cuvée' is a slightly Chardonnay-dominant 'party starter' according to Andrew: zesty, floral and vibrant.

Chinkapin Rosé is a fantastically rich yet elegant wine, with soft red berries up front and developing into a slightly tangy, gamey style. There's a touch more depth than the Englemann thanks to the additional Pinot Noir – a brilliant option with duck and even richer meats, but equally great on its own. The San Gabriel and Wainscot offer

Storm-salvaged and sculptured

the Blanc de Blancs and Blanc de Noirs alternatives, produced in tiny quantities in only the best years, and completely different in style: delicate, creamy Chardonnay versus beautifully rich and rounded Pinot Noir.

English Oak are realising this potential for a great cellar door culture, all built on quality of product and wider offering that's genuinely conscious of their environmental contribution. Best of all, if you happen to be at that particular Sandbanks restaurant, the wine is still cheaper than the major label Champagne alternatives, and just so much better.

Little Waddon Vineyard

@LITTLEWADDONVINEYARD

....

Winter's Ln, Waddon, Weymouth DT3 4ER
https://littlewaddonvineyard.co.uk

What: Vineyard stays, glamping, tasting and picnics
Recommended wines: Regent, Coastal White, Col Fondo

Touring the vineyards of Britain, it's quite easy to be instantly rather taken with the places and people I've met for the first time. Few more so than the Priestman family and their 3 acres of biodynamic Seyval, Phoenix and Regent.

The site was originally planted in 2004; current custodians Karen and Simon first laid eyes on it in 2018 and knew instantly where their future lay. It's easy to see why, nestled in a gently sloping sun trap, among natural windbreaks, just a couple of miles from the coast.

It's a minimal intervention approach that means wild yeast ferments, and next to no additions in the winery, the team having farmed the vines biodynamically. The goal is an ecological self-sufficiency of the vineyard as a cohesive, interconnected living system; a regenerative approach that will leave this patch of land in a better place than when it was found. In terms of the wine, it gives a truer expression of place and vintage in comparison to vines treated with herbicides and pesticides, or fruit turned into wine with commercial yeast strains and added preservatives. If wines have personalities, these are the most honest you'll find.

In practice, this means a 'nettle-tea' preparation, which according to Simon 'stinks, but works well', as a natural means of putting nitrogen back into the soil – vital in the plant cycle. Planting garlic and lavender increases site biodiversity, improving soil structure, water retention properties and attracting more nutrients for the vines' root systems. Fertiliser of seaweed and sheep manure helps crop productivity naturally.

It's the biodynamic practice of following a planting calendar that depends upon certain astrological configurations, such as the lunar phase, that seems to raise the most eyebrows and 'can get a bit druid' according to Simon. Vines are pruned on a new moon, but that lunar pull draws up the cane sap, making them much easier to cut. Harvesting fruit, too, according to this calendar, is followed, but with a dose of pragmatism at times. It's all about quality of fruit, and it just so happens that natural, centuries-old methods are the best source, and much better for the land.

Seyval, Phoenix and Regent are particularly attractive to winemakers like Daniel Ham, who makes Little Waddon's wines in a style he likes to drink. The range delivers natural quality straight to hearts and open minds alike, and are to me everything wine should be: seasonally expressive of place and practice, interesting, thought-provoking and above all, great fun to drink.

Col Fondo is the traditional Italian natural re-fermentation process that pre-dates the tank method for producing Prosecco. There are references to it as far back as the ninth century. Little Waddon's Phoenix sees spontaneous secondary fermentation on natural yeast lees in the then-sealed bottle, that has no riddling, disgorgement or dosage process. It gives such fresh, crisp, vibrant and aromatic complexity in flavours of honeysuckle, peach and a slight nuttiness. It can be served to your choice of *limpido*, 'clear', delicately poured from bottle to give a clear sparkling wine, or *agitato*, 'shaken',

gently mixing residual lees and enzymes to give the wine the Col Fondo classico taste.

The Regent is beautifully light, which belies a nose of rich herbs and spice, combined with a striking colour, and it has you pre-empting a much fuller-bodied mouthfeel than gracefully appears. Though it's quite earthy, its mid-palate spice marries perfectly with the ultimate overall elegance.

This is a genuine live-in experience too, with copper baths and wood-fired hot tubs on offer as part of 'The Hide' shepherd's hut glamping set-up, where you can watch the sun set over the vines that produce some very special fruit. People, practice and place. Little Waddon, to me, is everything wine should be.

A perfect piece of Dorset

Bride Valley Vineyard

@BRIDEVALLEYWINE

Stable Cottage, Court House, Litton Cheney, Dorset, DT2 9AW
https://bridevalleyvineyard.com

What: Tours, tastings and cellar door sales
Recommended wines: Blanc de Blancs, Crémant, Chardonnay, Rosé

One of the wine world's greatest adventurers, according to Jancis Robinson, is Steven Spurrier, with his contribution to the international industry that could only be understated by his own modesty. A genuine life in wine that began in 1954, aged thirteen, when he tasted a 1908 Cockburn Port at the family home. He would go on to establish France's first private wine school, and become an educator, merchant, international judge and latterly author, columnist and eventually grower. Finally, he became an English winemaking pioneer, at his Bride Valley home and vineyard in Dorset.

I have never known anyone, in any field, to be so universally respected within the industry they work in as he; Decanter Man of the Year in 2017 and IWSC Honorary Chair and WSET Honorary President, to name a few accolades. Steven Spurrier will probably be most fondly remembered for a tasting he organised through his Parisian shop and wine academy on 24 May 1976, that became known as the judgement of Paris.

Ever a champion of the underdog, as North American wine very much was then, he sourced the best of them from California and invited France's top critics, all of whom attended, to compare against the best equivalents of Bordeaux and Burgundy. With concern of a pre-judgement

Stable doors beneath the cellar door at Bride Valley

Down in the valley…

in Paris, he decided all wines would be tasted blind. Chateau Montelena's 1973 Chardonnay from California, with a release price of $6.50, came top of the whites, with six of nine judges awarding it their highest score. Stag's Leap Wine Cellars '73 was the top red, outscoring Mouton-Rothschild, Montrose and Haut-Brion.

In 1987 Steven and Arabella Spurrier bought Litton Cheney farm in Dorset, a former home of Reynolds Stone, wood sculptor and designer of the Breaky Bottom label. Spurrier was still running his Paris Académie du Vin at the time, where he showed leading French wine critic Michel Bettane some of the farmland's chalk soil that he had brought over in his pocket. Bettane said it was clearly from the world's most famous sparkling wine region, and on discovering it was in fact that of Dorset, said he should plant a vineyard.[vii] Top

Chablis producer Michel Laroche was impressed with the Bride Valley site and recommended planting Chardonnay and other grapes from the Pinot family. Had it not been for the wet summer that year, Pinot Blanc and Auxerrois might have been chosen. In the early nineties, Spurrier blind-tasted what he picked as Grand Cru Blanc de Blancs Champagne, that turned out to be from Nyetimber, and, ever impressed with the wines of Ridgeview in East Sussex, the desire to plant grew stronger and the direction it would take was decided.

Among the rolling slopes of the Bride Valley farm, the initial plan was to plant 30 hectares and produce up to 100,000 bottles a year. Site analysis suggested there were 10 to 12 hectares that ticked all the boxes, and with vines sourced from Burgundy's premier nursery, across the winter of 2008–9, 2 hectares were planted.

Vineyard manager Graham leading the tasting in the Spurriers garden

There were up to 42,000 vines by 2017. The huge 85-tonne crop in 2018 was a good twenty over estimate, and some of the Chardonnay was just too ripe for a sparkling base wine, so 3500 bottles of still were made and are now long gone.

The initial idea was to produce just one wine, a single vintage brut. At that stage there was no interest in variation of style and Spurrier was even less motivated by building up a range of reserve wines and producing a non-vintage. Georges Legrand persuaded him otherwise, on portfolio range at least, with the reasoning that a single wine invites a yes or no answer as to whether the drinker likes it or not. With a variety of wines, it's a question of which is your favourite.[viii]

Well into his seventies, Steven Spurrier was still regularly travelling all around the world under various guises, but would always take with him, wherever he went, two bottles of Bride Valley Blanc de Blancs, that he saw as the very essence of his home vineyard. The rest of the Bride Valley team would later learn where in the world he was currently located as the orders for that wine started coming in.

Behind the stables in the family garden is where the tasting part of the tour takes place, and the cellar door above is Spurrier's 'wine room', where many of his words were penned.

It's sometimes important to put emotion aside when tasting wine from a qualitative point of view, but, fortunately for me, the Bride Valley wines are absolutely sensational. As it's the house tradition to leave with a couple of bottles of the Blanc de Blancs, that's what I did, but would have done anyway. 100% Chardonnay, released in the summer three years after harvest, having seen twenty-four months on lees. Delicate and slightly creamy, super long with that melt-in-the-mouth texture, you could do far worse than leave with a lot more than two.

The Dorset Crémant came about following the damp and cool 2015 vintage that produced a wine that was a touch high in acidity, so was blended with the 2016 to soften out, and eventually bottled at a lower pressure. This is a classic approach of the Crémant style; the wine is crisp and citrus fruit-driven with refreshing salinity. The EU were soon on the case, however, and said that they couldn't possibly call it Crémant, as that's a French winemaking term to signify the eight French regions (and one in Luxembourg) producing wine in the Champagne method, from outside that region. Bride Valley applied for a PDO (Protected Designation of Origin), quoting their Dorset Crémant in the same terms as Melton Mowbray pork pies and Cornish pasties, which was duly granted, and the EU were obliged to let them continue.

Ultimately, Bride Valley are likely to become known for their Chardonnay. Their still version is stainless steel-fermented and slightly fleshy in style, bright in approach but with just a hint of creamy roundness which comes through, getting better and better with air. There's the sparkling 'Rosé Bella', named after Mrs Spurrier, with a third of the still Pinot Noir seeing a short time in American oak, which adds brightness and a touch of depth to the lighter style.

In the trade in Sydney I always thought someone knew what they were talking about if they referenced or asked about Steven Spurrier. What he did in '76 particularly resonates with those from countries outside Europe, or regions out of the mainstream. For most, planting a vineyard usually sits at the front end of a career in wine. For Spurrier, establishing Bride Valley was his swansong in a career that spanned almost six decades, during which he did, and his impact still does, so much. If ever you were to raise a toast to everything he achieved along the way, the greatest tribute of all would be to do so with a glass of Bride Valley.

Mr Steven Spurrier
October 1941–March 2021

MELBURY VALE WINERY
@MVWINERY

Foots Hill, Cann, Shaftesbury, Dorset, SP7 0BW
https://mvwinery.co.uk

What: Winery tours, tastings, glamping, vineyard gigs, picnics and bakery
Recommended wines: 'Grace' Sparkling Seyval, 'Elegance' Bacchus

Surveyor Clare Pestell and her engineer brother Glynn bought 28 acres of dilapidated farmland in the Dorset hillside near Shaftesbury in 2003. Other than some derelict buildings which would be converted into a new home the only thing visible, without sitting on her brother's shoulders, was the six-foot-tall grass covering much of the land.

With help from family and friends, and ably assisted by sixteen-year-old Australian Cattle Dog Mowgli, the pair set about clearing the land on which they would initially plant a 4000-native-tree woodland. Partway through the restoration project, they set up a prisoner reintegration programme. Most humbling was a new arrival who took off his shoes and socks to feel the sensation of walking barefoot across grass for the first time in six years. It's amazing the things we take for granted.

2013 saw the completion of a stunning on-site winery built into the hillside. Split into two halves, the wet room is for winemaking and the dry side for storage and bottle ageing. A couple of locals did take some convincing, expecting another thatch, rather than wildflower meadow, and rainwater harvesting roof, but the finished product has inspired the planting of a further 5000 vines in the local area.

As well as cellar door sales, part of the vineyard has been converted into the new home of Vale

First rows in the ground at Melbury

Not exaclty like the local thatch… Melbury Vale's hillside winery

Bakery, which was at risk of ceasing operations after losing its former site during the pandemic. Susan runs the bakery, sings in the band that play gigs at the winery and helps out with the vineyard tours. The latter come with a great lunch of cheese, local bread – flour sourced from Cann Mill next door – and the best falafel Scotch egg I've ever eaten.

The vines sit in an undulating site of sun traps facing different directions, some on chalk, some sandy clay. One block of Pinot Noir is accompanied by Solaris, Rondo and Seyval Blanc, which is complemented by fruit sourced from a total of 10,000 local vines in standalone vineyards such as Winborne and at Corfe Castle.

A variety of either estate-grown grapes, or those arriving from local growers, allows Clare the flexibility to make a range of vintage expressive wines. Sometimes lower alcohol and acid levels will dictate lean wines that make a great base for sparkling such as the aptly named and Seyval-based 'Grace', which is gracefully bright, fresh and light, with a touch of lees richness from secondary fermentation in bottle.

The grape- and season-driven approach resulted in a sparkling red 'Col Fondo' in 2020. Grapes like Rondo are perfect for this lighter, more natural style of sparkling wine, and Melbury Vale's was so attractive to one London distributor, they took the entire production.

The wines are predominantly lighter and vibrant in style, such as with 'Elegance': a blend of Bacchus and Reichensteiner. Never more than 20% the blend, much of the elegant structure shines through from the Bacchus, the traditional Germanic variety providing some uplift and brightness. What with the bakery, Scotch eggs and the tunes to go with them, would you need any more reasons to return?

BLUESTONE

@BLUESTONEVINEYARDS

. . . .

Amesbury Road, Cholderton, Wiltshire, SP4 0EW
https://www.bluestonevineyards.co.uk

What: Vineyard, tours, tastings, rare breeds farm and petting Zoo, cellar door and tasting room
Recommended wines: Classic Cuvée, Cuvée Rosé

Welcome to Wiltshire, where the bluestones brought from Wales to form Stonehenge in around 2500BC also inspired the naming of one of the region's latest premium wine producers. A peacock wandering around the car park, kids playing with alpacas and plans to turn the soft play area into a winery: you definitely don't get this in Burgundy. Diversifying the McConnell family's rare breed conservation farm and petting zoo into a vineyard and winery might not be the classic route to take, but in seeing the vineyard and tasting the wine, you'll soon see why it works. They're fast becoming less famous for the pig races, and more so the outstanding classic-method sparkling wine.

Brothers Toby and Nat decided there was more to life than working on boats in the Med and as a scientist based in Birmingham, respectively. Instead, they decided they wanted to combine the family business with their love of the outdoors, science, and the potential to create and nurture something. The answer came during an archaeological dig unearthing a Norman roundhouse, adjacent to what is now the lower paddock vineyard. A friend of their uncle's, who just happened to have some winemaking experience in Champagne,

recognised the potential for Pinot Noir and Chardonnay-based sparkling wine, given the pure, solid chalk soil in front of him. The chalk reaches 90 metres down to the water line. Seeing that this was combined with a south-facing slope and several very positive results of independent soil analysis, the team decided to plant the first vines in 2016.

With a view to a potentially multi-generational future, regenerative agriculture is a major desire of theirs. They want to be constantly improving soil health, rather than degrading it. This will integrate the farm animals in with the vineyards, as mob grazing is an effective way to maintain the no till-seeded cover crop. Introducing multiple plants and herbs among the vines improves biodiversity, benefiting soil health as their roots draw in greater levels of minerals and nutrients, which are particularly beneficial to vine health and quality of resulting fruit.

Ultimately, the vineyard's aim is to have one holistic site that exists in harmony through self-competition, rather than human intervention. There is a long way to go to achieving this, but the overall drive is for this philosophy to cover not just the vineyard, but the winemaking and bottling side of things, and it is an inspirational outlook.

To have the winery on-site will not just cut down on transport but enable the team to own a truly boutique production, curating small batch examples of the finest vintage-driven parcels of fruit, something that is currently hindered by contract winemakers' minimum press volume requirements.

The current release is a wondrous blend, aged for fifty-one months on lees and drinking well-rounded and impressively fresh; a textbook classic method. Meeting Nat and Toby, seeing their vineyard, hearing their vision and tasting the quality of fruit they're already producing, excites me massively for what they have ahead of them.

I can't wait to see the cellar door and tasting room, the underground barrel room and winery and, most of all, the ever-developing bio-diverse vineyard and portfolio of exciting and varied wines, but to be honest, they pretty much had me at 'Pig Races'.

Bluestone boy band's debut album due out 2022

Nat, Toby and Jack at Bluestone Vineyards

OFFBEAT

@DANIEL__HAM

Salisbury, Wiltshire
https://offbeatwines.co.uk

What: Not open to the public; visits by appointment
Recommended wines: Field Notes 1, Field Notes 2, Field Notes 3, 369, Wild Juice Chase

Daniel Ham and wife Nicola discovered their love of wine through Otago's Pinot Noir, on return trips from the region's ski fields while living in Dunedin. To use the name of one of his wines, they went full circle, and now, in a converted barn at Hugo Stewart's Downton vineyard, sits Offbeat Winery.

A marine biologist by trade, but a creative by heart, Daniel came back home to the South West to become a winemaker at Langham Estate. Given the set-up and their position in the fast-growing English sparkling wine market, a very nice long career *in situ* was laid out in front of him. So, he left, to do his own thing.

This, in short, meant moving in a more natural wine direction, sourcing fruit from different, largely biodynamically farmed sites. Daniel's still making classic-method sparkling wine under contract, and with a bigger interest in the provenance of produce and eating nutritiously, the same applied to his drinking. He wanted to make the kind of wines he likes himself, because what's the point in making wines you don't want to drink?

These are expressive, 'hands-off' wines that let the fruit shine and reflect the place and season from which they came. Offbeat are champions of

2018 Offbeat 'Skinny Dip', Solaris fermented in amphora on skins for three months

organic and biodynamic viticulture, a natural and honest philosophy that is of course consistent in the winery, with fruit at the fore and human intervention kept to an absolute minimum.

I met Daniel washing his 1970s hand-built Coquard press, and what a piece of kit it was. Only fifty in the world, and it is one of twenty square versions, and had been in a cellar in Champagne for the best part of the last fifty years. The minimal-intervention winemaking approach marries the best of old and new, originally championing grapes like Solaris, Phoenix, Orion, Madeleine and Rondo. Recently, greater access to quality biodynamic fruit of more classical varieties has shifted the focus to Pinot Noir, Meunier, Pinot Blanc and Chardonnay. The Coquard press is a much more oxidative process than those inert versions favoured for large-scale winemaking. Through a process called vicinal diphenol cascade, which hasn't yet had a wine named after it, introducing juice to oxygen from the outset sets up a positive feedback loop, which makes the wine far more tolerant in later life, so there's less need for additional preservatives. Micro-oxygenation also aids the binding of short-chain tannins, softening mouthfeel in the resulting wine.

Letting the fruit develop naturally in ancient vessels like Daniel's Italian terracotta amphora was partly inspired by trips to Italy, Slovenia and Georgia, where a band of new-wave winemakers have reverted to the traditional Qvevri, as their ancestors did thousands of years ago. Natural methods were

The fifty-year-old restored Coquard press… what a piece of kit!

Daniel, Jarvis and their 800-litre terracotta amphora

the only way then, and also the only way you could farm continuously for that long. It is a genuinely sustainable approach, because to be able to farm for a long time has to mean you're working with the land, rather than against it.

As Daniel says, 'What's to say everything we've learned over the last fifty years is the right way to do things?' It also means there's a better chance of fixing things, rather than being confronted with electronic error messages. Individual oak barrels might be good for twenty years, if looked after, but amphorae can be passed down through generations.

Producing classic-method sparkling wine by using fermenting juice from a current vintage as the tirage – the catalyst for secondary fermentation in bottle – is another, much more natural method. It is inspired by a few Grower Champagnes that, unlike the major houses, represent no interest in mass production or a regular style year after year. It's much less predictable or consistent, but it's a great example of the opportunity here in England, to follow the paths we choose rather than those passed down through the generations. Most of all, it's reflective of site and season, rather than using conventional and commercial methods.

This hands-off, natural approach is, in a reverse sort of way, a great reflection of Daniel's fingerprint. I'm in awe of this courageous, instinctive and challenging approach, with its understanding of process and in going against the natural human trait to want to constantly check and change things, rather than leave things be. These new wave winemakers are trailblazers in their own way. Production so limited, it's all on allocation – which is the industry's way of sharing it around as best as possible, because it's all sold before it's even released. So, you'll need to be quick, and there's likely to be an ever-changing array of wines every year.

Sometimes you taste wines so exciting you wish you could look into the future and taste them in twenty years' time. Daniel is a fine example of a winemaker I've met who I can't wait to see in twenty years' time too, to see all that he will have achieved and taste the kind of wines he's making with two decades' extra experience. However you refer to these wines, they represent possibly the most exciting future in the wine world. There is also a massive opportunity to do what craft beer has done, but become ten times tastier and mean so much more than good booze and good labels. They can actually make a stand environmentally, showcase regenerative farming and deliver an enormously important message to a vast audience via the medium of the popularity of wine. Aside from what natural wine can represent holistically, it can be such a great expression of grape, site, season and vision or fingerprint, which is the absolute epitome of wine. Daniel's are perhaps our greatest example; they're wines that are thought-provoking, conversation-generating and above all interesting and fun to drink, which is what wine should be. Natural and hands-off, Offbeat is wonderfully and absolutely on the pulse.

A wander among the vines with one of England's most engaging winemakers

Domaine Hugo

@DOMAINE.HUGO

....

Salisbury, Wiltshire
https://www.domainehugo.co.uk

What: Open by appointment only
Recommended wines: Domaine Hugo, Botley's Col Fondo

Growing up, Hugo Stewart spent many a weekend on his grandmother's Botley's Farm in Wiltshire. When he took what he thought was to be a year out in 2002, his friend Paul Old came to visit him in Corbières, and, intrigued by the workings of a vineyard, they set up Les Clos Perdus. Together they bought 20 hectares of existing vines, some over a hundred years old, from which they made biodynamic wine together for over a decade.

The driving force behind this natural approach is that Hugo wants as little as possible to intervene between soil and glass. From his point of view, using the same fertilisers, yeast strains and styles as everyone else defeats the object of striving for a terroir-centric approach in the vineyard. There's a sameness to it as a result, and Hugo wants his wine to be unique, distinctive and expressive. If the winemaking is more guided than hands-on, the result is the truest expression of site and season. Not working with supermarkets, who ultimately want a consistent product, is ideal, because in this marginal climate, much greater vintage variation leads to different wines each year, which is more interesting for both maker and drinker.

Returning home in 2015 he saw the potential for Botley's Farm's south-facing chalk downland, planting 4500 classic Champagne varietal vines a year later. In terms of the priority list at Domaine Hugo, it's quality wine first, organic and biodynamics second. As Hugo explains, so much of the biodynamic approach is incredibly practical. Pruning happens on a full moon, which lets people confuse themselves in all sorts of directions, but the gravitational pull on the ocean is fairly well-accepted. The same thing happens in a vine: moisture is drawn up it, pushing out any possible infection when the vine is pruned. Hugo says: 'You can't ignore the moon, especially as a plant is 90% water.'

Followed by additional plantings of Meunier and Pinot Gris, the beauty of all four varietals is down to the fact that if season ripeness dictates, they can produce great still wines as well as sparkling.

In 2018 Hugo took his first vintage to Langham winery, where the winemaker was Daniel Ham. Hugo's second winemaking partnership became a reality and together they designed and built the winery where both Domaine Hugo and Daniel's Offbeat wines are made. Daniel says they're both people who like to eat nutritiously and live healthily and sustainably, and that's exactly the approach they take to both drinking and making wine.

The first wines were released in 2021. 'Hugo' is a blend of all four grapes: Chardonnay, Pinot Noir, Meunier and Pinot Gris from the 2018 vintage and made by Daniel at Langham as a classic-method sparkling. It is so light, fresh and full of white flowers and peach, like the best Bellini you ever drank but with a touch of richness and additional complexity to keep it far more interesting.

The plan is for this wine to always be a field blend, with nature dictating the percentages.

2019's 'Botley's' is again a blend of all four, but one that went down a slightly different route. Inspired by JP Rietsch, some of the 2019 pressings were held back for a Col Fondo sparkling, to which was added some of the fermenting must from 2020, which sparked a secondary fermentation of the 2019 juice. This is real knife-edge winemaking, but from taking risks comes something special. Which, as Hugo says, is 'Both where the excitement and the beauty lie.'

From Corbières to Wiltshire: Hugo Stewart's Domaine Hugo Vineyard at Botley's Farm

MAUD HEATH VINEYARD

@MAUDHEATHWINES

Wick Bridge Farm, Wick Hill, Bremhill, Calne, Wiltshire, SN11 9LQ
https://www.maudheathvineyard.co.uk

What: Cellar door sales and tours by appointment
Recommended wines: Tytherton Red, Unoaked Chardonnay

Though you don't hear too much of the profession these days, the widow 'Maud Heath' was an eggler. Past the village of Bremhill and up to the market town of Chippenham she would tread to sell her bounty of eggs through the middle of the fifteenth century. On her death in 1474, she promised the sum of £8 a year forever, a staggering amount of money, founding a trust to build and maintain a causeway over the flood plain of the river Avon along her route. The original parchment, the sixty-four-arched raised path and the trust maintaining it all, still exist.

Overlooking the causeway in Bremhill, originally planted in 2006, is Maud Heath Vineyard. Dominic Bateman now has 6 acres of Pinot Noir, Meunier, Chardonnay, Bacchus and Rondo all in the ground across 6 acres of a natural ridge.

The 'Tytherton Red' is a blend slightly favouring Pinot Noir over Rondo, pending vintage variation. Up to six months in three- to five-year-old oak barrels adds a touch of depth and richness to the vibrant and approachable red. I love the hint of spice Rondo brings; married with light and bright Pinot, there's fragrance and elegance. A great example of a blend that works so well, it's a surprise not to see more of it.

The Chardonnay production to date has been motivated by a 'Chablis style', though the greatest wines of that region see some time in oak, the majority of which is fermented in stainless steel, with a focus on the crisp acidity. Maud Heath takes the latter approach, with a zingy little number that goes through no malolactic to keep the focus on the lighter, fresher style.

It's tucked away and has a super small-scale production, but Maud Heath's approach is as solid and as interesting as the history of the area it represents.

Barrel selection committee

Maud Heath reds are especially worth keeping an eye out for

Quoins Organic Vineyard

Little Ashley, Bradford-on-Avon, Wiltshire, BA15 2PW
https://www.quoinsvineyard.co.uk

What: Tours, tasting and cellar door sales
Recommended wines: Orion, Rosé

In 2002 Alan Chubb bought a 3-acre corner of a large, muddy field in Little Ashley, near Bradford-on-Avon. Previously, he had been travelling the world, advising others on growing a variety of tree crops – most recently oranges in Costa Rica. As a long-time champion of organic farming, he decided to see if he could succeed in organic viticulture himself, though in the early 2000s there were few other vineyards, fewer still following organic practices.

The name of the vineyard is pronounced 'coins', as a reference to the corner stones of a brick or stone wall, in this instance specifically referring to Alan's home on the end of a row. The desire was to produce quality wines to be proud of.

Alan says they also needed to turn a profit but that primarily: 'It was to be a family place, where we could have parties and barbecues, and where the children could earn some pocket money by helping out. We wanted to work in harmony with nature, using organic methods and creating a rich haven for wildlife.' The roe deer among the vines when I visited pay testament to that approach, as do the local sheep who mob graze the vineyard in the winter. Clover and dandelions growing naturally among the vines also add to the site's vast biodiversity.

Disease-resistant varietals Orion, Madeleine and Rondo were planted, and the first vintage was in 2005 and by 2013 the wines were being made at Britain's oldest organic vineyard, Sedlescombe in Kent. Producing between 3000 and 4000 bottles annually, they introduced a rosé to the range, made from the first pressings of the Rondo, to go with the other three single-varietal wines.

In 2019, following the sale of Sedlescombe, the 'Orion' was made by the hugely experienced Litmus in Surrey, and the rosé by Ben Wallgate at Tillingham near Rye. A touch of Madeleine was blended into the Rondo to give a lifted, brighter blush style with no added sulphur.

Alan is still passionately championing the practices which inspired him to produce quality fruit in the first place. The purity of fruit in the wines is absolutely good enough reason to visit, but as ever, the practices in place to create them are as thought-provoking and as interesting as the products themselves.

Autumn visitor to Quoins vineyard near Bradford-on-Avon

BOW-IN-THE-CLOUD VINEYARD

@BOWINTHECLOUDVINEYARD

. . . .

Noah's Ark, Garsdon, Malmesbury, Wiltshire, SN16 9NS
https://www.bowinthecloud.co.uk

What: Vineyard tours and tastings by special request
Recommended wines: Sparkling Seyval, Bacchus, Schönburger

On the outskirts of Malmesbury is 'Noah's Ark', the Willingale family's farmhouse and vineyard. A pretty apt name, given that a pair of vines made their way aboard the biblical version. Sophie Willingale now runs Bow-in-the-Cloud, organically farming an acre each of Bacchus, Seyval Blanc and Schönburger.

Following a career in the navy, her late father, Keith Willingale, purchased this special three-acre parcel of land in 1992. He wanted a retirement project that would keep him active, outside and among nature, though swiftly realised he was about 200 acres short of returning a profit via conventional farming.

Keith 'did a couple of courses' and decided growing wine grapes was for him. It was a good choice and a courageous one, especially given the early-nineties scale of the domestic industry, dwarfed by today's area under vine. The vineyard is surrounded by clay but sits on a little patch of sought-after Comanche and limestone. Initially intending to merely share the fruits of his labour with friends, Keith was soon at the local farmers' markets, making new pals throughout his retirement in the process. I love the connection these markets have between local produce, community and people like Sophie, who has

Cloud Nine

Sophie working the Cirencester markets

been behind the stall for the last fifteen years.

In at the deep end of the record-breaking and bumper 2018 vintage, Sophie – working alongside Keith's wife Esther – has taken over Keith's project and passion, merging both business and vine management. 'It became apparent very early on that the only way we could possibly survive was through a radical business rethink and relying on the support of the local community, which, in many cases, didn't know we existed. What we want to achieve is local people knowing who we are, what our values are, what our product is like and for them to be proud of us.'

There's plenty to be proud of, too. The sparkling Seyval shows off all that natural exuberance, freshness and acidity, and is ageing so well; at five years old, there is still so much time left to continue to do so. The still Bacchus is expressive and, although not down the super floral path taken by some, it is more refined and rounded than all-out fragrance. I

was delighted with the Schönburger – not a grape variety you're likely to see on the supermarket shelf anytime soon and all the more interesting as a result.

Producing around 1000 bottles across all three varietals annually, this is a very local product, but not only for local people – if you can get there quick enough, that is.

What I admire most about Bow-in-the-Cloud is not the quality of fruit or the strong sense of locality. Nor is it the emphasis on farming organically, or soil and wildlife welfare, though all are hugely important. What stands out is Sophie's adaptability while retaining a strong sense of the winery's quarter-century history, as she continues her father's legacy – from the vineyard where she has now planted Pinot Noir, something Keith always dreamt of, to the markets where she will carry on selling wine and making friends, just as he always did.

113

WALES

Gwlad beirdd a chantorion, enwogion o fri
Land of poets and singers, and people of stature
— 'Mae Hen Wlad Fy Nhadau'/'Land of My Fathers', Evan James

WHITE CASTLE

White Castle Vineyard
@WELSHWINES

Llanvetherine, Monmouthshire, NP7 8RA
https://whitecastlevineyard.com

What: Tours, cellar door tasting and sales Friday, Saturday and Sundays
Recommended wines: Siegerrebe, Regent, Pinot Noir

Wales, or 'Cymru' in Welsh, truly is a land of poets, singers and many people of stature who have made their mark in the wider world. Five of the first six presidents of the United States came from Welsh heritage, and Sir George Everest, former Surveyor General of India, after which Mount Everest is named was born in Crickhowell, Monmouthshire, in 1790.

The incredible Welsh language has also given us the word *hiraeth*. Much like 'terroir', there's no direct English translation, but it is best summarised as meaning a 'sense of place'; an almost nostalgic longing for home, for its traditions and culture, for the good old days. There is so much *hiraeth* in wine, which in itself is a great expression of place and the people who make that place so great – either those who make wine or those we share it with, celebrating good times, good days, good people and memories of good times.

Abergavenny couple Nicola and Robb Merchant bought the land that is now White Castle Vineyard in 1993. The dilapidated farm and 12-acre holding was up for auction and Robb, intrigued rather than seriously interested, wandered down to peer over the gate. When it didn't make the guide price, he called Nicola and told her to bring the cheque book. Two weeks later they received a letter from the local council, saying the sixteenth-

Robb Merchant at White Castle Vineyard

century barn that came with it was Grade II listed and therefore protected from modernisation.

Robb had been attracted to a job as a postman because it meant he could start early, finish early, and farm all afternoon. At that time the plan was to turn the farm into a wood yard, but Nicola's dream of a vineyard – which would grow to become Robb's obsession – only came to fruition in 2008. An adjoining, south-facing plot of land became available, and, following soil analysis, was planted with 4000 vines in 2009.

Knowing that competing with the supermarkets as a boutique producer was out of the question, they decided the way to go was via making high-class wines that are attractive to discerning drinkers and premium restaurants alike. With the knowledge that Pinot Noir and Chardonnay-based sparkling wines were a major focus for many British producers, including neighbours Ancre Hill, Robb and Nicola wanted to provide a point of difference and focus on still wines – primarily reds, if possible.

The unique site, based on sandstone soil, makes the ripening of Regent, Rondo and Pinot Noir – as well as the white grapes Siegerrebe and 2010's Seyval plantings – more than possible. Even if Robb had set out to source a local site specifically for a vineyard, I'm not sure he could have done any better than this place.

The prevailing weather comes from the South West, usually breaking over the Brecon Beacons or being diverted and depositing on Cardiff. Much drier than Glamorgan, their location is further inland and therefore warmer. You can feel the heat radiating up from the earth in the early days of summer. That wakes the vines up as soon as the warmth comes, so frost risk is a factor, and took out 70% of production in 2020. Everything produced under the White Castle label, however, will be estate-grown, even if that means in some years there's little or even no produce. The entire philosophy resonates on three main facets: provenance, integrity and quality.

Siegerrebe is wonderfully true to its part Gewürtz parentage – tropical melon, pineapple and signature lychee, but bone dry. Their Regent is all damsons and crunchy summer fruit; soft and velvety, and long with great depth and structure. White Castle's Pinot Noir – from Précoce – is one of those wines that was picked up across the national press, and I'm still fielding questions about it from all over the world. Deservedly so: a super expression of site ripeness, bright and exuberant fruit, softened slightly thanks to some old barrel time. Long and classy, it's all Abergavenny.

The production stays true to the quality-first approach that drew Robb to France's Loire Valley in 2018, armed with decades of zeroed-in climate data courtesy of the Institute of Biological, Environmental and Rural Sciences. Comparing the same weather information from specific sites in Reuilly, Quincy and Menetou-Salon, the hills around White Castle are increasingly similar. The mean temperature here tracks about 1 degree Celsius less than the average in the Loire, which has increased by more than that deficit in the last thirty years. Site, slope and soil permitting, there's no reason why White Castle can't ripen in the 2020s to the same degree as parts of the Loire did in the eighties and nineties.

Robb returned to France the following April, with soil samples in tow, and at a wine fair there discovered his love of Chinon's signature red grape, Cabernet Franc. So, in 2019, the slopes of Monmouthshire were planted with 1000 vines of the variety along with some more Pinot Noir.

Provenance, integrity, quality. Three important words, but only words, until they're given some meaning. Robb and Nicola do so gallantly, with humility and willingness to share their experience and vast expertise in a place as beautiful as it is capable of providing something amazing, and perhaps their most exciting results are yet to come.

Velfrey Vineyard

@VELFREYVINEYARD

Plas y Coed, Velfrey Road, Lampeter Velfrey, Pembrokeshire, SA34 0RA
https://www.velfreyvineyard.com

What: Cellar door tastings, sales and vineyard tours
Recommended wines: 'Velfrey' non-vintage and 'Velfrey' vintage

When self-employed publishers Fiona and husband Andy Mounsey were running a business with no geographical restrictions, they found the coast calling to them in 2014. Andy had visited Pembrokeshire as a child and took away with him fond memories, so they returned, initially without plans for a vineyard. Clearing the 'jungle' – a few acres of plot behind the farmhouse – was an investment in itself. Once complete, a shepherd's life brought twenty sheep, and with them the reality of the paraphernalia that would be involved. Fiona, Andy and son Ryan decided wine was a far tastier path to tread, in part thanks to Amanda at the nearby Jabajak vineyard, fifteen minutes up the road.

They employed the services of British viticulture royalty, Stephen Skelton, having read his introduction to commercial viticulture book (though the first chapter is basically every reason you shouldn't start a vineyard). Having made it to chapter two, Andy reached the crucial stage of site selection, but already had one chosen. Velfrey sits at 63 metres above sea level, 6 miles from the coast, gently sloping, almost due south, with a natural windbreak protecting the vines on three sides. Andy found himself wondering if his mind was seeing what he wanted it to as things fell into place and the vineyard dream became a reality.

A troubling element for Andy was where to put the fruiting wire: higher up and easier to tend at harvest, as recommended by a few people, or nearer the ground, closer to reflective soil heat, but potentially more susceptible to ground frost. Stephen's advice was pretty straightforward: 'The vines don't care about your back.' Lower trellis it was; close to the sea and its coastal breeze, which to a certain extent mitigates the threat of frost. Losing a few degrees as a result of the prevailing wind makes that heat emanating up from the soil all the more important.

With inspiration from a Burgundian brother-in-law, and a love of the wine from its many outstanding regions, Velfrey set out to specialise in one or two things – specifically in the realm of sparkling – rather than try to be all things to everyone. Which, along with the chalk soil, led to Pinot Noir and, in part motivated by Ancre Hill's version, meant Seyval got the nod as well.

Velfrey's first vintage was 2018, and just one wine was made, with a proportion of bought-in Chardonnay. This will form a regular release with increasing years' reserve wine, leaning toward a consistent house-style approach. The 2019 is an almost equal blend of Pinot Noir and Seyval, and is a classic vintage style; an equally great tribute to this awesome blend. It's fresh and approachable but seriously classy, and the Pinot Noir adds great depth, structure and red fruit weight. Some years will be lower in volume, and there will be greater vintage variation, but the two wines in the core range perfectly complement one another. There are also 500 hand-planted Solaris vines at the south-eastern edge of the vineyard, which may become an interesting made-on-site project – in 2021 some fruit was left on the vines for a late-harvest experiment.

The cellar door tasting room was delivered on a flatbed in two parts – quite a sight for the villagers, almost taking out a couple of telegraph poles enroute. Positioned at the northern end of the vineyard, it provides the perfect place to look out over the vines and enjoy a few glasses of Velfrey's finest. From here it's clear to see how well-suited this site is for vines, and you can taste what a good job the Mounseys have done in expressing it.

Golden hour at Velfrey in Pembrokeshire

Parva Farm Vineyard

Main Road, Tintern, Chepstow, Monmouthshire, NP16 6SQ
http://www.parvafarm.com

What: Tours, tastings, cellar door sales
Recommended wines: Ty Coch, Autumn Gold late-harvest Bacchus

The Wye Valley offers an amazing drive, winding its way up through Monmouthshire. At the southern end, in the village of Tintern, is Parva Farm Vineyard. Looking out over the river and village below, the Anglo-Welsh border follows the path of the snaking river, so that at the top of the vineyard you can see from Wales, into England, over the far river bank and back into Wales again. The view also takes in the historic Tintern Abbey, established in 1131, as well as a great riverside pub, The Wild Hare.

From Wales, over the River Wye into England, and back into Wales again

It's believed the Romans planted a vineyard on the site that is now Parva Farm Vineyard. The steep, sun-exposed slope is almost perfect for vine-growing, but one of the few in the area that's south-facing. The stone culverts built around a natural spring are classic Roman examples, supporting this theory. Monks from the Abbey would have almost certainly cultivated the land for grape production and, standing here among the vines, it's easy to see why.

The beginnings of the vineyard are almost as interesting as the land's historical past. Martin and Gay Rogers planted seventeen varietals in 1979, establishing Wales's oldest still-existing vineyard. Planting 1 hectare of Monmouthshire hillside to vines cannot have been an obvious thing to do, maverick even, but having travelled

'79-planted Monmouthshire slopes

around Germany it's likely that Rogers brought back a lot of what he saw to experiment with.

By 1996, however, when Judith and Colin Dudley bought the property, much of the estate had run into disrepair. The farmhouse and 60 acres of adjoining land was initially purchased for sheep, horses and breeding-stock Hereford cattle, though the couple of acres of vines were still very much alive. After several years of viti-rehab, the couple's first decent crop came along in 2001 and today, thanks to some additional plantings, it is still growing seventeen varietals across its 1 hectare. About 2000 Bacchus vines account for almost half of the vines in the ground, along with original Müller-Thurgau, Seyval Blanc and the Pinot Noir planted back in 1979 – making it some of the oldest in Britain. The one- and two-row plots of Kernling, Huxelrebe, Ehrenfelser, Reichensteiner and the rest are almost a museum-like tribute to those late-seventies days and the ancient history of the site, combined with the twentieth-century British viticulture industry as a whole.

As vines get older, generally their roots surge deeper, their yields reduce and their crop quality increases. Most of the Pinot Noir vines in the ground in Britain have been planted since 2010. Parva Farm's Pinot Noir is still a varietal for the warmer years, and currently blended into their 'Ty Coch' red, but the potential for these vines planted in the seventies in the coming years of increased warmth is staggering. Look out for single varietal Parva Farm Pinot Noir in the near future.

The vineyard is now under the stewardship of David Morris, son of Richard and Joy of Ancre Hill. Judith and Colin still run the cellar door at Parva Farm, with tastings and tours – you can wander back into the past in this incredible location. As custodians of this great site that looked as if it was about to run its course when they arrived here in the mid-nineties, the duo have done an amazing job in curating a path for its history to continue.

Vineyard crew at Parva Farm

Judith among her museum of vines in the parish of Tintern Parva

PANT DU

Caenarfon, Snowdonia
County Road, Penygroes, Caernarfon, Gwynedd, LL54 6HE
https://www.pantdu.co.uk

What: Tours, tastings, café and shop
Recommended wines: Gwin Coch (red), Gwin Gwyn (white)

Yr Wyddfa, meaning 'tomb' or 'monument', is known in English as Mount Snowdon. It is Wales's highest peak, and stands at 1085 metres tall. As legend has it, the mountain is a tomb of Rhita Gawr, a king-slaying ogre. Famous for apparently making clocks from the beards of those slain, the ogre's time was up when King Arthur supposedly climbed the mountain and killed him. Odd that a seemingly punctual, king-killing ogre had a passion for clock-making, when you think about it, but in the early 2000s, planting Pinot Noir and Sauvignon Blanc in the foothills of the mountain would have seemed almost as bizarre.

Not to Richard and Iola Huws, who transformed the slopes of the Dyffryn Nantlle valley in 2007, planting 9 acres of vines and twice that to cider apple trees. This special site is built on its pre-Cambrian rocks, making the soil here at least 541 million years old. Geologist Professor Richard Selley predicts that if the current global warming continues on the same path, Snowdonia will be ripening Pinot Noir by 2080.[ix] Well, it's happening already to a certain extent: Pant Du – pronounced 'pant dee' – have the early-ripening Pinot Noir Précoce in the ground. Largely due to the pre-historic rocks' heat-retention capability and the radiation of their warmth into those vine roots, it is possible. Crucially for Pant Du, the surrounding

Remarkable depth for the coolest end of a cool climate

122

mountains make theirs one of the driest spots in North Wales, maximising every minute of ripening potential through conducive soils.

There's even some traditional clone Pinot Noir, in part with a view to the future potential from the increasingly temperate slopes of the Nantlle Valley. As well as Sauvignon Blanc – another varietal you wouldn't necessarily associate with the cooler end of a cool climate – and Précoce, Seyval, Siegerrebe and Rondo are also planted. The Huws also produce five different ciders, honey (thanks to the bees transferring pollen between the apple trees) and, thanks to the rock formation beneath, perfectly pure spring water.

Pant Du are also Wales's first solar-powered vineyard, and aim to become fully self-sustainable. Two bore holes supply the water required for irrigation, drinking and cider production, and the forty-four solar panels on the south-facing roof of the café provide all the electricity required to power the equipment and buildings, and charge the electric car used for deliveries.

The wines are really well-made, soft and subtle – the Gwin Coch (red wine) especially. It's a blend of both Pinot Noir and Rondo, and there's a hint of spice to it that matches a suggestion of depth and attractive berry fruit composition. It's great value, and you couldn't get a better spot to enjoy them, too. Pant Du is 10 miles from the Snowdon summit, so if you're heading that way, do the amazing Mountain Rescue teams a favour by planning it properly and not calling them out. If the weather's good, avoid the Llanberis Path, it's the least interesting and the most popular. The Pig's Track from the car park at Pen-Y-Pass is much better. Just watch out for the ogre.

Vines at Pant Du, with a backdrop of Snowdonia National Park

Gwinllan Conwy Vineyard

@CONWYVINEYARD

Y Gwinwydd, Llangwstenin, Conwy, LL31 9JF
https://gwinllanconwy.co.uk

What: Vineyard tours, tastings and cellar door sales
Recommended wines: Period Sparkling Solaris, Regent Rosé

There are far worse places to be than sitting outside Dylan's restaurant in Criccieth, looking out over the sea and the thirteenth-century castle and tucking into an exceptional seafood platter. For those non-native Welsh speakers among us, there is a difficulty in pronouncing the wine you're ordering here, but the absolute stand-out fixture on the wine list is the fantastic Pefriog ('sparkling') Solaris from Gwinllan Conwy Vineyard. It's just super bright and, with tropical flavours shining through, it's great to pair with succulent king prawns.

Inspired by a shared passion for wine, Charlotte and Colin Bennett planted 300 vines in 2012 initially, with additional plantings taking the total to 3000 vines across 3 acres, with a further 3 acres under vine at Dwyran on Anglesey. Ortega and Phoenix accompanied Solaris to go with the cool climate red grape Rondo. Taking initiative from the increasingly suitable climate, they planted Pinot Noir and Chardonnay ahead of their initial crop from these vines in 2021. Ripening the Burgundian varietals on the north coast of Wales is a challenge, but there's a very specific set of conditions that makes this possible.

You can't really miss the slate in North Wales, which, combined with shale underneath the vines make for great drainage and heat retention. Thanks to the foehn effect (which is, in short, a

There are few finer spots in all of Britain

124

change from wet and cold conditions on one side of a mountain to warmer and drier on the other), the vines benefit from a long ripening season.

As well as the sparkling Solaris, there's a still version, a lively Regent rosé and oak-aged Rondo, plus a super easy-drinking 'Pydew' from Ortega and Phoenix. The latter is especially great with local restaurant Dylan's scallops: I honestly never imagined I would be sitting at a restaurant in North Wales marvelling at the local wine selection. But here I am, and I'm definitely coming back for more.

One of two great examples of Solaris by Gwinllan Conwy

JABAJAK
@JABAJAKVINEYARD

Banc Y Llain Llanboidy Road, Whitland, SA34 0ED
https://jabajak.co.uk

What: Cellar door sales, tastings, restaurant and stays
Recommended wines: Welsh Blush Sparkling Rosé, Jabajak White

Jabajak is an acronym for Julian, Amanda, Buddug and Joanna, Alexandra and Katie – the family at the heart of the vineyard, restaurant and boutique hotel. Amanda worked in the fashion and cloth industry and eventually moved to Morocco, before being drawn back home to West Wales. With no job to come back to, she bought a dilapidated farmhouse and a few outbuildings along with some empty fields.

Amanda's nan – who lived in the house next door – inspired her to open a restaurant based on serving local produce and seasonal dishes. The main farmhouse at Jabajak has it written into the deeds that it must always remain painted white, and as such lays claim to a slightly bigger, slightly more famous home…

As mentioned previously, five of the first six US presidents were of Welsh heritage, and the second and sixth – both called John Adams – were descended from a yeoman farmer from Llanboidy: David Adams. He grew up as a farmer on the drovers' estate at Banc-y-Llain, now Jabajak. They referred to the 'White House' on the hill as a place where legislation and governance for all the tenant farmers was administered from. Emigrating to the Americas, David Adams's grandson became the first president to reside in what we know today as the White House, and the first to refer to the

Jabajak vines planted in the heat-reflecting bluestone slate

building by this name, a place where governance was also administered, albeit on a slightly larger scale. It is seemingly possible therefore that the current president of the US resides in a place named after a humble Pembrokeshire farmhouse.

With her empty fields, Amanda was at a bit of a loss with what to do with them. Llamas and alpacas seemed to be the on-trend, slightly left-field option of the day, which Amanda considered. But then she thought, why not work with something she was genuinely passionate about? Like wine.

So, in 2004 Jabajak planted Phoenix and Seyval, followed by Rondo and Pinot Noir, on the south-facing slopes and bluestone slate. Best described by that Welsh word 'hiraeth', this nostalgic pride of home is a huge motivation behind the style of wine produced here, albeit by Three Choirs in Gloucestershire. The wines are super pure, bright and fresh; Jabajak white is a blend of Phoenix and Seyval, fermented in steel to retain freshness. It's delicate, crisp and refreshing meets slightly riper, more tropical fruit from the Phoenix.

The 'Welsh Blush' Sparkling Brut is the flagship wine, however: a blend of Seyval, Phoenix and Rondo, and super approachable and light in colour and weight. A stellar review from Oz Clarke sits framed in a glass cabinet in the bar – the bar itself a pretty good place to start an evening at Jabajak.

Sitting on the veranda outside the taverna-style restaurant in the late summer sun, you could almost be in Portugal. Add to this a very Welsh sense of relaxation so prominent around family-run food and wine establishments, and people so welcoming and friendly – with such an appetite for good tales. The nation is complete with its claims to the leader of the free world, and now its own wine.

The other White House, at Jabajak vineyard

127

The Sugar Loaf Vineyards

@SUGARLOAFVINEYARD

Pentre Lane, Abergavenny, NP7 7LA
https://sugarloafvineyards.co.uk

What: Cellar door sales, tours, tastings and restaurant
Recommended wines: Madeleine Maes, Deri Coch

The Sugar Loaf Vineyards' 5 acres of vines sit in the beautiful Brecon Beacons National Park, just outside Abergavenny. Up the winding single track lanes the vineyard, dissected by the stream winding its way down through the site, opens out offering awesome views of Sugarloaf Mountain opposite.

Family-owned and operated, and growing seven varietals, the vineyard has a pretty relaxed offering. There are self-guided walking routes through the vines and an often busy café kitchen and shop. The cheese platters go down pretty well with a tasting flight of four wines.

'Calon Lân' wins the award for the wine with the most Welsh name. It's the title of one of Britain's greatest hymns, and is also the label of Sugar Loaf's Reichensteiner. Crisp and long, its zesty acidity makes it a good opener, softening out slightly with a bit of bottle age – not that I would be putting it away for too long. 'Madeleine Mae' is more lifted and brighter in fruit structure, as you might expect given its varietal, but equally approachable. The Abergavenny medium-dry blend retains a touch of natural sugar, though it is more off-dry than genuinely sweet. Slightly honeyed, it's a blend of Seyval, Madeleine and Reichensteiner. Sugar Loaf blush blends Regent and Seyval, continuing the easy drinking theme, but with just a bit of added structure from the Regent – which also gets a run with some Rondo for the red offering, 'Deri Coch', meaning oaked red. This has some depth and richness too: bright, dark cherries up front and maintains that approachability, a hallmark of the entire range.

At the foothills of Sugar Loaf Mountain

Spring cover cropping

ANCRE HILL ESTATES
@ANCREHILL

Monmouth, NP25 5HS
https://www.ancrehillestates.co.uk

What: Cellar door sales, tours and tastings
Recommended wines: Blanc de Blancs, Blanc de Noirs, Pet-Nat, Orange Albariño

Richard and Joy Morris, together with son David, planted their first vineyard in 2006 on south-facing slopes surrounding their house near Monmouth. Today they're growing Chardonnay, Pinot Noir, Triomphe and – fascinatingly – Albariño.

Even more impressive is the Morris family's commitment to organic viticulture on their 12-hectare home vineyard. In 2011 they converted to biodynamic practices. 2016 and 2017 saw an additional 20 acres in the ground just up the road, planted exclusively to the big three sparkling varietals. The transition in the winery – itself probably the world's largest straw bale building at 4000 cubic metres – is equally impressive and reflective of their forward-thinking style. The 'Sui Generis' range – 'Latin for unique or 'in a class by itself' – is the greatest expression of the single site-growing style, and the selection of wines I'm most excited about.

Their Albariño is 100% whole-bunch macerated and on skins for anywhere between thirty to fifty days in the riper vintages. Fermentation is finished in both oak and steel, aging on lees for a minimum of ten months. The wine goes through malolactic fermentation or 'malo', softening its acid structure, and is bottled without any fining, filtration or the addition

Autumn leaves at Ancre Hill

In the ground in Monmouthshire since 2006

of SO₂ preservative, and finished off with an awesome *A Clockwork Orange*-inspired label.

The new winery also houses some Austrian oak barrels, seven relatively small concrete tanks – each named after the Seven Dwarfs – and 'egg' fermenters, and to go with the modern kit is a very modern sparkling. The Pet-Nat is 100% Triomphe, bottled during one long, continuous fermentation which captures the slightly softer fizz, resulting in a wine as bright and striking in appearance as it is in taste. Triomphe is such a great red varietal that seems to have been ushered out in favour of Rondo and Regent in most places, but it can produce a slightly fuller-bodied still red traditionally, or, in this case, a brilliantly bright and flavoursome lighter, sparkling version.

The more conventional Chardonnay and Pinot Noir-based sparkling wines are from vines grown on ancient mudstone – red loam and sandstone soils are slightly more classical in style, but, like the entire range, are just so well-made and distinctive. The Blanc de Blancs is from Chardonnay, usually produced from a single season in the better years and 100% fermented in oak and foudre. Up to five years' lees time adds toasty richness, and it's sensational stuff. Pinot Noir Blancs de Noirs usually sees slightly less time on lees, but is equally rich and powerful, fermented in a mix of oak, concrete egg and steel. It's also 100% Pinot for the sparkling rosé, just seeing steel and concrete fermenters, and maintaining a slightly more subtle style, also up to three years on lees.

Perifrog – Welsh for 'sparkling' – summarises the wider approach so effectively. It's designed to be super accessible both in style and price point, so lees time following secondary bottle fermentation is dialled right back to fifteen months, keeping a focus on attractive and aromatic fruit. Much of the flavour comes from the initial sixteen months on lees following first fermentation, with regular lees stirring. Reminiscent of

Nutbourne's 'Nutty Wild', this is exactly the kind of kit the wine rack could do with a lot of, and it hopefully inspires many more producers to make the kind of sparkling wine that takes the category out of the 'celebration only' mindset.

There's lees contact for all the stills too – a Chardonnay, a Pinot Noir and a rosé which is occasionally a blend of the two grapes. Interestingly, the rosé is made from the final 15% from the press of the Blanc de Noirs production, having seen a brief five or so hours on skins, adding a touch of texture but not at all overdoing it. Fermented in steel and concrete egg, and on lees for a mouthfeel-accentuating six months, this is exactly the style of rosé that sings – great for summer afternoons but equally food-versatile and interesting, and most of all it's demanding of another glass.

This is as distinct an approach as it is fascinating to witness, and best of all taste. Perhaps not a style for everyone, but what wine is? I'd far rather see people going after what they believe in than conforming to the norm. It is so worth a trip to see Richard and Joy in person and get a glimpse of what they're up to next.

Former cellar door at Ancre Hill

MONTGOMERY

@MONTGOMERYVINEYARD

....

Montgomery, Powys, Wales, SY15 6LR

What: Cellar door sales by appointment
Recommended wines: Sparkling Rosé, Solaris

One of the more recent arrivals on the Welsh wine scene, but certainly a force to be reckoned with, Montgomery has made a very strong start to life as a premium producer. The modern branding and bright, expressive wines have earned them a serious following, of clearly well-informed drinkers on both sides of the border.

The driving force behind Montgomery is Woody Lennard, who, together with his family, planted Solaris, Bacchus, Pinot Noir and Rondo in their vineyard in 'the garden of Montgomeryshire', back in 2014.

At a huge 275 metres above sea level, the south-facing 3 acres of vines are believed to be the highest in Britain. Glacial shift over millennia and the flint that sits beneath the vineyard today aids ripening and drainage, and also add a freshness that's true throughout the range.

Made at Halfpenny Green in Staffordshire, the sparkling rosé is a blend of Pinot Précoce and Seyval. The early-ripening Pinot provides bright, approachable red fruit and goes so well with Seyval, which is also very fresh and fruit-forward, long, zingy and super precise. Solaris lends the ripeness for the floral single varietal white – we're not at all likely to be lacking in any vibrant acidity here but it's balanced perfectly with the exuberant variety's natural character. The

Some of Britain's highest vines

Rondo is super approachable too, and, frankly, at this height above sea level, producing wine at all is impressive, let alone in the red department. The red is pretty juicy too, but classically light and fantastic after twenty or so minutes in the fridge.

Super-small quantities are available at Montgomery, given the selective area under vine. This coupled with an ever-growing following means you might have to be quick on the release list here, but it's a list well worth keeping an eye on.

Picking fruit at the Lennard family's Montgomery vineyard

WEST MIDLANDS

HALFPENNY GREEN WINE ESTATE

RODINGTON VINEYARD

@RODINGTONVINEYARD

Rodington Road, Sugden Lane, Telford, Shropshire, TF6 6ND
http://rodingtonvineyard.co.uk

What: Cellar door sales
Recommended wines: Ortega, Solaris Dry, Seyval Oaked

Ram Dass Chahal and Nirmala Devi emigrated from Punjab to 1970s Shrewsbury, then during their retirement they bought 8 acres of land on the edge of Rodington village, which they suspect was sold to them because it was 'no good for growing anything'. This dry, arid, sandy patch of land pretty swiftly ended the long-time dream of farming an apple orchard, based on professional advice that one or two fruit trees would probably be fine, but commercially speaking it was nowhere near viable. That specialist's parting shot was: 'Could try some grape vines instead.'

This is because a slightly stressed vine is a potentially profitable one: burrowing deeper in search of moisture, vine roots take up greater amounts of nutrients and minerals as they're forced into trying harder to propagate. More established vines generally pull out greater depth of flavour from beneath, and better-quality fruit to go with it. Visiting Rodington vineyard on a warm day, you absolutely get the sense of how unique this place is, with its warmth emanating up from the ground beneath the vines. Sloping gently due south, with nothing but vines growing down to the oak tree bordering the vineyard, the land then rolls upwards into the north-facing slope opposite which, in complete contrast, is luscious, green and plentiful. The land is protected from the south-westerlies

Tending the vines at Rodington Vineyard

by the Shropshire Hills, the weather is broken and sent around the vineyard, the sandy soil stores up heat and the southerly aspect maximises sun hours: all contribute to some great ripening. Harvest takes place as early as the second week in September; given the Loire Valley's average start date between 2010 and 2020 was the end of September, you get a sense of how special this piece of land really is for ripening grapes.

Ripeness is absolutely translated into the wines: the 2009 plantings of Ortega, Seyval, Solaris, Bacchus and Rondo were latterly joined by Pinot Noir, all benefiting from a brighter and richer composition. They're all amazingly well-priced, too, and sold direct from the shed-turned-cellar-door-shop next to the family home. It's nice to see some Seyval with a bit of oak ageing – ripe enough to stand up to a few months in old French – but not losing any classic English fruit freshness. Solaris is the most tropical of the stills; intensely rich fruit is softened slightly by some extended bottle ageing. There's an Ortega Seyval blend and a few versions of Rondo, including rosé and both an oaked and unoaked version.

Mrs Nirmal Devi explains that her family has always worked hard, that when they wake up there's nobody waiting there to help them but themselves. It's a family built on respect for everyone, working together and sharing things. Most recently it seems, this is their success, with their multiple award-winning wines. Here's a family originally from Punjab growing grapes and making wine in Shropshire, to a philosophy built on toil and graft. They just happened to land on an incredible little patch of land to do so – otherwise known as making your own luck – and are making some great wines while they're at it.

Rodington was formerly known as Blue Tractor Wines: Ram Dass Chahal with the old blue tractor that inspired the original labels

KERRY VALE VINEYARD

@KERRYVALEVINEYARD

Pentreheyling, Shropshire, SY15 6HU
https://www.kerryvalevineyard.co.uk

What: Vineyard tours, tastings, cellar door sales, café and bakery
Recommended wines: Shropshire Lady Solaris, Reserve Rondo

Within a stone's throw of Wales on three sides, this little pocket of England is surrounded, and well-protected, thriving on the land of Kerry Vale.

The Ferguson family established the vineyard in 2010, buying a dilapidated farmhouse and a few outbuildings known as Brompton Smithy, which formally belonged to the local blacksmith. Preserved to this day is a well in the cellar door café, now covered over with glass and illuminated; it probably dates back to the site's Roman times. A recent visitor actually lived here as a child in the thirties and forties, and told of the local circus and its parade of elephants passing through. Being walked between venues in those days, the elephants would all of a sudden get excited, trumpeting as they sensed the approaching bore hole and water reserve beneath. In an amusing parallel to the future of the venue, they would stop here for a well-earned drink, furiously pumped up by the blacksmith.

The vineyard is owned by Russell and Janet Cooke and run with the help of Nadine Roach, daughter of the original owners. What they've all achieved is a huge credit to her parents' work along with the influence of the site's heritage, Bronze Age, druid funerary monuments and the eastern side of the Pentreheyling Roman fort included. There are now 6000 vines across 5 acres: Solaris,

Tasting room and shop by the vines, complete with well

A stone's throw from Wales

Phoenix and Rondo recently joined by Pinot Noir.

The vineyard sits in the vale beneath the ancient drovers' path of Kerry Ridgeway. Red kites keep pests including the rare hare at bay, both of which have a wine named after them. Sparkling white wine made from red grapes Pinot Noir and Meunier – either blended with Chardonnay or in Blanc de Noirs form – dominates the British market, but Kerry Vale have taken this white wine from black grapes approach, instead using Rondo to make the still white 'Illusion', which to my knowledge is the only example of its kind. Point of difference is great, but only if it makes a good wine, which this absolutely does, with a fragrant, tangy redcurrant and lemon zest zing quality to it.

'Shropshire Lady' is the most popular of the range; with classic ripe Solaris tropical fruit underpinned by a citrus core, I could drink a lot of this on a sunny day perched up next to the equally attractive lavender bed here. Along with a classic-method sparkling red made from Rondo, the versatile variety offers a strawberries-and-cream style light rosé under the Rare Hare name, and two stand-out still reds. The 'Red Kite' is a slightly softer, lighter cherry-driven, easy-drinking number that would be equally good on said sunny day, especially after twenty minutes in the fridge, Portuguese style. Saúde!

The Rondo Reserve is slightly more serious. Delicate and well-handled oak integration supports the slightly darker core, and a richer dark cherry roundness, not full-bodied, make it a touch bigger and more complex.

You might not see any elephants drinking from the well these days, but there's a tastier source of thirst quencher *in situ*, along with lots of other local produce in the shop, including Jan's hugely popular home-baked cakes.

HENCOTE

@HENCOTEESTATE

Cross Hill, Shrewsbury, Shropshire, SY4 3AA
https://www.hencote.com

What: Cellar door sales, tastings, tours, restaurant and stays
Recommended wines: Evolution Sparkling, Chardonnay, Mark II

Originally mentioned in the Domesday book as 'Hencot', the Ice Age glacial shift north had cut a burrow in the land, on the ridge of which existed a few medieval settlements. This became 'Hencote', meaning 'high on the hill'.

Mark Stevens runs Hencote Estate vineyard and winery, taking over after his parents acquired the site in 1997. His mum originally planted 200 'hobby vines' in 2009, to go with 60 varieties of fruit and veg. Despite the rain in 2012, they were so pleasantly surprised by their 300-bottle yield, made partly with an old cider press, that the family looked more seriously into a vineyard as a commercial operation. Analysis of the sandy loam site came back positively, so 18,000 vines were planted in 2015, followed by a further 4000 a year later.

Over half of the site is planted to Pinot Noir, followed by Chardonnay, Meunier, 1000 Pinot Noir Précoce vines and the balance made up of Solaris, Seyval Blanc and Rondo. The natural bowl of the vineyard maximises sun exposure to those slope-side vines, and it sits in a relatively dry little pocket: their annual rainfall is almost 1000mm below the national average. Airflow down the slope helps counter spring frost which is, as ever, a concern; it meant they lost 45% of their crop in 2017. That year motivated the purchase of a

Storm incoming at Hencote vineyard

cold air drain that's hooked up to a tractor engine, pushing the cold air up to 50 metres where it mixes with the warm air and raises the overall temperature of the site. There are also the loyal bougie candles, of which you need about 500 per hectare, at 9 euros a candle, that last for about eight hours, or one night. You also need people to light them, who usually don't work for free, especially at 3am in below-freezing temperatures.

The winery was completed in 2015, adjoined to which is 'The View', a glass-fronted restaurant and bar overlooking the vines out towards the cathedral city. Somewhere between a Prosecco style and a richer classic method is the 'Evolution Sparkling', a two-thirds Pinot Noir to Seyval blend. It works so well: it's super fresh and approachable, drinks classic English orchard coming from the Seyval, but the Pinot adds a bit of structure and red fruit. At just three months on lees it is an early-release, Friday-afternoon kind of wine that's worth having a few of in stock in the wine rack.

Vivienne blends the bright and tropical Solaris with 50% Chardonnay for a touch of palate-broadening from the latter. Mark's other sister, Suzanne, is the naming inspiration for the 100% Pinot Noir rosé, which is super light and easy, and another prime candidate for getting stuck into on a Friday.

Winemaker Gavin Patterson has got some serious toys to play with, and he saves the best of them for the Saturday night duo. From the top pick of fruit in the best years, the Chardonnay is fermented on natural yeast and aged for ten months on lees in terracotta amphorae; it is bright and lifted but retains such a freshness and natural acidity. The pick of the Pinot Noir from the best years is fermented in amphorae before being pressed off and back into terracotta for ten months. Still super light, but so pure, it's expressive and elegant, and well worth sticking away either in the rack or for when there are not too many others around to have to share it with.

Hencote's vines with Shrewsbury on the southern side

Ripening sunlight approaching harvest at Hencote

Black Mountain Vineyard

@BLACKMOUNTAINVINEYARD

··

Turnastone, Herefordshire
https://blackmountainvineyard.co.uk

What: Not open to the public
Recommended wines: Col Fondo White, Col Fondo Red

Though not from a farming family, Mark Smith always wanted to become a farmer. From Birmingham, his vocation led him to working on a dairy farm in Hamilton, New Zealand. Returning home mid-foot and mouth crisis, there weren't many jobs going, so he ended up taking a few shifts with a mate in a wine shop back in his home city.

One wine often leads to another. He left retail and went to Plumpton College, completing the degree in viticulture and oenology, following which he was able to work at a winery in Montpelier and be back home in time for later harvests at Bolney and Davenport.

Despite never really planning on having his own vineyard, at just about the time he was looking for what to do next, a friend's mum inherited a small hillside next to a nature reserve in Herefordshire. She liked the idea of seeing it planted with vines, so asked if Mark would like to rent it from her.

Both Mark and his wife Laura worked full time jobs for the first six years of the vineyard's life. The 2-hectare site was initially planted to the big three sparkling wine grapes, but as time went on, instinct and creative desire took over. Now down to about 300 Chardonnay vines, the remaining land has been replaced with Phoenix, Solaris and the lesser-seen Cabernet Cortis. Having gone through organic conversion, these hybrid varieties are disease-resistant and also allow greater cover-cropping, in turn benefitting soil structure and vine roots. The more natural approach was inspired by a desire to look after the soil – which is predominantly made up of loam and heavy clay over a red sandstone bedrock. The pure fruit it produces lends itself perfectly to naturally fragrant and site-expressive wines, the best showcase of which is through a continuation of this philosophy via a hands-off approach in the winery.

Mark is now favouring Col Fondo sparkling – as opposed to potentially masking fruit quality with long lees time in the classic method. It's this point of difference that enables wine to be so interesting, but the wine has to be good, which is fortunate for Mark, because in his little green shed at the base of the vineyard – with no electricity – he's crafting some of my favourite wines from this entire trip.

Both Col Fondos are made by adding some fermenting must from the current vintage to barrel-aged base wines up to two years old, sparking a secondary fermentation in bottle.

The white is a blend of Meunier, Pinot Noir, Pinot Gris, Solaris and Siegerrebe. It's super energetic in acidity and has incredible texture, but shining through is outstanding, precise fruit quality, and such a long, long finish. As with the red – Meunier, Pinot Noir, Cab Cortis and Siegerrebe – both wines are aromatic and crunchy but all in perfect, delicate balance; thought-provoking but not overworked. They are edgy in a good way, but not trying too hard, and about as handmade as it gets: a tiny 90-litre press and bottles topped up with a kitchen jug, capped and hand-labelled too.

They're exactly the kind of wines – made in the kind of way – that inspires excitement in fans of the slightly left-field varieties, but are so approachable and above all just so well-made that you don't need to be in a natural wine bar in Hackney to be able to enjoy them. However, this might be the best way to get hold of some, as the entirety of Mark's production is on allocation with London-based distributor, Under the Bonnet – the same outfit that look after Daniel Ham's Offbeat wines. Good company, great booze.

Mark at Black Mountain managed the vineyard alongside a full-time job for the first six years

Levelling up… living, drinking proof that some of the country's best wines are not confined to the south-east

143

ASTLEY VINEYARD
@ASTLEYVINEYARD

Hampstall Lane, Stourport-on-Severn, DY13 0RU
https://astleyvineyard.co.uk

What: Tours, tastings and cellar door sales
Recommended wines: Old Vine Kerner, Orange Kerner, Sabrinna

Astley celebrated their fiftieth year in 2021; a family-run business ever since the first Madeleine and Kerner vines were planted. The Haywood family became the third set of owners in 2017, and from the outset took it on as a custodianship of the land, embracing organic farming for best-quality fruit and soil health. Sitting less than a mile from the Severn Valley, 2 miles from the river and protected by the surrounding hills, you can feel the warmth among the 5 acres of gently sloping vines.

Initially planted by the Bache family, the vineyard has a colourful history, to say the least. With its swimming pool and plentiful supply of booze, it was a legendary party spot throughout the seventies. Bought by Jonty Daniels – a Cambridge-educated agronomist and farm manager – for £1 in 1993, the site's potential was recognised and Jonty transitioned it into a professional operation. His wines made their way onto the Michelin-starred restaurant wine list at Sketch in Mayfair, and were championed by Rick Stein and Jancis Robinson. But he 'didn't believe in publicity' so never mentioned this to locals, instead selling the wines for £4 a bottle in the local pub.

According to local legend, Jonty made a guitar from Kerner vine wood and tamed some local badgers, who he fed peanut butter and jam sandwiches to. Before retiring to Thailand, he

Bev Haywood, head of the third family to take custodianship of Astley Vineyard

eventually agreed to pass on the vineyard to the Haywood family – renting a house nearby for six months and helping them with the transition.

Tim and Bev Haywood's son Chris, together with wife Matleena and ably assisted by Finnish Lapphund Otso, has embraced the winemaking role, an approach that marries tradition and modernity with fruit from some amazing old vines.

The most attractive element to his winemaking is Chris's pragmatism to do what's best for the final product; most wines are wild-yeast fermented, but not at all costs. In the on-site winery there's plenty of small batch action – as little as sixty-eight bottles of Sauvignon Blanc in 2020 and a 189-bottle release of Pinot Noir – but most famously, several contrasting versions of hero-varietal Kerner. A crossing of Riesling and red grape Trollinger, Kerner is a hardy varietal and capable of thriving in much less favourable conditions. It was an inspired choice in 1971 and, thanks to five decades of careful stewardship, Chris is now able to work with some incredible old vine fruit.

There's a young current release that's crisp, slightly saline in character and so refreshing. The old vine bottle-aged version, however, is the greatest expression of these gnarly old vines, with more developed aromatics – and at five years old, it is still drinking vibrantly and with loads of time left. It is so true to its Riesling parentage, with a prominent but well-integrated acidity and lime citrus that meets a slightly smoky hint of kerosene. Riesling can be so varied in style, is incredibly late ripening and naturally high in acidity and as a result – notable efforts from Charlie Herring and Beacon Down aside – it's next to non-existent in Britain. If you're a fan, then it's worth getting hold of some Astley Kerner, not as a replacement to Riesling, but as an amazing expression of varietal in its own right.

Skin contact is embraced with some Kerner seeing just four days' worth in 2020, which took all the benefits of texture, flavour and richness, but according to Chris, 'none of the scary element of skin contact'. Even the natural 'Orange Kerner' is an example of an approach that always comes back to quality of the fruit, which is at the fore and still perfectly balanced with 20 days' skin time. 'Sabrinna', an 'accidental rosé', took some colour from Siegerrebe skins and is blended with 2% Madeleine to produce a blush, ripe and floral rosé that turned into a bestseller.

At entry level there are maybe England's best value wines: 'Severn Vale' – a field blend of Bacchus, Madeleine, Kerner and Siegerrebe, which is a fruit-forward easy goer, and the ripe, stone-fruit 'Peach Bomb' from Madeleine. A couple of sparklings complete the set – Freya's secondary ferment ceased at around 18 grams of sugar and so is embraced in the 'sec' style, and a classic method that was initially intended as a Pet-Nat but as an example of his approach, Chris felt was better suited to a traditional style.

The labels and cellar door offerings are as attractive as the wines, too; I honestly don't think the Haywoods have missed a single beat. If the next fifty years are as good as the first half-century, it's shaping up to be a very entertaining few decades at Astley vineyard, and going by the winemaking, there couldn't be a more fitting tribute to the vineyard's illustrious heritage.

Astley's Old Vine Kerner is so reminiscent of the grape's Riesling parentage – a must-try

Halfpenny Green Wine Estate
@HALFPENNYGREENWINEESTATE

- -

Tom Lane, Halfpenny Green, Bobbington, Staffordshire, DY7 5EP
https://www.halfpennygreen.co.uk

What: Cellar door sales, tours, tasting and restaurant
Recommended wines: Penny Red, Penny Black, Classic Cuvée, Sparkling Seyval

Looking out from the balcony at Halfpenny Green, you could be in the Alsace, rather than Staffordshire; a remarkable site, as is the operation within. Diversification of the family farm inspired Martin Vickers to plant a trial half-acre of Reichensteiner, Seyval Blanc and Müller-Thurgau, yielding 100 bottles that were all consumed in one post-harvest 1985 weekend.

By 1989 Martin's son Clive was back from Harper Adams, planting 20 further acres and moving production away from Three Choirs to their own on-site winery by 1994, also hosting tasting evenings. From the outset, the intention was growing and trialling varieties – which continues today – as well as offering contract winemaking with a large focus on events and experience. Their first brand-new winery was built in 2005, complete with automated bottling and labelling line, and word spread. Now up to 600-tonne capacity – and no plans to curtail growth – Halfpenny are producing for around seventy separate growers. Around thirty of these are co-ops, like the Urban Wine Co. whose members pool their grapes and get back a balance in bottle accordingly. Even so, this is an incredible feat of logistics, especially given such huge vintage variation in yield size in this marginal climate of ours.

A view from the vines

Working with so many growers all over the country puts Halfpenny in a very strong position to see a wide variety of fruit and source for themselves accordingly. They've worked hard with the reds especially, planting Rondo and Divico – the latter with a view to filling the slight void of a fuller, richer, more tannic English variety, but also working with trial planters EMR in Sussex.

Producing at scale also enables them to create their own range of wines that are about as cost-effective as English wine gets. Halfpenny supplied Aldi's first English red, 'Bowler and Brolly' in 2021, 10,000 bottles of which lasted less than a week. The signature Halfpenny-labelled version on this front, however, is 'Penny Red', a blend that changes depending on season, but is normally based around Rondo, Regent and Dornfelder. Super subtle and approachable, there's tannin, structure and dark fruit from the latter two and Rondo throwing in a bit of customary spice and fragrance, which, for £10 at the time of writing, is pretty impressive in a climate that is so costly to grow in, whatever the scale or operation.

The Classic Cuvée blend gets a Seyval-led addition for Halfpenny's 'Brut Sparkling', and the result is a beautiful freshness leading the way into eighteen months of lees time, and resulting partial-richness. Still Chardonnay and Pinot Noir is sourced from Essex, 'always Essex' in Clive's words, such is the ripening potential and fruit quality coming from this part of the country. In 2014 the first Champagne varietal Classic Cuvée was made, but ever since their first sparkling wine in 1994, the portfolio has never been more than 20% fizz. With six million people within an hour's drive, the vast majority want still, so that's their focus. Most of them will have been to Halfpenny, too, by the sounds of things – the café, shop, craft centre, deli and butchers see 300,000 visitors a year, and the best spot to pay a visit to is the balcony, accompanied by a tasting flight.

View from the tasting balcony at Halfpenny Green

The 1988-planted 'Triangle' Vineyard

WOODCHESTER VALLEY
@WOODCHESTERVALLEYVINEYARD

· ·

Convent Lane, Woodchester, Stroud, GL5 5HR
https://www.woodchestervalleyvineyard.co.uk

What: Vineyard and winery tours by appointment, tastings and stays
Recommended wines: Reserve Cuvée, Pinot Noir, Atcombe Red, Bacchus Orpheus

In 2007, on some of the steepest vineyard slopes in Britain, Fiona Shiner first planted Bacchus vines in Amberley, Gloucestershire. On a clear day, from the highest point of the vineyards, you can even see Wales. More beneficially, viticulturally speaking, steep slopes generate air flow, both cooling grapes mid-ripening and fighting spring frost. In the soil beneath these slopes, vine roots pull out greater flavour potential as they tunnel deeper through the rocky, well-drained limestone.

On the site of an old dairy farm, barns have been turned into vineyard-view accommodation and a very modern winery. There's a lot here that winemakers the world over would be envious of, not least the ambition behind it all. The Shiners now have 55 acres planted across three separate sites, growing twelve different grape varieties. It's family-owned and operated: the vineyard's 2020 vintage was picked almost entirely by Fiona Shiner, her daughters and their partners.

The 'big three' sparkling wine grapes – Pinot Noir, Chardonnay and Pinot Meunier – are the hero varietals. Nothing says future vision like planting an additional 20,500 still and sparkling clone Pinot Noir vines, which will take the annual winery production to around

Hardy vines enjoying some winter sun

Postcard from Stroud

150,000 bottles. From speaking to winemaker Jeremy Mount, however, it's pretty clear that quality rather than quantity is the major motivation. Despite the great site, winery investment and vision, this is no easy job.

From the adjacent woodland, 'midnight badger raves' are cited as one of the bigger threats, specifically the omnivore's taste for ripening fruit. Vines are resistant to low temperatures through winter, but new-season growth can be destroyed by late-season frosts. Lighting up to 3000 bougie candles among the vines in the early hours helps disperse these frost pockets. Quite a sight, and quite a job, at 3am in the freezing cold. It's agreed, also, that they'll try and remember to let the local fire brigade know in advance.

The premium 'Orpheus' Bacchus, produced from the original 2007 vines, is a nod to their ambitions at the quality end, and is especially good to see alongside a leaner and more floral entry-level version. Ortega ripens well, and with good fruit weight, it more than stands up to some barrel maturation; it's textural and interesting, in a good way. The Reserve Cuvée – a blend of the Chardonnay, Pinot Noir and Meunier – is a classic marriage of finesse, rich biscuity lees and super length. Releasing the Blanc de Blancs sparkling after additional ageing is a good move reputation-wise, the wine having developed into a truer reflection of quality through extended maturation in bottle.

Like the wider UK wine industry as a whole, the future is bright for the Shiner family and Woodchester Valley. Having worked at wineries all around the world, winemaker Jeremy has a lot to smile about too… minus the badgers.

Little Oak Vineyard

@LITTLEOAKVINEYARD

Paxford Road, Chipping Campden, GL55 6LA
https://www.littleoakvineyard.com

What: Vineyard tours, tastings and lunch
Recommended wines: Sparkling Seyval, Siegerrebe

Pulling into Little Oak Vineyard feels a bit like driving into someone's back garden, probably because that's exactly what it is. After a trial planting of Siegerrebe in the top corner of a slight north-to-south-facing slope, these vines bore inaugural fruit in 2008. That first vintage yielded just six bottles for Steve and Gemma Wilson. The juice, however, was so good that Steve drank all six in one go (presumably in the company of at least one or two others). On the back of this extensive quality check and as English sparkling wine gleaned more column inches, a further 900 Siegerrebe and 400 Seyval Blanc vines were planted.

Twelve years on from the first vintage at Little Oak, there are plans for a second vineyard, which may see some lesser-known red grape varieties like Divico, but also more Seyval. The latter is producing large yields of good-looking, tightly packed bunches, though it is susceptible to botrytis rot as a result. Milder winters and spring frosts, as late as the second week of May in 2020, decimate any new vine growth, and can leave one end of the vineyard ripening weeks behind another. These challenges are living proof that there's more to climate change than simply higher temperatures and easier ripening. Steve

Winter vines mid pruning season

and Gemma hand-tend their two-and-a-half acres, leaf stripping to aid air flow, mitigating rot and spraying a seaweed solution – rich in iodine – to give those nutrient-deficient vines the few weeks' hurry-up they sometimes need.

Deciding to not plant 'more fashionable' grapes is a nice insight into their philosophy. They'll continue to produce fruit from varieties according to quality potential, rather than mainstream popularity. Tasting three separate vintages of Siegerrebe provided a brilliant example of how different the wine can be from contrasting years, which is exactly how wine should be portrayed: as an expression of individual site and season. All three wines opened with a freshness, as varying degrees of riper stone and tropical fruit developed.

Little Oak sparkling Seyval Blanc is a crunchy green apple, yet it's fresh and easy-drinking in style. It hits a really good spot for a sparkling wine: easy enough to be ultimately crowd-pleasing yet interesting enough to never get boring.

What started as a retirement project, providing a couple of hundred bottles a year for thirsty family and friends, turned into Gemma and Steve harvesting 18 tonnes of fruit in 2018, a truly remarkable haul from land that is not even 3 acres. There's now a specialist tasting room, where alongside a local produce lunch you're able to sample the range in what is an entertaining insight into marginal-climate grape growing. You can even join the club and lease a vine that not only provides personalised bottles but comes with an invite to the annual vineyard summer party. In my experience, a vineyard is a pretty good place for a party.

Cold start at Little Oak in Chipping Campden

Three Choirs Vineyards
@THREECHOIRSVINEYARD

Baldwins Farm, Newent, Gloucestershire, GL18 1LS
https://www.three-choirs-vineyards.co.uk

What: Cellar door sales, tours, tastings, restaurant and stays
Recommended wines: Blanc de Noirs, Noble Harvest, Pinot Noir Précoce, Bacchus

Three Choirs Festival is the world's longest-running classical music festival, celebrating its 300th year in 2015. It was also the inspiration behind the name of one of the oldest vineyards in Britain, originally planted to a test half-acre of vines in 1973.

Almost fifty years later, it seems a commercial vineyard was a more than viable option for Three Choirs, who now have over 75 acres planted, both here in Gloucestershire and, as of 2014, taking over Wickham in Hampshire. Winemaker Kevin Shayle has been at the helm since 1987, overseeing a considerable winemaking operation, with thirty different varieties in the ground. Experimentation has been a hallmark of Three Choirs since the outset, and given the heritage of the plantings, those seventies favourites – Madeleine, Müller-Thurgau, Seyval, Bacchus and Siegerrebe, among many others – are yielding some impressive fruit and benefiting from a concise re-planting programme, meaning most of the vines are between ten and twenty years old.

John Oldacre took the vineyards forward, having acquired the site in 1984 from founder Alan McKechnie. The former installed – for the time – a modern winery in 1990

Traditional views that provided new label inspiration

and adopted the Three Choirs name, which remains largely in the hands of his family today. He also installed a visitor centre, which continues to be at the core of the operation, and eight bedrooms that were added in 2000.

Classic Cuvée is Seyval-led, and super fresh despite twenty months on lees, which adds richness to go with additional structure from Pinot Noir, rounded off with some bright Phoenix. Another traditional style – as you might expect given the history of the site – is the Bacchus, a lively, zesty and floral offering, approachable in both style and price point, which is consistent through the entire range. Siegerrebe is true to its parentage of Gewürtz and Madeleine, ripe and tropical bordering exotic fruit and spice, a point of difference wine in some ways but not at all overpowering or too distinct to be polarising. Rosé sales have exploded at Three Choirs, in-line with the wider market, so production has dramatically increased as a result. Blending Phoenix, Seyval, Triomphe, Pinot Noir and Madeleine offers complexity, but is ultimately fruit-forward and fresh in style, citrus and red berry fruit-driven, subtle and easy-going summer drinking. This is the advantage to Three Choirs; lots of varietals in the ground and a good, historic understanding of site.

The sparkling range at the premium end of the portfolio is perhaps atypical to the otherwise classically approachable, accessibly priced still wine range, but it adds some real class. The Blanc de Noirs especially, at a minimum five years on lees and usually bottled with a dosage around 8 grams of sugar, is drinking superbly seven years down the track. No need for any malolactic fermentation as sugar and time softens out a naturally persistent acidity. It's still super fresh, but throws in those classic toasty, brioche and creamy flavours, and is a great example of why this style is still the number one pairing for a proper chip butty.

It's great to see a traditional producer of largely classic English varietals adapt to the modern day in terms of packaging and cellar door experience, and with the latter especially, they've been at the forefront of what they do here.

The restaurant completes the set for visitor offering at the Gloucestershire site, with Hampshire having more of a focus on weddings. Regular shop hours for the former mean you can drop in and taste some real history, from a library of varietals and resulting wines. Eat, drink or stay – or take a relaxing combination of the lot.

Views from the self-guided trail at Three Choirs

EAST MIDLANDS

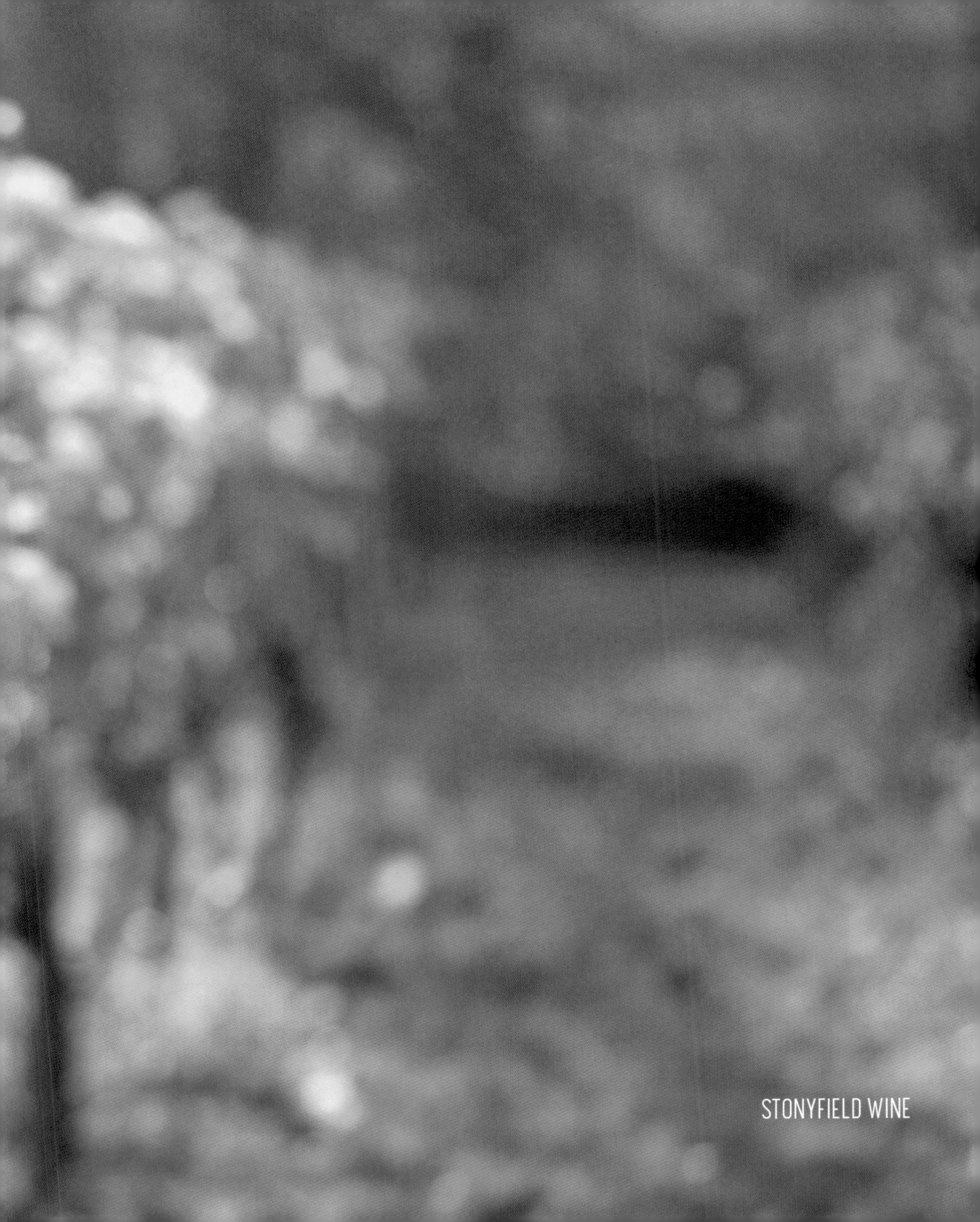

STONYFIELD WINE

Stonyfield Wine

@STONYFIELDWINE

30a Stoke Road, Blisworth, Northampton, NN7 3BZ
https://www.stonyfieldwine.co.uk

What: Cellar door sales, tours and tastings
Recommended wines: Sparkling Seyval

Roman era vine-pruning hooks were found at both Grendon and Wollaston, which contribute to the theory that second- and third-century viticulture was practised in modern-day Northamptonshire on sites up to 11 hectares in size. Today, twenty minutes to the south-west is Stonyfield vineyard, which was planted in 2011.

During the late eighteenth century engineers started work on what was to be the longest tunnel in England, the Grand Union Canal. They spread the ironstone rocks from the creation of the tunnel onto the field above, creating what is now the aptly named Stonyfield.

Belinda Brown and her brother John inherited the land, but it was Belinda's husband, Michael, who always said it would make a great vineyard. Given the stone content, regular ploughing was impossible, but the natural rocky topsoil is ideal for vines, storing heat and aiding drainage.

Belinda's grandfather tried his luck, but moved over to farming free-range pigs instead. Her parents then grew wildflowers for their seeds, but when Michael died in 2010, it seemed like a perfect memorial to him to see his vision through.

With the ground cleared at the end of

Seyval leaves falling at Stonyfield

2010, 1000 vines were planted producing the first harvest in 2013 from an equal split of Pinot Noir and Seyval Blanc. If I had 500 vines of two varieties to plant, I would be incredibly tempted to choose these two – both capable of fantastic expression in both still and sparkling – but it's the latter that Stonyfield have specialised in. The sparkling white is 80% Seyval, and is beautifully fresh, zingy and precise. It's a super classy wine, fragrant and approachable but with just a hint of red fruit depth coming from the Pinot.

The rosé almost reverses that blend, and with three years on lees is a touch richer and more opulently red fruit-forward. Still elegant and crisp, both wines are made at Halfpenny Green, continuing on from the area's almost 2000-year wine-based legacy.

Pest control in safe hands

Eglantine Vineyard

Ash Lane, Costock, Loughborough, LE12 6UX
https://www.eglantinevineyard.com

What: Cellar door sales, tours and tasting
Best wine: North Star, Sparkling Seyval, Madeleine

Tony and Veronica Skuriat initially planted Eglantine vineyard between 1979 and 1984, also establishing an incredible vine trials collection of 200 different varietals. A true pioneer, Tony set up the Mercian Vineyards Association in 1994 and was also involved in the formation of the UK Vineyards Association, serving as the first treasurer of what was to go on to become WineGB.

Veronica has been here for thirty-six years, helping Tony make wine, mead and cherry wine. The family operation has gone one step further, as their daughter Helenka went on to plant Hanwell vineyard just down the road in 2012, largely so that her children could have the same lifestyle she had. Tony, Veronica and Eglantine are now possibly most famous as makers of what they modestly refer to as 'the country's best dessert wine', the Eglantine 'North Star'. During harvest the best bunches of Madeleine Angevine are selected and taken into the freezer room where the grapes are gently pressed when frozen. Similar to ice wine, famously made in Canada, this concentrates flavour and sugar, resulting in natural sweetness. North Star is only made in the riper vintages, where enough sugar is present and has only been produced six times in the last two decades.

Tony even made his own gyropalette, which mechanically rotates classic-method sparkling wine bottles during production, prior to disgorgement. 'Gyros' have become commonplace in both Champagne and Britain, largely replacing hand 'riddling' techniques, but few can claim to have done so with such a unique, bespoke creation.

Seyval is blended with Madeleine for one of the two classic-method sparkling wines, the other made exclusively from Pinot Noir. There's even some Malbec in the ground here, used for bending in the reds and imparting colour and tannin, but they're several degrees and possibly a couple of hundred years away from being able to fully ripen it for a single varietal version.

It's the very definition of a parent vineyard: into their fifth decade and showing no signs of slowing down yet.

Tony Skuriat, a pioneer of viticulture in Britain with over 200 varietals planted since the late seventies

NORTH OF ENGLAND

DUNESFORDE

DUNESFORDE

Upper Dunsforth, York, YO26 9RU
https://www.dunesforde.com

What: Cellar door sales (Monday–Saturday), tours (Thursday–Saturday), tastings and bar (terrace and cellar bar open Fridays and Saturdays)
Recommended wines: Blanc de Noirs, Solaris, Sparkling Pinot Gris, Bacchus

You don't have to be in England's biggest county long before someone tells you where Yorkshire placed on the latest Olympic medal table. There's a sense of regional pride here, and now the residents can add wine to the long list of things to be proud of.

Ian and Mandy Townsend were in search of a career change, and the vineyards of Tuscany were calling. Their son James, who is now making wine under Henry at Harrow and Hope, was then at Castello di Potentino, just south of Montalcino. Just about everyone makes wine in Italy. There are over a million vineyards producing more wine than any other country in the world. While struggling to see what their unique selling point might be, it then appeared close to home, specifically, in the pony field next door in Upper Dunsforth, North Yorkshire. Here is a place of vast Roman heritage – nearby Aldborough was the 'capital' of the period's largest tribe, the Romanised Brigantes. The town was a major Roman administrative centre, complete with forum, temple, amphitheatre and, most probably, several vineyards. The main Roman road between Aldborough and York passes what is now Dunesforde vineyard, named after Dunsforth's entry in the Domesday Book.

Taking inspiration from the location's Tuscan beginnings and Roman influence, Bacchus (aptly named after the Roman god of wine) was

Pinot Noir Précoce at Dunesforde near Aldborough

planted in 2016 alongside Solaris, Pinot Gris and Pinot Noir Précoce. Choice of varietals – alongside every other element of Dunesforde's establishment – was calculated professionally, according to site and soil and the potential to make the best possible wine. The naturally protected 4 acres slope gently to the south, and additional drainage was built into the sandy loam and clay prior to planting. There's below-average rainfall through the growing season, and with bud burst naturally a few weeks behind the south, spring frost is slightly less of a threat. As the days are longer, additional sunlight helps ripening, but it's not as strong, hence the choice in having the majority of grapes that classically ripen earlier.

Having travelled extensively through the cellar door cultures of Australia and south Africa, Ian and Mandy planned from the outset to recreate that experience in Yorkshire. The tasting room and cellar bar sit at the bottom of the slope, complete with vine-side terrace. Inside, a Roman cellar has been re-created, and upstairs there's a 27-foot wall-long mural depicting the scene at Aldborough as it would have been at the end of the third century.

The wines, too, pay tribute to the site's heritage. Queen Cartimandua formed a pact with the invading Romans and ruled until 69AD. 'Queen of the North' sparkling rosé is named in her honour, and is a blend of classic-method Chardonnay and Pinot Noir. The core of the range, however, is all single-site, single-varietal reflective of a premium, boutique producer. The Blanc de Noirs was one of only fifteen wines, out of 155 in total, to pick up gold at the 2021 Independent English Wine Awards – a well-respected show employing a diverse range of judges representing everyday drinkers as closely as possible. It is great to see individual sparkling expressions of Dunesforde Solaris and Pinot Gris, too, and their quality is testament to the professional approach in site,

varietal selection and application. Sparkling is a good choice, too, as a touch less ripeness is required for fruit going into still wine prior to secondary fermentation in bottle. The Gris is slightly crisper and more citrus-driven to the Solaris's expressive and floral character.

Solaris is early ripening yet so exuberant; Dunesforde's still version is bright and characterful, bordering tropical fruit and – as you would expect at the cooler end of a cool climate – not at all lacking fresh acidity. Bacchus is also down the expressive route: floral, zesty and fresh.

Youngest son and head of wine Peter Townsend might get 2500 bottles from Pinot Gris and Précoce across one half of the site, and as many as 4500 of Solaris and Bacchus from the other 2 acres. These are young vines and their yields will increase as the vines establish themselves, but across such a relatively small site a huge focus has also gone into the cellar door operation, with the upstairs having the capacity and kitchen to host modern-day banquets. The vine-side terrace is an awesome addition, too, especially enjoyable during the summer months.

For now, the wines are being made at Halfpenny Green, but one day there might be a winery here, too, with James going full circle and finishing off what he started.

Dunesforde vineyard and cellar door

CARLTON TOWERS
@CARLTON_TOWERS

High Street, Carlton, Goole, DN14 9LZ
https://carltontowers.co.uk

What: Walled garden vineyard tours
Recommended wines: Not yet released

Carlton Towers has got to be one of Britain's most striking vineyards. At the epicentre of the 1500 acres of farm and woodland, 250 acres of parkland and an 11-acre lake is the Grade I-listed Yorkshire Manor that was once held by Robert de Bruce. Backing onto it is the walled garden vineyard.

The vineyard is now owned by Lady Emma and Lord Gerald Fitzalan-Howard, who, having enrolled on an RHS walled garden course, got talking to a fellow participant with South African vineyard experience. Furnished with the knowledge that within a walled garden there's additional heat and therefore ripening potential, the Howards were inspired.

Most vineyards are partly protected from the elements by topography, trees or hedgerows. The Howards used their house. Gerald took his JCB to both the inside and outside of the garden, testing soil structure and installing weather stations on both sides of the walls. The analysis brought confirmation of additional degrees within, plus positive results in drainage and heat retention of sand and stone that was revealed beneath.

Built in 1773, and briefly providing grazing pasture to Carlton Tower's Oxford Sandy and

Carlton Towers… and a back garden befitting the residence

Black pigs, in 2017 the area was planted to 2500 Auxerrois and Pinot Noir vines. Gerald also laid 70 tonnes of slate chippings that, like the walls around them, store and radiate heat.

The plan is to produce a single sparkling wine called Duke Miles in honour of Gerald's father, which is expected to be released in 2024. Until then there are vineyard tours, stays and fine dining to be had, at one of the most aesthetically remarkable vineyards in Britain, if not the world.

Carlton Towers and walled garden vineyard

LAUREL VINES
@LAURELVINESVINEYARD

Aike, Driffield, East Yorkshire, YO25 9BG
https://laurel-vines.co.uk

What: Cellar door sales, vineyard picnics
Recommended wines: Madeleine, Ortega

Ian Sargent planted a 'test' of 2000 vines in the paddock behind his home in 2011. Searching for a specific site to do so, he found it when the renovated house at Laurel Farm came up for sale. Ever since, Laurel's first vintage wine has always been made on-site, previously in an old stable and, since 2017, in a winery built from the same brick as the farmhouse.

Initially favouring Solaris, Rondo and Ortega, the vines took so well they were followed by Madeleine and later, in 2018, Pinot Noir Précoce and Chardonnay. There's also some Seyval, which will be incorporated into one of the two sparklings, and plans for another 5000 vines – taking the total to 17,000 – and maybe some Bacchus, depending on the results of some high-level talks between Ian and his wife Rebekah.

One of the best things about the ever-growing British wine industry is how it helps bring communities together. When the harvesting date and time sign goes up on the gate at Laurel Vineyard up to seventy neighbours arrive to pick grapes, including police officers, medical staff and the local vicar. In 2021 Driffield women's cycle team tried to out-pick their rivals at Beverley; it's pretty serious competition. Bringing people back to rural communities and supporting countryside

Ian at Laurel Vines

economies also gets people outside and among nature, pulling together, developing relationships and generally having a good time. Ian says the vineyard belongs to the community; how rewarding it is, therefore, for locals to help produce the wine they can, eventually, share with others.

But this isn't merely a community project: the site is a fantastic one. Gently sloping south, varietals have been well-chosen, and the vineyard is professionally managed, maximising the sun's ripening effect. We're on sandy loam and the same band of solid chalk that stretches down through the 'Wolds' into East Anglia and down underneath the South Downs and – you know the rest. We're far enough east to get some warmth, but far enough from the coast to avoid the worst of the coastal breeze. Crucially, it seems to be a dry spot, too.

The winery is in three parts: grape processing and bottle store; wet room and winemaking; and equipment storage. It's a seriously professional set-up, and the wines do more than justice to everything at Laurel. They're well-priced too; this is Yorkshire, after all.

Ortega is all linear and green apples upfront but has an ever-attractive developing savoury roundness. Madeleine is bright and floral but restrained and elegant. There's a funky little 100% Rondo rosé – and when I say 'little', I mean pretty punchy, bucking the trend of light and soft, much to its credit, by throwing in some liberal rural aromas.

If there's an element of intrigue driven by perceived novelty in English wine, it's even more evident when you connect the words 'wine' and 'Yorkshire'. But like the wider industry, whatever brings that first experience, if it's not a good one, there's no future. Like much of the wider industry too, a first experience at Laurel is likely to be far better than good, and if you're in time for harvest, you might just drop in on the region's largest fancy dress party.

Almost good to go: Pinot Noir Précoce

Ozzy the black lab

167

LITTLE WOLD VINEYARD
@LITTLEWOLDVINEYARD

Comberdale Hill, South Cave, Brough HU15
https://www.littlewoldvineyard.co.uk

What: Cellar door sales, tours and tasting
Recommended wines: Poppy Hill Rosé, James View, Three Cocked Hat

Market Place Farm has been in the Wilson family for over 70 years. It was initially bought in 1947 by Robert Wilson when the 'Cave Castle' estate was split up. Farmed traditionally, the Wolds – a range of hills usually rising from chalk or limestone – which make up nearly half of the acreage, were in permanent grass, supporting beef and dairy herds. Cattle turned to poultry, but by the late nineties, the farm diversified once again, to renewables, planting 150 acres of energy crops.

In search of further diversification, Henry stumbled across the idea of a vineyard while in South Africa. Engaging a local specialist, the site got the thumbs up, and planting began in chalk-laden slopes during the spring of 2012. Every one of the initial 3000 vines went in the ground by hand, with Pinot Noir and Chardonnay joined by Rondo, Madeleine and Solaris.

After their first harvest in 2016, the following season yielded more than 6 tonnes, and following success with the early releases, an additional 6000 vines were planted in 2018, and a further 6000 in 2021. As well as being host to an ever-popular wedding and events business, the tasting room built in 2019 provides an occasionally required shelter for tours.

Going to the chapel and we're going to drink some fantastic York

Barley Hill is a blend of Seyval and Phoenix; concentrated and bright stone-fruit and a touch of residual sugar make it a great match for spice. The 100% Rondo provides a red-summer-fruit-driven, easy-going rosé: distinct yet elegant, clean and crisp, it's named after the poppies that would grow in the hillside chalk if it wasn't slightly busy doing other things.

Rondo is also the sole varietal in the 'Three Cocked Hat' red, and one of the cellar door's most popular wines. Light and unoaked, Beaujolais Nouveau in style, such is the fragrance and fresh, it's light fruit-forward in character, but it's got a slightly darker fruit-driven core, and just a touch of spice keeping it nice and interesting.

There are a lot of things going on at Little Wold. It's an ever-expanding operation and one built on diversification, ingenuity and, since 2012 at least, Yorkshire wine.

ze

Yorkshire Heart Vineyard & Brewery

Pool Ln, Nun Monkton, York YO26 8EL
https://yorkshireheart.com

What: Cellar door sales, tours, tastings, camping and glamping, brewery
Recommended wines: Eleanor White, Winemaker's Choice, Eleanor Red

In 1999, Gillian and Chris Spakouskas planted thirty-five experimental vines in their garden, across seven varietals. Though this was born from hobbyist beginnings, it came with a professional approach – no crop was taken for the first three years and the couple took their initial wines along to what was then the UK Vineyards Association annual competition to see how they compared. Renting an initial acre of well-protected local farmland, vineyard life worked well alongside early morning milk rounds, leaving all afternoon and evening to tend the vines – thirty-five of which have become 22,000, planted in two 7-acre paddocks either side of the Wine House Café.

The motivation has always lied in Gillian's winemaking abilities, so naturally an on-site winery was a must. It processed 35,000 bottles in 2018, with a capacity of 20,000. There's a brewery too, run by son, Tim, and 2020 brought the opportunity to re-trace the former milk rounds with far more interesting alcoholic products, albeit through necessity rather than choice.

Yorkshire Heart represents its location in the middle of this great county combined

Bottling in progress in the winery at Yorkshire Heart

with a very passionate approach to what they do. Seyval, and the sparkling wines it dominates, represents a third of total produce. With some second-hand kit bought from Bolney in Sussex, everything for classic-method production is done on-site – currently the only winery in the North able to do so. A touch of Pinot Noir is added to the wine for the rosé version, but it's great to see a sparkling red from 100% Rondo, because they'll be out barbecuing up here whatever the weather, and this style is a perfect match.

There's a strong presence of blends across the remaining still wines, showcasing both craft and individual season, with the specific blend of grapes changing as required each year. 'Eleanor White' is usually comprised of Ortega and Siegerrebe, but currently takes fruit from four very interesting rows including Pinot Gris and – accidentally sold to them – late-ripening Chardonnay clone vines.

Among those rows also is Cabernet Franc – you heard that right, the Loire Valley's signature red grape, in Yorkshire. This is not a drill. Gillian says they've been speaking Yorkshire to it for some years now, and, while she considered learning French to see if it would understand that, they eventually cropped some fruit from the vines and blended it into 'Eleanor Red', alongside Pinot Noir and Gamay. Rich, structured, savoury and, frankly, remarkable.

There's smart barrel use too, largely for oxidation, texture and a hint of tannin rather than flavour, in both whites and reds, taking the same blends and producing a completely different wine with four or five months' softening time in wood. Latimer Red is a great example; currently a blend of Rondo, Dornfelder and the lesser-seen Acalon varietal. Acalon itself is a part-crossing of Dornfelder, providing depth, structure

2013-planted Regent vines

and dark fruit in both oaked and un-oaked versions, slightly brighter in the latter plays a touch richer and chewier in the former.

All grown and made on-site in the heart of Yorkshire, it's such a great and varied range that all started through a trial of what might work. Which turns out to be quite a lot, most of all the calibre of winemaking.

171

Renishaw Hall

@ENGLISHWINEPROJECT

Renishaw Park, Chesterfield S21 3WB
https://www.englishwineproject.co.uk

What: Cellar door sales, tours and tastings
Recommended wines: Vintage Cuvée, Walled Garden Rosé, Madeleine

Until 1986, the Guinness Book of Records included Renishaw Hall's 1 hectare of vines as the world's most northerly vineyard. Planted by Sir Reresby Sitwell in 1972, in part to replicate his Sicilian estate at Monte Gufoni. The walled garden was once providing year-round decadence in produce thanks to the heat-retaining stone and its greater ripening potential. This, along with wine industry links, convinced Sir Reresby to plant Pinot Noir, Reichensteiner and, presumably motivated by the Italian connection, the only British example of Trebbiano I'm aware of. I'm not sure how successful the latter was especially, but it sounds like he had a good time at least, serving rent-paying farmers a glass of his 'finest', while he drank something entirely different from apparently the same bottle.

In 2001 and eight years prior to Sir Reresby's death, Kieron Atkinson was at Sandhurst Military Academy, later deciding during his third tour (to Afghanistan, after two in Ireland) that his future lay in winemaking. He studied at Plumpton, and having volunteered at Renishaw in 2010, took on the vineyard and winemaking the following year under his 'English Wine Project' brand. With

English Wine Project's Kieron Atkinson, winemaker at Renishaw Hall

an urban winery in Darley Abbey, Derby, a trip to see him and taste his wine – and cider – comes very highly recommended. He's also a published author – 'Grow Your Own Wine' is a great read for anyone motivated to put a few vines in the garden or spare bit of land.

With over a decade's experience in a variety of roles alongside Renishaw – including three years at Halfpenny Green – here is a great example of the modern band of skilled British winemakers. A big fan of oak, specifically for oxidation as much as the flavour potential, but also experimenting with oak chips, too, sourced from premium Bordeaux cooper, Seguin Moreau. 'Oaked' Madeleine Angevine is big, rich and full of creamy, candied sweet fruit that replaces sugar in balancing acidity, though the considerable fruit weight more than stands up to the wood. The traditional barrel regime is a pretty solid one too, in part utilising refurbished oak that's shaved and re-toasted and at a quarter of the price of a brand new one, makes the final product more price approachable.

Vintage Cuvée is a great example of classic method, Chardonnay and Pinot Noir that at eighteen months on lees, benefits from the slightly richer autolytic influence but above all the focus is on the zesty citrus and elderflower fresh fruit. Further, with full malolactic fermentation softening natural acidity, it's right in the sweet spot for classic-method sparkling – I'm not sure there's such a thing as a 'sparkling for everyone', but as classic method goes, this is as close as it gets.

Walled Garden Rosé is England in a glass – Seyval-inspired rose garden freshness meets redcurrant, textural Pinot Noir, but without losing any of the summer's afternoon attractiveness these pale rosés so overwhelmingly represent.

I'm not sure there's likely to be any more Trebbiano planted in Sheffield, with Renishaw now favouring aromatic varietals like Rondo and Solaris that benefit from reduced disease pressure, but the experiments are ongoing. In 2018 a foot-pressed, wild fermented on-skins Pet-Nat sold out just about as soon as it hit the shelf at Renishaw Hall. Which is where most of the 4000 to 5000 bottles a year are picked up, as well as the Darley Abbey urban winery too, of course. A great day out.

A variety of new, old and refurbished barrels in use

173

HAMPSHIRE

HAMBLEDON

BSIXTWELVE, LONE FARM VINEYARD

@BSIXTWELVE.WINE

....

Lone Farm Lane, Itchen Abbas, Winchester, Hampshire, SO21 1BX
https://www.bsixtwelve.co.uk

What: Cellar door tastings and sales by appointment
Recommended wines: Pinot Blanc, Pet-Nat, Skin-Contact Pinot Blanc

Given the column inches it generates, you could be forgiven for thinking that the band of chalk stretching from beneath Champagne, under the English Channel and on into the South East of England, accounts for almost all of what lies beneath Kent and Sussex. But Hampshire holds more chalk as a percentage than either of these counties, accounting for around 70% of the major soil type. It is, therefore, home to a vast array of some of our greatest sparkling wine producers, those led by saline-fresh Chardonnay especially. Also true of the wider industry is that there's so much more to see: Britain's oldest commercial vineyard planted in 1952; one of our greatest winemakers in Emma Rice; some Riesling in a 1-acre walled garden near Lymington and several versions of incredible Pinot Blanc at Bsixtwelve.

The 2-acre vineyard at Lone Farm is home to Balbina Leeming, known as 'B,' probably English wine's most engaging and entertaining personality. Her 2 acres of Pinot Blanc – and the wines they produce – take their name from Antoine de Saint-Exupéry's novel *The Little Prince*, set on an asteroid that's 2 kilometres in diameter, called Bésixdouze.

Born in Spain (though half Venezuelan and having grown up in Venezuela), B says her love

True love… and a glorious terracotta amphora

of wine began around the family dinner table. She toured vineyards in Argentina, Australia, South Africa and Europe while working in London. Together with her husband David she acquired a then-derelict old threshing barn in Hampshire and they have restored it outstandingly. It is now a great tribute to the site's history and former custodians, and equally just about the perfect example of a home and base to plant a vineyard in front of.

When she was walking her Hungarian Vizsla Lola, B's interest in creating a vineyard was piqued by nearby vines at The Grange. She had already planted 1000 trees and restored a meadow further up the hill, so that when she looked out of the window one day at a spare couple of acres before her, B knew there and then that a vineyard was meant to happen. Sparkling wine was never the initial desire, despite the gently sloping, heavily chalk- and flint-laden site, and despite the quality produced nearby.

So, in went the vines, planted exclusively to Pinot Blanc – largely motivated by a tasting of Simon Woodhead's version at Stopham. The desire and excitement B brings to everything she does is enough to excite anyone, seemingly instinctively knowing the best way forward and steadfastly setting out to achieve it, while retaining a humility and generosity to share with others.

Looking down the slope from her 'bench of thanks' onto the grazing sheep and valley beyond, it's very easy to feel grateful for such beauty and to see one's small place in the grand scheme of things. This notion was part of the motivation behind the conversion to organic viticulture. The entire 2019 crop was lost to powdery mildew, but 2020 yielded 2.5 tonnes of good fruit that is now expanding the range in small quantities of hugely attractive wines that are the very embodiment of Balbina's approach and charm in bottle form.

The core release is the straight Pinot Blanc.

It's rounded and rich but not overly so. It's bigger than your easy-drinking crisp white. Not so full it needs food, but it is equally great alongside it. There's a three-weeks-on-skins version, which lets all the pure, ripe fruit and varietal character shine as it is supported with great texture and a slight elevation in body. The ancestral-method sparkling, where the wine is bottled during one long continuous, fizz-capturing fermentation, shows a great synergy with the others in the range: it is just as ripe and rich, elegant yet vibrant and, best of all, incredibly top-up enticing.

There's a winery being built into the natural slope, an amphora *in situ* already – and, based on the first few wines B has made, I can't wait to see what's next. It's an amazing place, full of superb wine and great people with an invigorating approach. Fortunately, in Britain we're a multicultural industry of travellers, gastronomes and creators, and B is absolutely the epitome of this.

2 acres of vines and a seventeenth-century threshing barn

LADYHILL VINEYARD

Ladyhill Estate, Lovington Lane, Ovington, Winchester, Hampshire, SO21 1DA

What: Sales and events, boutique stays
Recommended wines: To be released

Dominique first realised the potential for English wine, having tasted some sparkling made by Chapel Down, twenty-three years prior to planting her own vineyard in Hampshire. In May 2021, while still running a business producing and selling children's toothbrushes, sparkling variety vines went into a glorious hillside near Winchester.

Black Chalk's rosé, and Dominique's desire to emulate this style, ultimately inspired her to do so. Given the sloping chalk and flint soil, an equal split of the versatile Pinot Noir and Pinot Meunier were a good choice for producing both still and sparkling wines, though 60% of her 18,000 vines are Chardonnay.

We don't expect to see the first wines until 2024 at the earliest, but this is one to look out for. It's a stunning spot, with maximum sun exposure and natural airflow rolling down the slope. Glamping and events will also form a large part of the offering, with the site already gifted a woodland hideaway in place.

The most recent addition to a premium collection of vineyards around Alresford

Britain's latest vineyard manager

HATTINGLEY VALLEY

@HATTINGLEYWINES

Wield Yard, Lower Wield, Alresford, Hampshire, SO24 9AJ
https://hattingleyvalley.com

What: Tours, tastings and cellar door sales by appointment
Recommended wines: Classic Cuvée, English Gent, Blanc de Blancs

When Simon Robinson acquired Hattingley Farm in 2000, it was a collection of chicken sheds and Land Rover workshops. Concerned about its future, and with family in the area, after hearing a piece about Nyetimber on Radio 4 he decided to turn it into an ultra-modern winery instead.

Because the land sits at 200 metres above sea level, the plan was always to work with other local vineyards, both in terms of sourcing regionally diverse fruit and contract winemaking. An eye for supreme talent led to Simon's career-best masterstroke after meeting Emma Rice, who was promptly brought on board as director and head winemaker, and who is now possibly the country's greatest.

Aged fifteen she worked as a glass collector in the White Horse at Chilgrove. Struck by the sheer size of the wine list and the price of some of its contents, her lightbulb moment came after working a dinner celebrating the inn's twenty-fifth year. The deal was that she could taste anything that might be left in the bottles, which included Haut Brion 1982, d'Yquem '47, and Krug '79, from Jeroboam, and she can still remember the taste of the latter.

From retail to wineries in Nelson, New Zealand, then back in London with Burgundian importer Domaine Direct, she became editor

Emma Rice in the Hattingley barrel room; there are now around 250 barrels

of Hugh Johnson's pocket wine book. Emma signed up for the first offering of the full degree at Plumpton, with five others, and after stints with wineries in California and Tasmania, she returned to Britain once more in 2008. It was clear where the most exciting place to be a winemaker was and, all of a sudden, she became one of the country's most experienced.

Emma set up her consultancy business just as Simon was planting his vines and asked her if she 'fancied a little winery on the side.' The opportunity to build a winery and brand from scratch was pretty unique and exciting, and from the outset she had a 'fearless belief' that they could do it. Few others were embarking on a project of this scale and nature at the time, so it was courageous, but also a vision built on total confidence.

Emma is making some of the best wines in the country for labels like Roebuck, Raimes and Alder Ridge to name just a few, best expressing their outstanding fruit and using some of it in the Hattingley range, which you can absolutely include in that list. Whether sourced from Hampshire, Kent or East Anglia, every batch offers something different, and Emma is in a great place to oversee regional differences and skilfully blend accordingly, adding layers of complexity.

Like the wider industry, Hattingley have built their reputation on classic-method, long lees-aged wines of great class and calibre, but continue to evolve while staying true to their strengths. Epitomising the opportunity at the approachable end of the market, both stylistically and by price, is the 'English Lady': a sparkling red, Précoce-dominant and a third Pinot Noir. Six months in old oak, more for depth and structure than flavour, and a year on lees before being disgorged with a minimal dosage of 4 grams per litre. The 'English Gent', a two-thirds Bacchus and Pinot Gris blend, is tank-fermented and initially on lees for three months, before secondary fermentation in bottle and a

further twelve months on lees. Fresh and aromatic, as these grapes are, there's a hint of richness, but the focus is on the bright and expressive fruit.

The 250 oak barrels are almost as impressive in sight and smell as the core range itself – Hattingley's Classic Cuvée is exactly that, and one of my favourite expressions of this non-vintage style. It's 15% initially barrel-fermented, a blend of 50% Chardonnay, 30% Pinot Noir and a balance of Pinot Meunier. Then 25% of reserve wines were added to the six-year-old base vintage, where four years on lees followed, adding that classic toasty complexity to creamy, rich and crunchy fruit.

The Blanc de Blancs, 100% Chardonnay, is from exclusively chalk vineyards in Sussex and Hampshire and aged for five years on lees, exuberant in the fresh salinity that the best chalk-based Chardonnay tends to express. The vintage 'Kings Cuvée', named after the farm that makes up the rest of the estate, was initially made by accident when an old barrel was forgotten about and is now an equal split of Pinot Noir and Chardonnay, with just over 10% Meunier. It is 100% barrel-fermented and in oak for seven months, prior to bottling on lees for somewhere between four and five years. There's also a still Chardonnay, in the lean and fresh bracket, a tiny proportion of which sees some time in a 500-litre puncheon.

The Hattingley label is served in British Airways first class cabins and the brand has an ever-growing presence in the US and Scandinavia; there was also an exclusive 'Team GB' bottling of the Classic Cuvée created for the Olympics. Hattingley are a top five producer in quality, scale and commercial success and we need these flag bearers in this industry. Best of all for us, and especially for those drinking their wines, is the 'who' behind it all. In this case, it's Emma Rice, with a fantastic career behind her that started when she collected glasses in a pub.

RAIMES FAMILY VINEYARD
@RAIMESVINEYARD

Grange Farm, Tichborne, Alresford, Hampshire, SO24 0NE
https://www.raimes.co.uk

What: Stable yard cellar door sales and tastings, tours
Recommended wines: Classic Brut, Blanc de Noirs, Blanc de Blancs, Vintage Rosé

Saturday is 'turn up and drink' day. Not my words, but those of the voice coming from the barn-turned-cellar door at Raimes Family Vineyard in Tichborne, about one minute past opening time.

The fifth generation Raimes family farm covers 1800 acres, from the slopes of the Winchester South Downs to the ecologically diverse water meadows and grasslands at the north-eastern end of the River Itchen.

As the British industry was going through the modern shift to ultimate professionalism in the late 2000s, current custodians of the family farm at Tichborne, Robert and Augusta, were approached by an agent working on behalf of a landmark Champagne house, who weren't interested in any of their barley, wheat or pedigree-horned Hereford cattle. They were politely told to look elsewhere in their search for desirable, chalk-based land, but thanks to the friendly heads up 10 of the Raimes' 1800 acres went under vine to the same varietals the Champagne house would have planted: Chardonnay, Pinot Noir and Pinot Meunier. Robert was already a professional agronomist, studying soil science and disease resistance for their existing crops,

As British as it gets… and it just got better

and Augusta enrolled at Plumpton studying viticulture to hone the relevance and existing expertise in the direction of their new vineyard.

There was a time when lots of people were needed to farm land on this scale – now, tractors are the size of a house and can cost as much as one, and are satellite guided and don't even need steering – a seismic shift to mechanisation. Working the vineyard requires quite the opposite; even across just 10 acres, each vine needs hand tending all year round, involving the entire family once again, quite nostalgically, with products and places, full of character. Not that the latter is at all lacking – few cellar doors have quite the charm or authenticity as Raimes's stable-yard version, with the family serving tasting flights for a tenner, along with apple slices and pork pies, all while a beautiful grey pony called Starlight keeps a watchful eye on the tasting notes.

The wines are made by Emma Rice just 7 miles up the road at Hattingley Valley, and she takes some of the fruit for her own blends. Being so close to the winery not only makes it easier for the whole family to participate in blending trials and dosage decisions, during harvest the Raimes family can pick early in the morning, getting their grapes to the winery and straight into the press a good few hours ahead of the rest of Hattingley's contract clients.

If the toughest job you have on the day you visit is choosing your favourite of the four wines, then it's going to be a nice little afternoon. You'll probably find that you have your work cut out in picking a preference nonetheless, such is the quality throughout. They're all quite different, but there's a consistency to the range, one of depth, structure, purity of fruit and just great length.

The Blanc de Noirs is classically rich and full of vibrancy, red fruit and texture. The Blanc de Blancs is just so long, with the partial barrel fermentation and forty-two months on lees adding a creaminess to the lemon sherbet fruit and lingering acidity. Vintage Rosé is predominantly Pinot Noir-based, with the remaining third being an equal split of Pinot Meunier and Chardonnay. It tastes of strawberries and cream and makes for easy drinking, but is not at all light on complexity, trademark richness and slightly more fresh summer fruits. The wine I kept coming back to, however, was the Classic Cuvée, a blend of 55% Chardonnay, 28% Pinot Meunier and 17% Pinot Noir, that saw forty-two months on lees. It's all sea spray freshness and approachability up front, with a creamy mouth-feel and crunch like apple crumble – the autolysis not at all masking such precise fruit.

Both the fruit and the winemaking here are a credit to one another, and the makings of a great relationship. If it's a relationship you're after, I can't recommend Saturday afternoons at Tichborne highly enough, especially when you follow the site's advice. You'll be joining the Raimes family for a very long time to come, and all you need do is turn up and drink.

One of my favourite cellar-door experiences: ponies, pork pies and proper booze

HAMBLEDON VINEYARD

@HAMBLEDON_VINEYARD

Hambledon, Hampshire, PO7 4RY
https://hambledonvineyard.co.uk

What: Cellar door tastings, sales, visitor centre and restaurant, dine in the vines
Recommended wines: Classic Cuvée, Première Cuvée, Classic Cuvée Rosé, Première Cuvée Zero Dosage Rosé

The village of Hambledon, though small in size, is mighty in stature, and not just in terms of wine. It's the home of Britain's oldest continuous commercial vineyard, and to the second-best thing to get involved with on an English summer's afternoon, cricket. On this very spot, 250 years ago, the legendary Kent and England bowler, 'Lumpy' Stevens, beat the great Hambledon batsman John Small three times to no avail, the ball going through the middle of the two-stump wicket of the day. Thanks to Lumpy's protests a middle, third stump was introduced, and written into the 1774 code of the Laws of Cricket.

Of an equally great British name, Major General Sir Guy Salisbury-Jones is said to have acquired his love of wine having shared a ration of it with two French soldiers in a First World War trench. He spent much of his career in France, fought in the Second World War and, after his role as military attaché at the British Embassy in Paris, retired to Hambledon in 1952 when he established his vineyard on the chalky south-facing slopes beneath his home.

The house and winery changed hands several times following his death – the vineyard running into a state of neglect, until 1999, when the property was bought by Ian Kellett.

Nestled away in Hampshire: a view from behind the vines at Hambledon

Looking forward with future vision as much as respecting the site's history, under Ian's stewardship Hambledon has been transformed.

A biochemist, financier and geologist, and champion of Hampshire's chalk soils and majority south-easterly facing slopes, Ian's in-depth research and Plumpton studies convinced him that premium sparkling was the future. In 2005 he planted a 10-acre 'test bed' of Chardonnay, Pinot Noir and Meunier across twenty-seven different combinations of clones and rootstocks. Ian also revived a partnership between Hambledon and Champagne House Pol Roger, initially established through Salisbury-Jones during his time at the Embassy in Paris.

As a lover of Chardonnay, and a huge fan of Krug, I feel that there are a few interesting parallels between the two producers, not least in style and approach, which ultimately means Hambledon aim to be curators of the best multi-vintage sparkling wine in the world. It's a bold ambition, but if you visit Hambledon and see the gravity-fed winery, tasting room, restaurant, and half a million bottles storage facility, it doesn't seem so farfetched. Great wines are served in restaurants, rather than made there, but the calibre of fruit coming from their 80 hectares planted in Newhaven chalk suggests they've got both ends of their wine's journey well covered.

The dramatic slope of the 'Home Vineyard' below the family home and winery drops 60 metres from top to bottom, and as much as 6 degrees Celsius as it does so. At the lowest point is the early ripening Meunier, in the middle is Pinot Noir, and Chardonnay occupies the rows closest to home, which seems fitting. Windmill Down vineyard to the west and a third site, East Vineyard, plus two others in the village, provide the balance of grapes, with all three varietals planted in each. Recommended by Pol Roger, former Duval-Leroy chef-de-cave Hervé Jestin heads up the winemaking team, accompanied by Felix Gabillet and Tobias Tullberg, plus consultant Didier Pierson, totalling a combined experience of over 100 vintages. The additional cellar space built in 2021 is crucial to the multi-vintage approach, capable of storing a library of reserve wines. Chardonnay dominance and small-percentage base wine barrel-fermenting are also familiar hallmarks.

Around 20% of tank-aged reserve wines – dating back a decade – are blended into a five-year-old base vintage for the Classic Cuvée, just over half of which is Chardonnay and around a quarter Pinot Noir with the balance of Meunier, all of which comes from the Windmill Down site. Thirty-five months on lees and classically lower dosage around 4 grams per litre add to the richness, crunchy green apples and precise acidity, and, like the best non-vintage wines, develops so well under cork.

The flagship white, Première Cuvée, takes the Classic Cuvée approach and goes up a notch at every level, from a seriously impressive start. Two-thirds Chardonnay, around a seven-year-old base vintage and blends of barrel-aged reserve wines, with a minimum of sixty-two months on lees, and a still lower dosage of around 2.5 grams. It's richer and rounder, yet super elegant and structured.

The two rosés follow the same concise pattern: the classic is 90% Chardonnay with 10% red Pinot Noir added, with forty-five months on lees and an uplifting 10 grams dosage. Premiere Cuvée Rosé gets really interesting: zero dosage, 100% Meunier at thirty-five months on lees. Conservative style this isn't. It's vibrant and rich in texture, a game-dinner's dream pairing, and my kind of rosé.

Ian Kellet's custodianship of Hambledon is a great and important tribute to the history of the site, as well as to the work and devotion of Sir Guy Salisbury-Jones, a true trail-blazer; if only he could see it now and, better still, see where it is going.

A dramatic slope at Hambledon's home vineyard

Jenkyn Place

Hole Lane, Bentley, Hampshire, GU10 5LU
https://www.jenkynplace.com

What: Tours, tastings and cellar doors sales by appointment
Recommended wines: Blanc de Noirs, Classic Cuvée, Blanc de Blancs, rosé

Property entrepreneur Simon Bladon moved into Jenkyn Place house in 2003. With a couple of spare rooms at the new family home in need of furnishing, he went off to a furniture auction where he was hugely impressed with the glass of Champagne he was handed, asking of its origin. 'That, sir, is not Champagne, it's estate-grown Sussex sparkling wine,' came the reply. No furniture was bought that day, Simon having headed straight home to put plans in place for a vineyard instead.

The land next door was then made up of hop fields, but as American imports of the freeze-dried version were taking over, the farmer wanted out. Like much of Kent, hop fields make great vineyard sites – both plants are suited to well-drained, heat-retaining and south-facing sites, of which Jenkyn Place absolutely hits the sweet spot, with its green sand and marlstone on chalk. Protected by the South Downs and with natural windbreaks all around the two vineyards, it's home to 13 acres of Chardonnay, Pinot Meunier and Pinot Noir, sitting about 100 metres above sea level.

With now well-established vines in the ground since 2004, they're providing a full representation of the site's quality, and, equally crucially, have wines aged in bottle for serious time too. The 2010 Blanc de Noirs is an incredible wine and is just

Making the Jenkyn Place wines since the beginning, Dermot Sugrue

absolutely hitting its straps: equal split Pinot Noir and Meunier, separately whole-bunch pressed and aged on lees for forty-two months and time on cork too, has done so much for the wine's evolution. It's rich, gamey and earthy, but soft acidity remains, along with crunchy, slightly dried red fruit and just a hint of the best parmesan you ever smelt. Its complexity and development are things of pure delight and are a brilliant example of bottle-ageing. Just how good the 2018 version of this might be in 2028 is fairly mind-blowing, as is the potential we're seeing from this special site right now.

Dermot Sugrue has made the Jenkyn Place wines since their first vintage. 2015's Chardonnay looked so good he bottled some as 'Cuvée Boz', under his own label, Sugrue South Downs. If the country's most talked about winemaker put his own name on the bottle it tells you all you need to know about the quality of Jenkyn Place fruit.

In contrast to Cuvée Boz, Jenkyn's 2015 Blanc de Blancs vintage saw some base wine barrel fermentation, as well as forty-two months on lees, after full malolactic fermentation – so there's less of that hallmark Sugrue acidity zing – though still present, it's richer, rounded and fatter in style. It's a third cheaper, too.

Hampshire might not get the column inches bestowed to Kent or Sussex, but make no mistake, the quality of wine coming out of here is as good as any. Jenkyn Place are right at the top of the Hampshire tree: their wines are as good – and as good value – as any others I've had on this trip, in part thanks to that first glass of sparkling… from Sussex.

Golden bubbles of great quality

189

The Grange

@THEGRANGEWINE

Burge's Field Vineyard, Hampshire
https://www.thegrangewine.co.uk

What: Tours, tastings and cellar door sales
Recommended wines: The Grange Classic NV, The Grange Pink NV

In the south-west corner of the 3500-acre Grange Estate, in 2011, Zam Baring and his siblings planted 52,000 vines to Chardonnay, Meunier and Pinot Noir on the sheltered, south-facing slopes of Burge's Field.

The Estate itself was first bought by the current family's forebear, Alexander Baring, in 1817. Changing hands in 1932, the house was later requisitioned as an HQ by the American 9th Army prior to the D-Day landings, with Winston Churchill visiting to receive a briefing from supreme commander Dwight Eisenhower. The estate returned to Baring ownership in the 1960s under Zam's father, John Baring, and is now home to The Grange Festival and a 570-seat opera theatre.

The vineyard slopes southward, down towards the River Itchen. Here the clear chalk streams are famous for their fly fishing – and with a brace of trout in the bag, there's now some equally local, super premium produce in vinous form to go with.

This part of Hampshire is becoming increasingly prominent for its concentration of high-quality wine producers. Pommery have plantings on either side, Bsixtwelve have 2 acres of Pinot Blanc just down the road, and Raimes are just the other side of the A31. The biggest of the lot, Hattingley Valley, are 20 minutes to the north-east, where The Grange wines were made from their second vintage by legendary winemaker Emma Rice. Tasting new releases from The Grange defines why this area is so sought after. There's no way I can choose my top pick from producers close to Winchester – let alone the entire country. But The Grange are right up there, in both stakes.

Zam planted in 2011, with the first release not until 2018. In 2022 he built a 200-tonne capacity winery, complete with a cellar big enough to store half a million bottles. Commitment to quality was accentuated in the signing of winemaker Harry Pickering from Gusbourne to lead that side of the operation, where he'll also set up a small but premium contract winemaking service. Zam has spent much of his career in production of another kind, producing Hugh Fearnley-Whittingstall's River Cottage TV show, among others, and, in his words, 'If you're going to do it, you may as well do it big.' In his case, big means high quality, rather than huge production.

Both 'The Grange Classic NV' and 'The Grange Pink NV' genuinely define 'precision' in wine – concentrated fruit and striking, energetic acidity through both, the former with slightly more crunchy green apples and linear to the latter's rich yet approachable red fruit. Both are rounded and so refined – or, you could say, just so well-balanced and complex. This is clearly an incredible part of a special little pocket, and best of all for The Grange, this is just the beginning.

Zam Baring at Burge's Field, home to The Grange

CHARLIE HERRING
@CHARLIEHERRINGWINES

Yaldhurst Lane, Lymington, Hampshire, SO41 8HE
https://www.charlieherring.com

What: Annual open day
Recommended wines: Any you can get your hands on, Sparkling Solera Chardonnay, Sparkling Chardonnay, Riesling, Skin-Contact Sauvignon

Visiting a winery for the first time, much like tasting new wines, comes with excitement, intrigue and slight trepidation of what might be. None more so than turning up to Charlie Herring, which, in Tim Phillips's own words, is a place with a 'set of values… Come here to see it, and then you're part of it.' You'll have to go there too, if you want to buy any of the extremely low-production, high-demand range, all sold at the annual open day.

Coming from an economics background he figured that looking back on some old accounts wasn't much to take with you, so in 2002 he moved to South Africa and embarked on a career as winemaker in Stellenbosch and latterly Australia, with the legendary biodynamic producer, Julian Castagna.

Visiting his parents near Lymington in 2005, he cycled past a sign that said: 'Walled garden for sale.' Built in 1805 as a kitchen garden for the adjoining stately home, the brick walls act as a windbreak, storing and radiating heat so the landed gentry didn't have to eat swedes and turnips for six months a year like everyone else.

'Le Clos du Paradis' – the walled vineyard of paradise – was planted to three varietals in 2008: Chardonnay, Sauvignon Blanc and the notoriously late-ripening, high-acidity Riesling. In a naturally later-ripening, high acidity-producing marginal

Traditional-method cider in progress; either you're already in th

climate also known as Britain, Denbies planted some in 1986 and could never get it to work; Rathfinny tried and dug it all up a few years later. Beacon Down have 500 'cloched' vines in Sussex, and make a medium-sweet style, with sugar going some way to attempt balancing acidity.

But inside these Lymington walls there's 30% more growing degree days than outside it; the rows are planted north to south, but to best maximise the hotter afternoon sun at a slight tilt just off due south. Tim read a paper calculating the exact aspect to plant his vines only to discover the garden built in 1805 was almost exactly to the degree required. The glasshouse was nearest the house kitchen, but sat at a strange distance from the garden gate. On the shortest day in the middle of winter, Tim realised why. The sun's shadow just about kissed the very bottom edge of the glass wall closest to the house, amazing proof those early-nineteenth-century growers knew exactly what they were doing.

Underneath the vines is a mega mix of gravel soils made up of alluvial, granite, sandstone and flints, all well-draining and heat-retaining. Ripening the Rizza and restraining its acidity leaning is

get some of this and you soon will be

perhaps aided further by Tim's South African-inspired approach to trellising. Permanent cordon, as opposed to single shoot training, means the thicker branches can store more water which may in turn increase pH levels, resulting in fruit with less acidity. He found this out quite by accident, training the vines as he learnt to in South Africa, where water retention in branches is preferable because it's hotter.

Chardonnay and Riesling have always been varietal 'royalty', but Tim planted Sauvignon for one main reason. Just down the road you can get locally caught dressed crab for £3.50 a serve, and he thought, how good would this be with a glass of locally sourced Sauvignon?

Farming passionately and organically for the good of site, soil and grape, rather than for green stickers on bottles, there are biodynamic principles incorporated here, but as a chemist, Tim does things based on science, rather than faith. In the wild meadow by the vineyard that is also home to Tim's apple orchard, nettles and yarrow grow. These native plants have evolved to be resistant to mildew, which is ever a concern in a wet climate and especially inside the walls where there's reduced airflow. So, Tim extracts salicylic acid from them, which is prepared into a 'tea' and applied to the vines as a replacement for sulphur.

The approach marries the best of tradition and current understanding, and is therefore maybe the most modern of all. Has he got it right? Tim says come back in 300 years and we'll know by then. He's motivated by a custodianship of the land that will leave it able to produce fruit for the next three centuries and beyond, but also by the fact that if you're not making booze that people want to drink, what's the point? It's his livelihood, so there has to be a commercial element to it, and he can survive two weather-wiped-out vintages a decade. He could plant disease-resistant varietals instead, but on this tiny scale – as much relevant to the wider domestic scene as it is Tim's 1 acre – it has to be about quality.

According to his self-branded 'peasant economics', £100 goes into the vineyard annually. Glass, labels and crown caps come to less than a couple of quid per bottle, which means he can earn a living and you can drink his wines for what is, frankly, a ridiculously accessible price. The only trouble is demand far, far outweighing supply. There's not even one bottle of Riesling per customer; each release is done by ballot.

For the first couple of years, Tim blended the Riesling in with the Chardonnay and 'hoped that no one would notice.' To soften acidity, a sparkling has been made since, that after three years' lees ageing and resulting time softening, was looking great, and after four it was, in Tim's words, 'absolutely epic'. In 2020, for the first time, it went on skins for three months as a still wine. The wine is so dense and concentrated, but tight, compact and restrained, which is perfect in preparation to see some air as it's bottled and developed over the time following. It's so powerful yet so elegant, so well-rounded and balanced, which is really a hallmark of the world's greatest wines. Skinsy texture and richness is there, but it's all so in sync, biding its time. Truly remarkable stuff.

Tim's also making cider from the 150-year-old apple trees. He saved five trees with two different and completely unique apple varietals from a curtailed EU-funded trial, naming the varietals Bronwen and Red Iris after his wife and daughter, pressing in Chardonnay skins that might amount to a third of its entire crop and otherwise would just be mulched back into the soil.

Refusing to release his first few vintages of Sauvignon Blanc because he wasn't happy with the quality, Tim describes that concern as like having an IT issue and the person on the helpline telling him, 'There's a problem between the keyboard and the seat, and it's you, mate.' A touch of self-deprecating humour is amusing, but unlike everything else he does, it is in no way accurate. More recently, possibly as the vineyard has established itself – given also that the vines are planted on original roots rather than grafted root stock which tend to establish themselves in the ground a bit quicker – he's incorporated skin contact. Sauvignon takes to skins so well that five days' worth might taste like next to none, the textural influence imparted can support the fruit so attractively in much the same way a Fumé Blanc might with oak and lees ageing.

Of the two sparkling Chardonnays there's a three to four years on lees version and a very special Solera system blended offering that sees five to seven years in bottle before release. Inspired by the Austrian Schloss Gobelsberg, the Solera is a blend of multiple vintages, added to each time some juice is taken from it and bottled. That way some of the very first vintage will always remain in the master blend, adding complexity as time evolves and new wine is added.

In the winery, two old basket presses do the job wonderfully – there are no electronic error messages here. Hyper oxygenation is encouraged through this part of the process, which makes it more capable of handling oxidation post-fermentation, instead of achieving this through sulphur. Slow fermentations are preferable to hold onto varietal character and delicate flavours – this happens quite naturally when fermentation stops as the temperature drops to below 6 or 7 degrees in the winter after harvest, restarting again in February or March when it warms, gradually.

I said to Tim that having been fortunate enough to be only the second person other than him to taste the 2020 Riesling from barrel, I feel like I should be at the back of the queue in his Riesling ballot. What I meant by that was: I really hope I'm at the front of the queue in his Riesling ballot. But who is Charlie Herring? I suppose we'll never know.

Tim and his chooks in their 1-acre walled garden vineyard near Lymington

Exton Park
@EXTONPARKVINEYARD

....

Allens Farm Lane, Exton, Hampshire, England, SO32 3NW
https://www.extonparkvineyard.com

What: Cellar door sales by appointment, tours and tastings
Recommended wines: Blanc de Blancs, Blanc de Noirs

The first 12 acres of Exton Park's vines were planted in 2003, but since 2011 have provided fruit for a contrasting approach to classic-method sparkling wine. The familiar varieties of predominantly Chardonnay and Pinot Noir, as well as some Meunier, are planted across the 60-acre, single-vineyard estate. Each of the nine blocks within are subject to different climate patterns, grape clones, vine age and even pruning methods and altitude, dropping from 175 to 65 meters above sea level. These variables provide fruit for a multitude of unique base wines, all of which play their own part in producing wines of huge complexity, further added to by changes in season and development of reserve wines.

With Corinne Seely as head winemaker and their own winery on-site, Exton take the traditional non-vintage approach and turn it on its head. Blending wines from several different years is common in classic-method production, but normally the majority of a blend is from a single 'base vintage', to which is added a smaller proportion of reserve wines. With a reserve wine library evolving for more than a decade, each season all nine plots are picked and pressed separately, and each of the final wines released is normally at least 80% blended from these back

An innovative approach yielding super premium results…
Exton Park 'RB|32 Brut'

196

vintage reserve wines, all of varying age and style.

Every label is stamped with 'RB' – reserve blend – and states the number of wines that have been blended inside that bottle. It's an innovative approach to a very traditional process, motivated by complexity in the final product. As each wine ages its naturally vibrant acidity softens, bringing something different to the table. It's not the most cost-effective approach, but it negates the odd bad – or zero – crop vintage that could well be a factor in such a marginal climate.

'RB 32' is a blend of predominantly 60% Pinot Noir to a balance of Chardonnay, and contains the oldest reserve wines, ageing on lees for three years. It's rich, structured and precise, but that chalk-based Chardonnay adds a supreme nutty, saline edge, maintaining a subtle savoury roundness. The rosé, 'RB 23', is two-thirds Pinot Noir to Meunier, again on lees for three years with a richness to it, and a flavoursome orchard pear and red fruit taste that means it doesn't lose any of that classic rosé refreshing approachability. The Blanc de Noirs gets an extra year on lees to soften further, and a dosage of around 10 grams to uplift fruit and help balance acidity. The Blanc de Blancs is absolutely where it's at for power and structure, however, with baked apples and a creamy richness, yet it's so elegant and with precision in acid line – made from forty-five reserve wines, additional lees time and a touch of barrel ageing.

Exton Park was relaunched in 2021 with modern branding, packaging and huge attention to detail – all so important in an increasingly vibrant and relevant industry – including a landscape shot of the vineyard on the inside of the bottle-neck foil that's gradually revealed as you peel it back.

It's been a ten-year project just to get to this stage, but here there's a fresh and exciting approach, and best of all some seriously good fruit and skilled handling in its showcasing in unique bottles. At the top of the vineyard the centrepiece of the entire operation is the stunning new HQ, a sentence which, quite frankly, doesn't come close to doing the building justice. Unfortunately it can't be open nine to five due to the small village locality, so it is kept as a hub for showcase events, largely for 'The Vault' – Exton's wine club. It's probably the best of its kind anywhere in Britain – so much effort, thought, detail and investment has gone into its building. This mirrors the approach to the range of wines, and both ends of the operation absolutely complement each other.

Welcome to English wine in the twenty-first century: take a seat… and get yourself a glass

Black Chalk

@BLACKCHALKWINE

. . . .

The Old Dairy, Fullerton Road, Andover, SP11 7JX
https://www.blackchalkwine.co.uk

What: Cellar door sales, tours and tastings
Recommended wines: Classic II, Wild Rosé, Dancer in Pink Rosé

In 2009, Jacob Leadley left his 'comfortable' London-based finance job to retrain as a winemaker. Seven years later he was working at the multi-award-winning Hattingley Valley. In the heart of Hampshire's Test Valley, Black Chalk started off as a conversation among family and friends who were sourcing fruit from local growers to produce small-scale, high-quality expressions of classic-method sparkling wine.

But two years after that first release – and with the support of an EU fund as well as additional backing – they built an ultra-modern winery, tasting room and shop. Within a mile radius, they acquired four separate plots of pre-planted vines: Hide, Rivers, The Levels and The Circle, growing their own Pinot Noir, Meunier, Chardonnay, Pinot Gris and Pinot Noir Précoce over a total of 12 hectares of premium chalkland location. The prior owner's wines were made at Hattingley, so having seen the quality of fruit coming off these vines, Jacob knew the opportunity to acquire them for his Black Chalk label was too good to turn down.

The investment didn't stop there – Zoë Driver worked with Jacob as assistant winemaker at Hattingley, having originally been selected over 200 others to be their first

A vision built on talent, experimentation, great fruit… and awesome teamwork: Jacob and Zoë

198

winemaking apprentice. Her first ever wine won a silver at the WineGB awards – an ice wine where the grapes were frozen before being continually pressed over seventy-two hours – so she slept at the winery and set an alarm for every three hours to restart the process. Both Jacob and Zoë recognised the mutual opportunity, and Zoë joined Black Chalk as one half of an awesome winemaking team.

Meunier features so prominently in the Black Chalk blends, which is so good to see; it's flavoursome and bright in character and adds approachability and extra layers of interest. The entire range is built on small batch experiments, straight-as-an-arrow acidity and complexity in wines that celebrate the naturally brilliant fruit. There's just under a third of Meunier in the Chardonnay-driven 'Classic II' blend, with a balance of Pinot Noir. Barrel and twenty-eight months' lees time adds richness, complexity and further roundness, but it's linear, fragrant, fresh and super enticing. The 80% malolactic fermentation adds further softening so Classic II was released ahead of Classic I – the latter seeing much less malo and developing in bottle for longer before release. Meunier takes the lead role in the Wild Rosé, at almost half, to an equal split of Chardonnay and Pinot Noir. Two years on lees retains a classic, crisp and red-fruit-forward style, but there are layers of elegant complexity.

They added a still rosé in 2020 – their first still and the first wine released from their own vines, made in their own winery – the concentration and purity of fruit from 'Hide' vineyard especially lending itself to this category. 'Dancer in Pink' was so well-received by Dominique at Lady Hill that it inspired her to plant. An initial trial blend of Pinot Noir, Précoce and Pinot Gris worked so well, it was stuck with – and hits the nail on the head for premium English rosé. It's bright and super easy-going, with lots of enchanting red fruit, yet – like the entire range – it is layered and full of ample texture, depth and structure. Perfect for a picnic in the park yet there's so much to unpick and intrigue.

The constant striving to experiment and be creative makes Black Chalk's journey one that is very much worth following. Two Blanc de Blancs were added to the range, both celebrating and expressing wonderful fruit and acidity, again through differing amounts of malo and fermenting yeasts. There's a Blanc de Noirs based on the illustrious 777 Burgundian Pinot Noir clone, and more still wines to come, too.

There is some serious investment at Black Chalk, in both buildings and vines but best of all people. It's a relatively young producer, but one which belies its years in the wines it has already released.

Black Chalk are making some of the best kit going and the quality is testament to site, process and teamwork. Jacob and Zoë are a talented duo but even stronger together – seemingly only disagreeing when it comes to choice in winery music.

Utter precision, exceptional expressions of classic-method sparkling and English rosé

SURREY

ALBURY ESTATE

GREYFRIARS VINEYARD
@GREYFRIARSVINEYARD

. . . .

The Hog's Back, Puttenham, Guildford, GU3 1AG
https://www.greyfriarsvineyard.co.uk

What: Cellar door tasting, sales and events
Recommended wines: Sparkling Rosé Reserve, Blanc de Noirs, Still Pinot Gris

The vineyards of Surrey Hills, with their proximity to London, make them a very viable day trip for millions of people. The North Downs Way is popular with walkers, cyclists and, previously, pilgrims. Seventeenth-century gunpowder mills were built along this droving route, as monks and friars trod their path to Canterbury.

'Grow great grapes, make amazing wine and sell it at an accessible price.' Easier said than done, but that's the charter laid out by Mike Wagstaff at Greyfriars, on the south-facing chalk slopes of the 'Hog's Back', near Guildford.

In 2009 Mike was running an oil company in Aberdeen, a pretty hefty commute from the family home in Surrey. Already aware of the vines at the Hog's Back, Mike and his wife Hilary found their dream home in the same village shortly after. An inquisitive call discovered the sale of the vineyard had fallen through that same week, so there and then Mike reduced his commute by about 598 miles.

Bill Croxon and Phil Underwood planted the initial 1500 Pinot Noir and Chardonnay vines in 1989 on original rootstock. Veterinarians first and vignerons second, passion probably explains their approach in the midst of the amateur era. Though they had some success, it's thanks to these pioneers

Winemaker and owner Mike Wagstaff at Greyfriars cellar door

that Mike and Hilary's generation are able to take these vines forward today, professionally. This original block now produces about 1.5 tonnes of the site's most interesting Chardonnay especially, and there's still an on-site vet's practice, too.

Having recruited Hilary's brother-in-law, Plumpton graduate, singer and London bar manager, David Line, as vineyard manager, they acquired an additional site less than a mile from the original. Plantings over the following five years took the total area to about 40 acres under vine, all on a narrow band of chalk. About half of which is Chardonnay, a third Pinot Noir with about 10% Pinot Meunier, and also a small holding of both Pinot Gris and Sauvignon Blanc.

The on-site winery moved to the second site in 2013, which also enabled the development of the chalk cellar, now capable of storing 250,000 bottles. This increases the depth of reserve wines for blending, also allowing flavour development across the range as the wines age gracefully, being released when quality dictates.

Pinot Gris from the warmer end of the site is blended with almost a third of Chardonnay for 'Noor', the first release in a series celebrating local history. On the other side of the Hogs Back, at Wanborough Manor, Special Operations Executives were trained during the Second World War. Noor Inayat Khan was a radio operator dropped into Axis-controlled France to link up with local resistance. She was eventually captured, and escaped, twice, before her demise in a concentration camp in 1944.

Two weeks after the wines' release, the cellar door had a visitor whose grandmother trained with Noor at Wanborough. Half of the Gris was barrel-fermented, the touch of whole bunch Chardonnay adds uplift and a hint of texture from some short skin contact. The ripe fruit is evident but this is delicate, fresh and rounded. The Blanc de Blancs from Chardonnay sees

five years on lees in bottle before release, and there's also a barrel-fermented version of the same wine with almost three years on lees before release after some additional time on cork. The 10-year anniversary wine, 'X', is a striking Blanc de Noirs from 100% Pinot Noir, that sees forty-eight months on lees. Just 5 grams per litre dosage complements the rich yet crisp, awesome Pinot Noir fruit that increasingly seems to be at the forefront of the most interesting Greyfriars releases. An equal split of Chardonnay and Pinot Noir from the 2011 plantings – seen as the label's finest – were whole-bunch pressed and aged on lees for a minimum of twenty-four months before being disgorged and labelled as the Cuvée Royale.

The most popular wine of the range at cellar door, however, consistently proves to be the Vintage Rosé Reserve. Made up of predominantly Pinot Noir with 10% Meunier, the 2014 edition won the International Wine Challenge Trophy for best English sparkling wine in 2019. It's a third oak barrel-fermented, and only 450 bottles of the late-disgorged were released in June 2021 at six years on lees, so it would be well worth keeping an eye on the Greyfriars mailing list to try and snare some if they decide to delve deep into that chalk cellar of theirs for a second library release…

Roll down the hill and load up the boot

203

Chilworth Manor Vineyard

@CHILWORTHMANORVINEYARD

Halfpenny Ln, Chilworth, Guildford, GU4 8NN
https://chilworthmanorvineyard.com

What: Tastings and tours by appointment from 2023, cellar door sales
Recommended wines: Rosé, Sparkling Rosé, Blanc de Blancs

If you thought we were at the marginal end of the climate for viticulture, then spare a thought for the vines of Skåne, southern Sweden. But if it's possible to ripen grapes for wine production in her home country, surely we can do so in the Surrey Hills, thought Mia Wrigley, co-owner of Chilworth Manor, in the late 2000s. Husband Graham remembers helping his father plant a small vineyard in Kent in the seventies, and when he was given a few 'plant-in-the-garden type' vines for a birthday in 2012, it seemed as though things were falling into place to look more seriously at establishing a commercial vineyard.

The 50-odd acre estate at Chilworth Manor has a fairly colourful history: once owned by William the Conqueror and recorded in the Domesday book, through the seventeenth century the owners were also at the centre of the local gunpowder mills that were in production at that time. Just above the site runs the North Downs Way, where Augustine monks ministered the pilgrims en route to Canterbury at the ancient church of St Martha-on-the-Hill. Supposedly, the secret underground tunnels still run from the manor up to the church, though the vineyard, planted in 2013 just below the main house, is a touch easier to find.

Legacy preservation was a priority of the

The vineyard at Chilworth Manor

Wrigleys on their arrival in 2006, but so was taking the estate forward, especially in terms of produce. Head gardener John MacRae-Brown's job spec soon included vineyard manager; his garden got a bit bigger, and as of 2013, included 11,000 vines.

On the south-facing slopes of greensand below the North Downs, John stood above 'a load of stalky vines in a big patch of dirt' and realised things had just got very real, and the steep learning curve had just got a bit steeper. No surprise the professional advice was to plant the region's big three varietals, intending to make premium, classic-method sparkling wine.

2017 saw the first release of the debut still rosé, with every vintage selling out following the May release. An all but equal split of Meunier and Pinot Noir, it's vibrant and youthful – classically Provençal pale in colour – but rich with aromatics and summer red fruit, and easy, long and crisp.

There's a sparkling rosé, available annually from June, followed by an autumn unleashing of the Classic Cuvée – both dates are worth noting due to the focus on quality and small-quantity approach to production. A classic-method Brut rosé sees two years on lees for the Meunier, Pinot Noir and Chardonnay blend. It's equally delicate in colour and appearance. But like the still version, there is a lot of elegant yet interesting red fruit at its core, and a long, rich and slightly creamy finish.

The vineyard borders an extensive area of protected woodland along the Tillingbourne River, with plenty of wildlife, and beehives in the vineyard. The Manor also continues their tradition of supporting charities by opening their gardens for various events, including 'Picnic & Pimm's'. It's a stunning spot, and immaculately maintained with lots on – and the drinks list just got a whole lot better, too.

Decent spot for a Pimms, and an even better one for some sensational rosé

ALBURY ORGANIC VINEYARD
@ALBURYVINEYARD

Silent Pool, Shere Road, Albury, GU5 9BW
https://www.alburyvineyard.com

What: Tours, tastings, cellar door sales and events
Recommended wines: Classic Cuvée, Sparkling Seyval, rosé, Wild Ferment Sparkling Chardonnay

'Children, dogs and muddy boots all welcome' at Albury Organic Vineyard and cellar door. Nick Wenman's passion for wine stems from winning a school prize and being presented with his book of choice by the head, which he chose as The World Atlas of Wine. Following school he joined an IT firm as a trainee salesman, and left as a divisional board director.

Enrolling on the WSET's Diploma course, he was introduced to legendary vineyard consultant Stephen Skelton, whom he promptly took out for a few lunchtime wines. The lightbulb moment came on that very afternoon break – here was England's most experienced viticulturist telling Nick in 2007 that it was absolutely possible to make great wine in England. So, having negotiated a thirty-year lease with Albury Estate, in went 5 acres of vines across two blocks in 2009, followed by 8 further acres the following year. Two elements have been instrumental in the rise of Albury Estate Vineyard: they've been organic from the very outset of planting, which led to biodynamic conversion a couple of years in. The second is vineyard manager Alex Valsecchi. During her ten years at RHS Wisely, where she planted the small vineyard, Alex's passion and viticultural expertise grew, and she has absolutely thrived alongside Nick at Albury.

A lone poppy among the vines at Albury Estate

For both, there are three fundamental reasons behind their biodynamic approach. As well as the obvious environmental benefits, without a sustainable business model, there's no platform from which you can use the vineyard to positively impact the soil, biodiversity or wider environment. Nick foresaw the increasingly competitive sparkling wine market and felt that this approach, which focused on quality and provenance, would provide them an edge. Finally, having travelled the world and tasted organic and biodynamic wines from all sorts of different regions, the passion shown by these producers, the quality of wine they were making and the sense of place these wines were expressing ultimately inspired him to follow his instinct. From the beginning, they have never once broken any of the principles or stipulations required to be certified organic and biodynamic producers.

There's an abundance of bugs and butterflies, and half a million bees that help pollinate wildflowers and increase biodiversity here, benefiting soil, vine roots and the resulting fruit. The bees are also helping to spread indigenous yeast strains around the vineyard, crucial in the 'Wild Ferment' Chardonnay, of which just a few hundred sparkling bottles are made from initially hand-crushed fruit. Fresh and funky – in a very good way – that distinctive cider apple-like natural yeast aroma supports the pure, zesty and zingy Chardonnay fruit.

Classic Cuvée goes down a slightly more traditional route, and is a great example of biodynamic producers being purveyors of great fruit first, and biodynamics second. Pinot's Noir- and Meunier-led, blended with Chardonnay just fifteen months on lees keeps the focus on that superior, rich, red fruit with supporting richness and a slightly creamy, classy Chardonnay subtlety. Seyval is added to Chardonnay for the Blanc de Blancs – and with it comes great fragrance and English orchard fruit. Seyval

also forms part of Nick's 'lockdown cocktail' made with some Albury Sweet Vermouth that was distilled from a blend of Sauvignon and Pinot Noir next door at Silent Pool Distillery.

With a focus on local distribution, don't expect to see Albury taking on the growing export market anytime soon. It's an all-encompassing approach to environmental benefit, which goes far beyond the tending of the vines. There's a desire to grow the already thriving experience-based events at cellar door. Think children, dogs, muddy boots, amazing fruit and great wines.

Possibly the best view in the Surrey hills

207

Litmus Wines

Dorking, Surrey
https://www.litmuswines.com

What: Not open to the public; online cellar door only
Recommended wines: Orange, Element 20, White Pinot

However long your CV is, I doubt it's as long and as well-travelled as Adelaide-born John Worontschak's, head winemaker at Denbies and Founder of Litmus Wines. Previous job titles held include: carpenter, floor sweeper, sauerkraut maker, hardware store assistant, bedsprings maker and postie, before working the 1977 and 1978 vintages with South Australian legends, Petaluma. More Australian vintages followed before he headed to Burgundy and eventually, in 1988, the Thames Valley. Travelling back and forth between hemispheres and being able to work two vintages a year, he was well ahead of his time.

During the flying winemaker era – through the mid-nineties and early 2000s – John made wine for Tesco in the Czech Republic, and consulted for wineries in other places including, but not limited to: England, Canada, California, Peru, Mexico, Turkey, Uruguay, Chile, Hungary, Bulgaria, Russia, Ukraine, Romania, Germany, India, France, Spain and Italy. Eventually partnering with Sam Harrop to form Litmus Wines in 2008, he was still at the front end of the professional movement.

Taking over the winemaking operations at Denbies in 2010, John and Sam moved the Litmus base there the following year,

continuing the consultancy and contract winemaking services. Four decades after that first vintage at Petaluma, they finally have a market to share all that experience with. Matthieu Elzinga fronts up the winemaking team with John, sourcing fruit from sites across Essex, Surrey and Sussex. The range has always been about championing still wine that moves away from the amateur era of simple fruit-forward and one-dimensional wines. The elegant, pure fruit we can grow here is the base for the Litmus range, which is all about promoting balance, complexity and length of flavour across the range of four wines, where older barrel-ageing and lees contact has become a bit of a trademark.

'Element 20' was first produced in 2010. The current release is an almost equal-part blend of Essex Chardonnay and Pinot Blanc and a final third of Surrey Pinot Gris, all fermented separately in one- to five-year-old French barriques, being left on lees for eleven months before bottling. The richness and texture as a result is so rounded and rewarding, and it's an awesome food wine – as the whole range is intended to be – with lengthy acidity also suggesting gastronomy as well as further flavour-development potential.

Litmus Orange is maybe the very definition in bottle of why John likes it here so much. Fragrant, aromatic English fruit from 90% Bacchus, aged on skins for eighteen weeks, blended with 10% Pinot Noir that was fermented without skins, and aged in older oak barriques. Its bright, concentrated fruit is backed up with layers of savoury, nutty spice.

The White Pinot leads the way in this increasingly popular category; incredible ripe stone-fruit is rounded with mouth-filling texture through nine months on lees in barrel. The honeyed, slightly smoky character is such an asset to the ripe Essex fruit, full of traditional red Pinot flavour and hallmark elegance and complexity.

From Tasmania and Adelaide to the Thames Valley and Dorking, via just about everywhere in between, here is the result of four decades of experience making wines as modern as they come.

White wine from skinless Pinot Noir grapes is something Britain excels at and there are few finer than this 2016 Litmus

Denbies Wine Estate
@DENBIES_WINE_ESTATE

. . . .

London Rd, Dorking, RH5 6AA
https://www.denbies.co.uk

What: Cellar door sales, events and tastings, hotel and restaurant
Recommended wines: Greensands NV, Pinot Noir

Most London-based cyclists will have given Box Hill a crack at some point, winding their way up into the Surrey Hills and eventually overlooking the vines of Denbies Wine Estate. If running is more your thing, then the Mole Valley Park run actually takes place right here among the vineyard. Or you could just take the real athlete's choice and forget both, and instead hit the tasting bar. In 1986, when Adrian White announced he was planning on planting in Dorking, there wasn't even an official record of hectares under vine in Britain. Approximately 500 was the total,[x] which, during 1986 to 1989, Adrian single-handedly grew considerably, putting 100 hectares in the ground.

Advice came from the Mosel Valley at a time when almost all of the vines being planted were the early ripening, disease-resistant German hybrids, but fascinatingly Riesling was included. The famously late-ripening, high-acidity varietal was later pulled out and re-planted in a warmer pocket. Apparently it was only ripening 'once every five years', which I would say was still a relatively good result.

Planting such a volume of vines, when they did, makes Denbies a true pathfinder of the modern, professional industry. Despite bringing a new-world, almost American

Inside the heart of Denbies Wine Estate

approach to technology, the early pioneers at Denbies hadn't reckoned with the almighty power that exists on this side of the Atlantic – the local council planning department. Huge, frost-dispelling propeller fans were installed in the vineyard at a reported cost of £250,000, but, following the first few very early morning alarms – and noise of the props firing up – with no planning permission sought as required, they were just as quickly told to get rid of them.

Several of the initial plantings were later replaced with Chardonnay, Meunier and Pinot Noir, as the potential for classic-method sparkling wine in England gained pace. Rondo, too, with a view to additional reds, went in. Eventually they got on the right side of the council and the stunning winery and visitor centre was built. There's not much you can't do at Denbies today. It's got weddings, hotel stays, the 'Hatch on the Lane' restaurant and a 'vineyard train', which is better than a train because it's essentially a Land Rover Defender that tows you around the best viewpoints of the estate. If recorded voice commentaries and the general public aren't your thing, there are 7 miles of footpaths through the vines for a slightly more relaxed wander, far away from Denbies' 350,000 annual visitors.

The range is huge: I counted eighteen different wines including a sub-ten-quid rosé which goes to show that single figure price points are possible in Britain, but only really from scale producers, and I dare say those well-versed in diversification.

Golden hour at Denbies

211

WEST SUSSEX

BLACKDOWN RIDGE

Trotton Estate Vineyards
@TROTTONESTATE

Gatehouse Ln, Rogate, Petersfield, GU31 5DA
https://trottonestatevineyards.com//estate

What: tours, tastings, cellar door sales
Recommended wines: Spectacular Sparkling, Brilliant Bacchus

Carolyn and Robin Butler spent many happy afternoons down at nearby Cowdray Park Polo Club, prior to establishing Trotton Estate. Robin retired from the sport and Carolyn decided soon after that it simply wasn't as much fun without him. But as the ponies retired with them, or went to other stables, they had a few spare fields that they wondered what to do with.

In 2012 llamas were pretty popular, and cattle and sheep were probably more work than they were viable, but it was driving between Petworth and Midhurst past vineyards owned by Nyetimber and Roebuck Estate, combined with Carolyn's long-time passion for wine, that convinced the Butlers to look a little more closely at the possibility of planting a few vines. It's a good thing they did, because they sit on the same belt of greensand soil that stretches all the way down to those landmark estates, through classic south downland chalk.

I imagine there's the odd bottle of Champagne consumed at polo events now and then, so from the outset a premium quality English sparkling was their desired style. Classic method leads to classic varietals, so goes the traditional tale, so in the ground went Chardonnay, Pinot Noir and Pinot Meunier.

Trotton Estate Vineyards' 'Spectacular Sparkling' and 'Brilliant Bacchus'

There's a bit more creative freedom in the naming of animals than to children, and names of favourite ponies certainly make for much better titles of vineyards. 'Treehut' was planted in 2013, the initial fruit from which was so promising that in 2015, they planted 'El Duke', Carolyn's favourite, along with 'Fat Boy' and 'Gringa'. From their 25,000 vines, they could produce around 30 to 40,000 bottles a year if they so wished, but that's not so much the desire as it is to keep a focus on quality and continue to hone a place that can be passed on down through the generations.

There are just two wines produced currently, one being the Sparkling Brut currently made at Hambledon just over the county border in Hampshire. Predominantly Chardonnay, almost a third Pinot Noir and the balance of Meunier. It's a pretty classic approach, and sees almost three years on lees. Creamy Chardonnay and toasty richness combine nicely; the acidity is just starting to soften but it's still very approachable, in a very nice place indeed. The same can be said of the floral, zesty 'Brilliant Bacchus', which with 5% Pinot Gris adds a touch of rounded stone-fruit complexion, made by Simon at Stopham winery.

Tours end up at the 'tasting shed', overlooking the vines from the middle of two vineyards, and are run by English Vineyard Tours, on which you'll probably see a few very content looking ponies trotting around the vacant paddocks. Not the worst place to retire to.

Trotton Estate Vineyards, named after Carolyn and Robin's favourite polo ponies: Fat Boy, El Duke and Gringa

TINWOOD ESTATE
@TINWOODESTEVINEYARD

Tinwood Farm, Halnaker, Chichester, West Sussex, PO18 0NE
https://www.tinwoodestate.com

What: Cellar door sales and tastings, eco lodge stays
Recommended wines: Blanc de Blancs, Brut NV, rosé

The family of Tinwood Estate's second-generation custodian, Art Tukker, has farmed this patch of Sussex countryside since 1983. As relationships with supermarkets became increasingly tough, his father's enthusiasm for growing iceberg lettuce waned and so, for Art's 21st birthday in 2006, he was given a 250-acre farm. Having just completed a degree in Agriculture at the University of Kent, where his dissertation was on the viability of planting a vineyard on an English farm, the importance of site and soil was not lost.

Some spend years looking for their perfect place to plant, but Art's was right underneath his feet all along. As it happens, iceberg lettuce prefers loose, well-drained yet moisture-retaining soil – so it made sense to grow it here on this chalk and flint.

Despite site suitability, it was still a courageous move in what was then still a pretty niche industry, planting 46,000 vines in 2007, with additions in 2008 and 2015. About half of the 100,000 vines are Chardonnay, almost a third Pinot Noir and the balance, you guessed it, Pinot Meunier.

At the start of the Tinwood journey there wasn't much local vineyard support, for the pretty good reason that in 2007, there wasn't any. Most of the equipment was imported from Germany and came with instructions in German, too.

Vine-side eco-lodges

Tinwood's cellar door

Partnering with Ridgeview Estate was a smart move, as they were able to lend guidance and also make the wine. In return, as a measure of the calibre of fruit Tinwood are growing, they're now the majority provider for Ridgeview's own labels.

Much of what Tinwood do in the vineyard and winery is French-inspired, but the cellar door is very much a tribute to Art's eight months working at a winery in Blenheim, New Zealand. Easy-going and welcoming, it's Kiwi-style-culture at its best. An amazing set-up, complete with vine view eco-lodges, tasting flights, cheese boards and good times.

The range itself is as sleek and as stylish as the ultra-modern, wood-panelled tasting room and accompanying veranda. There are just three wines made here; all vintage-sparkling expressions of the site and season and all extremely classy. The Blanc de Blancs is super refreshing and citrus-driven, and there's a nice touch of sea-spray salinity. At eighteen months on lees, the focus is very much on the approachable style of classic method, but there's a lot of elegant complexity, and it's absolutely superb with some oysters.

The vineyard plantings are reflected in the blend of the Brut, normally around 45% Chardonnay, 35% Pinot Noir and a balance of Meunier. A touch richer than the Blanc de Blancs, more rounded red fruit and additional time on lees adds to the toasty complexity.

Chardonnay dominance to the tune of about 60% brings freshness and finesse to the rosé, sitting nicely with the red fruit-forward character of the two Pinots. Like the wider range, there is a lot to unpick in terms of complexity in the final blends. And these are brilliant to drink from one of the eco-lodges or the tasting room.

STOPHAM VINEYARD
@STOPHAMVINEYARD

Stopham, Pulborough, West Sussex, RH20 1EE
https://www.stophamvineyard.co.uk

What: Cellar door tastings, sales and tours
Recommended wines: Pinot Blanc, Pinot Gris, Barrel-fermented Pinot Blanc

The merging of creativity and science in the production of wine is one of its very many attractive facets. Scientific understanding and precision, I would imagine, also ranks highly in the world of F1 engineering. Which is exactly where Simon Woodhead – owner and winemaker at Stopham – worked until a little Spanish career-siesta back in 2004. Taking a bit of time out in sunnier climes inspired him to take on a career based purely on passion, which led to his enrolling at Plumpton college, studying viticulture.

At a party in the village of Stopham he got wind of a spare bit of land that, due to its dry, sandy soil, was no use for growing regular crops. So, in 2007, the 15 or so acres acquired were planted to Bacchus, Pinot Gris and, fascinatingly, Pinot Blanc. A love of aromatic, still whites inspired these Alsatian varietals – I'm not sure there were many other plantings of Pinot Blanc pre-2010; Stopham's has gone on to be a flag bearer, inspiring plenty of others to follow suit. Slightly more common sparkling desires led to fellow partygoers Pinot Noir and Chardonnay, too.

The range is built on craft, passion and precision. It's all about purity of fruit, complexity in blends and, above all, a focus on pristine and delightfully fragrant varietals. Small batches

Former F1 engineer turned Pinot Blanc pioneer Simon at Stopham

of barrel ferments add further complexity that is carefully handled as Simon isn't big on oak, keeping the focus on the delicate fruit instead. Having said that, my personal favourite of the wines is the tiny-production, barrel-fermented Pinot Blanc, with just a small run of 600 cellar door-only bottles from 2019. The additional texture and ever so slightly oxidative, fleshy style lends itself so well to food, but doesn't lose any of the trademark freshness and crisp acidity.

The most popular wine at cellar door is the Pinot Gris, which, depending on vintage, occasionally has some Bacchus blended in, providing a very expressive, floral uplift. Ever so slightly off-dry, though not obviously so, the added brightness softens out the naturally zingy acidity and makes it easy drinking, but again, precision is key in the high-quality, cool-climate fruit.

A tasting of the Pinot Blanc with Simon inspired Balbina at Bsixtwelve to plant it as her sole varietal, to great success. Though I'm a massive fan of the barrel-fermented version, Stopham's stainless steel version is the purest example of the varietal there is. Just so fresh and flavoursome, it's rich, ripe and rounded but zesty with just a touch of subtle spice; succinct in every aspect.

There's a three-quarters Chardonnay to Pinot classic-method sparkling too, and why not? Sampling it makes a great start to a tasting in the converted, Grade II-listed barn at the former farmyard. Speaking of which, tours and tastings run most Saturdays during the summer months, and you can even tag on a pub lunch by the river, at the equally historic White Hart at Stopham Bridge.

Vintage '21 at Stopham, good times all around

Blackdown Ridge

@BLACKDOWNRIDGE

Blackdown Ridge Estate, Lurgashall, West Sussex, GU27 3BT
https://www.blackdownridge.co.uk

What: Tours, tastings and cellar door sales
Recommended wines: Triomphe, Primordia, Sparkling Rosé

Professor Martin Cook is a world-renowned histopathologist, specialising in melanomas, and sponsored by Cancer Research UK. At the back end of his seventies, he's still travelling the world, sharing his expertise, but on a rare day off at home in Blackdown Park, he doesn't mind the odd glass of wine.

It just so happens he's lived on the estate at Blackdown for the last twenty-five years, beneath the ridge of the same name, which is the highest part of the South Downs. During a wine-fuelled dinner with an Italian family friend – and if you're going to have a wine-fuelled dinner, it may as well be with an Italian friend – Antonio suggested to Martin that the south-facing slopes on which the estate sits would be perfect for planting vines. The vineyard was planted at 130 metres above sea level, which, in 2010, would have been considered too high, but now makes them well-placed looking forward, with frost and drainage rolling down the hill, which is especially beneficial given the part-clay makeup of the soil.

It was planted to Pinot Noir, Meunier, Chardonnay and Pinot Blanc, largely inspired by the wines of Champagne. These vines were joined by Bacchus, Triomphe and, latterly, Sauvignon Blanc, for the range of Blackdown stills. It's a striking spot, and tucked away to the side of the vineyard is the purpose-built winery, where English Wine Project's Kieron Atkinson and business development manager-turned-2020 winemaker, Lucinda Colucci, make the wines.

Primordia – meaning first created – is a classic-method, classic blend of Chardonnay, Pinot Noir and Meunier. At just fourteen months on lees but with several years in bottle, the focus is fresh and fruit-forward, with citrus zest and liveliness at the fore but ageing that has rounded it all out and let the ripeness shine. Pinot Noir with a touch of Meunier makes up the sparkling rosé; it's bright and crisp but classy and defined – red summer fruit abounds and is and backed up by toasty background richness.

As well as a rosé and a seriously well-priced Sauvignon Blanc that is fragrant yet attractively subtle and rounded, the headline in the still bracket is the Triomphe red. Ten months in French oak, this is voluptuous and generous in body, dark fruit-driven and with wood-derived smoke and spice, a genuine by-the-fire English red.

Lucinda worked with Martin in the NHS and, when offered an opportunity for a career-change, she jumped at the chance and just kept going. She also transformed the labels with a modern re-brand – the artwork inspired by the old goose that lives on the estate's pond. The setting is a really unique part of West Sussex, as attractive as the wines the site is producing.

Winery at Blackdown Ridge

Roebuck Estates
@ROEBUCKESTATES

Upperton Farm, Tillington
https://www.roebuckestates.co.uk

What: Cellar door sales, tastings by appointment
Recommended wines: Classic Cuvée, Rosé de Noirs, Blanc de Noirs

Site and soil, sun hours and supreme professionalism. These are the metrics on which the potential for world-class winemaking has been realised by those paving the way for others to follow. Roebuck Estates are the living, breathing, growing epitome of this, and standing at the top of the home vineyard, you can see exactly why. Founded in 2016 by Mike Smith and John Ball, and run by James Mead and Danielle Whitehead, the Roebuck brand is a relatively new one, but the full story goes back much further and much deeper.

The sweeping South Downs stand tall in the distance, protecting much of the region from the cold south-westerly weather fronts. On the gentle slopes opposite are Roebuck's five premium vineyard sites, which combine a total of 80 hectares and around 200,000 vines. Five separate sites mean five different microclimates, five unique soil structures and five contrasting growing seasons, every year. Across the big three sparkling grapes – Chardonnay and Pinot Noir and Meunier, and a mixture of Champagne and Burgundy clones of these varietals – there is vast potential for stylistically contrasting batches of fruit from not just each vineyard, but even from certain blocks and rows of vines – the 40-acre Hazlehurst vineyard is split into eight distinctly

A range of wines as good as any

different blocks alone. Take all these variables and multiply them by various winemaking techniques – be it oak maturation and to what degree, plus whole bunch-pressing, or not – and you start to see how Roebuck can actually produce scores of different small-batch wines every vintage – almost numbering 100 in 2018 – each with their own fingerprint. Blended from these base wines are a final stable of just three, such is the focus on quality and complexity in the resulting range.

In the vineyard itself is a nifty bit of kit called Sectormentor, providing real time and seasonal-comparative data on individual vines via a quick scan of the tags in the app. It tracks everything from soil biology to biodiversity levels, ripeness, alcohol and yield predictions, harvest tracking and synced weather station info. Ultimately this alone won't ensure grape quality, but it will allow for increasingly informed decision-making, which absolutely will be to the continued benefit of the crop.

Roebuck's 'home' vineyard was planted in 2006 on well-drained sandy soil slopes by neighbours Upperton Vineyards at their Tillington site. On the other side of Petworth – itself full of so much olde English charm, and where you can pick up some of the Roebuck range at Hennings wine merchants, and kilos of cheese at the Hungry Guest Deli – is the equally attractive Roman Villa vineyard. Originally owned by Nyetimber who planted it exclusively to Pinot Noir in 2007, it is just 13 acres and some way away from the centre of operations. Their loss was very much Roebuck's gain as it provided all of the fruit for the 2015 Blanc de Noirs.

Throughout the range there's a depth in complexity, structure and class, which is a tribute to the multi-site, multi-batch approach. Partial premium Burgundy barrel-fermenting of base wines adds a touch of textural attractiveness and a slightly fleshy development which is added to by almost four years on lees for the Classic Cuvée. It's a richer style, layered and ever improving with air, so worth giving it some breathing time or – if you've the self-discipline – cellar time. With 100% Pinot Noir from the Roman Villa vineyard, the Blanc de Noirs is rich but superbly balanced, ripe-stone-fruit-driven yet super complex and savoury, and so long and silky, with limited availability in magnum format, in what is the single best ageing format. The aforementioned cellaring self-discipline was considerably lacking here, however, as my mag of Roebuck Blanc de Noirs lasted all of about forty-eight hours.

The Rosé de Noirs is also sourced from the Roman Villa vineyard. Again, part barrel-fermentation and extended lees ageing up to three years underlines a sense of consistency across the range. There's a touch of Précoce added to the blend here too, an approachable brightness uplift that very much complements the vibrant, expressive red fruit-driven rosé, that's not at all lacking in richness and longevity.

Of all the premium producers, it's only at the very best do you come away thinking about the great value that the entire range represents; as ever a mark of sheer complexity and of the most interesting wines. This is outstanding kit that any fan of sparkling wine needs to see, and I'll definitely be back for more of all three. I might just have to ask someone responsible to cellar them for me next time.

Super-premium vines at Roebuck Estates, in the heart of the Sussex South Downs

NUTBOURNE VINEYARDS
@NUTBOURNEVINEYARDS

· ·

Gay Street, Pulborough, RH20 2HH
https://www.nutbournevineyards.com

What: Cellar door tastings, tours, sales
Recommended wines: Chardonnay, Nutty Vintage, Nutty Wild, Pinot Noir

This really is West Sussex wine country. There are five vineyards in walking distance from the vines at Nutbourne, including one beginning with N – and ending with timber – that makes more wine and gets more coverage at royal weddings, but none who encompass the very essence of wine as fully as the Gladwin Family.

This is grape-to-glass and paddock-to-plate philosophy so completely that if you're going to anyone's home for dinner it will struggle to beat their offering. Absolutely everything from a winemaking perspective is done on-site. From the 24 acres of nine varieties, to the making, bottling, ageing and packaging. Even the label artwork is painted by mum and co-owner Bridget, who also makes her own feta and blue cheese.

With three sons struggling somewhat at a city school, Peter and Bridget decided country life was calling, and craved being outside and growing things. So, for the last thirty years, that's exactly what sons Richard, Oliver and Gregory have been doing.

Chef Oliver and restaurateur brother Richard run the restaurants The Shed in Notting Hill, Rabbit on the Kings Road, Chelsea, Nutbourne in Battersea, Sussex in Soho, and, the latest addition, The Fat Badger in Richmond. They source ingredients from brother Greg, who farms Sussex cattle, sheep and

Robin 'Freanovino' disgorging Nutty Vintage

pigs back in West Sussex. True to the restaurants' 'local and wild' approach, all of the ingredients come from the family farm and what can't be produced themselves is either foraged, or sourced from other local producers. The farm itself runs along the river Nut, and the woodland at the tributary spring is the 'Bourne', but when the Gladwins arrived in 1990, there was already a ten-year-old vineyard on-site. Then an importer of wine, Peter thought he would just grow and make it himself instead, thinking running a vineyard surely couldn't be that hard.

There's a great tour at Nutbourne, starting in the 'wine lodge' mid-vines, and wandering through the wildflower meadows and wetlands, past the alpacas. Best of all it's a tour immersed in four decades of history. Peter remembers those early Nyetimber wines with Stuart and Sandy Moss, and the Nutbourne range is an amazing expression of all of that experience, blended with a very contemporary feel, reflective of this wonderful, naturally farmed, mostly greensand site.

'Nutty Wild', the non-vintage, predominantly Pinot Noir sparkling, is classic method in production but far from it in style – fermented to 10% alcohol – it's light, fresh, young and easy. With super attractive, tangy red summer fruit, it's about as good a sparkling as any to have plenty of stocked in the wine rack for just about any occasion. Nutty Vintage Brut is much more traditional in approach and sees three years on lees in the vineyard's underground cave, which is carved out of the land next to the winery. Like the entire range, serious bang-for-buck quality is absolutely epitomised in the still Chardonnay as well. This ripe site is evident in the generous fruit-forward style, added to by full malolactic fermentation and six months in French oak. It's still the crisp, zesty green apple-upfront Chardonnay we'd expect, but its richness and complexity frankly make a mockery of the ridiculously generous price.

Nutbourne Pinot Noir is another classic. Dark, cherry-driven and with some depth and structure added to by delicate handling in both French and American oak. 'Sussex Reserve' is a field blend encompassing the German varietals and is sold in a flute bottle as a nod to its composition – which also includes some skinless Pinot Noir. Super accessible in every respect – and on all of the family restaurants' wine lists.

There's a lot going on at Nutbourne, a lot to see and a great deal of quality to taste. Their approach revolves around family, friends, eating and drinking, summing up many of the things that make the British wine industry so great.

Lunch at Nutbourne Vineyards in West Sussex

NYETIMBER

@NYETIMBER

. . . .

Gay Street, West Chiltington, RH20 2HH
https://nyetimber.com

What: Ticketed open weekends
Recommended wines: Classic Cuvée, Blanc de Blancs, Tillington Single Vineyard

From the Domesday book and Henry VIII to pioneers of premium sparkling wine in Great Britain – Sandy and Stuart Moss – the Nyetimber estate's history dates back at least 1000 years.

Nyetimber, derived from the Anglo-Saxon word 'Nitimbreha', meaning 'new wood', was latterly given by Henry VIII to Thomas Cromwell. The restored fifteenth-century barn is a sole relic, still standing today. Anne of Cleves was given the estate as part of her annulment from Henry VIII – with the notable bonus of being allowed to keep her head – and, a little over four centuries later, American couple Sandy and Stuart Moss arrived and bought the property.

They will forever be remembered as true pioneers of the shift to professionalism in the history of Great British winemaking – especially in the field that the industry's become most famous for: classic-method sparkling. Most other producers in 1988 were growing hybrid Germanic grape varieties, so to the Anglophile couple from Chicago, it seemed there was an obvious gap for quality sparkling wine. Although the first English classic method from the big three Champagne grapes had been made five years earlier – the Mosses planted Chardonnay, Pinot Noir and Meunier, and

Chardonnay vines at Nyetimber Estate, planted in 1988 by Sandy and Stuart Moss

A former residence of Henry VIII, including fifteenth-century barn: Nyetimber Estate

invested in a hugely professional operation, with this premium style exclusively in mind.

Their first wine, from Chardonnay planted in 1988 and made in 1992, won best sparkling wine in England. Their second, a blend of all three from 1993, won best non-Champagne sparkling wine in the world at the International Wine & Spirit Competition in 1998. But what they did was worth so much more than awards. Classic-method sparkling is a timely, costly and skill-heavy process, but by meticulously managing vines and cropping small, finely tuned yields with the help of Champenois consultancy, in both personnel and equipment, they showed the country – and the world – the results that could be achieved.

When they returned to the States in 2001, songwriter Andy Hill bought the property and, within a couple of years, current cult figure

Dermot Sugrue, now of Wiston Estate, was making the wine. Eric Heerema bought the property in 2006, and the range now consists of seven wines from 350 hectares under vine and counting, across eleven vineyard sites and the three counties of Sussex, Kent and Hampshire. West Sussex is home to the majority of six sites, then there are three in Kent and two in Hampshire, where most of the Chardonnay comes from chalk, though the wines are actually made at their processing facility in Crawley.

When Eric Heerema took over, winemakers Cherie Spriggs and Brad Greatrix were on the west coast of Canada and were pondering the potential of quality sparkling wine in England. Cherie genuinely emailed info@nyetimber.com, asking if there was much of a wine industry around them and if so, if there were any winemaking gigs

Nyetimber Blanc de Blancs in the park

going. Turns out the answer to both questions was yes. Fast forward a decade and in 2018 Cherie not only became the first person outside Champagne to win the International Wine Challenge's award for best sparkling winemaker in the world, but also became the first woman to claim the coveted title.

Within their hundreds of hectares, Nyetimber own more vines than most of the major label Champagne houses. They're able to source vastly contrasting parcels of fruit, producing as many as 115 batches of base wine across their three county holdings. Most of the range – 'Tillington' single vineyard aside – is a multi-site blend, and all see extended lees ageing as standard.

At the top end is the '1086' pair, a nod to the Domesday book and the estate's history. They are also, currently, the most expensive wines you can buy that are of British origin, at more than £300 for the duo in regular 750ml format.

Following the consistent 'house style' route, thanks to the multi-vintage blending, the Classic Cuvée is predominantly Chardonnay, up to about 60%, with most of the rest from Pinot Noir. Reserve wines – up to a third of the final wine – go back just over a decade, whereas the base vintage is normally of about half that age. Yet there's a great freshness to it, which is slightly saline sea spray and refreshing.

The vintage Blanc de Blancs is sourced from a mixture of chalk-based vineyards in Hampshire, normally around a third, and greensand in West Sussex. A small amount – less than 5% – is fermented in new Burgundy barrels, which adds a touch of extra complexity, as does the five years on lees. It's still so fresh but has a developing richness and noticeable oak influence. It is also super elegant and slightly creamy with loads of time left on it yet.

Nyetimber aim to be producing two million bottles annually within the next decade. To put that into context, Moët make about thirty million across their range each year. But don't compare the two, not least because the wines of Nyetimber are a million miles apart, and going in a much better direction. With the ability to source great sites and fruit accordingly, they're still able to continue what Stuart and Sandy Moss started, in exclusively producing high-quality classic-method sparkling wine in an ultra-professional way. Just like the wider modern British industry – the early days of which they played a huge role in shaping – they are now doing so on a much bigger scale.

A good day's tasting

AMBRIEL

@AMBRIELSPARKLING

Nutbourne Ln, Nutbourne, Nr Pulborough, RH20 2HS
https://ambrielsparkling.com

What: Cellar door sales and events by appointment
Recommended wines: MV Classic Cuvée, rosé, Blanc de Noirs

Barrister and banker Wendy and Charles Outhwaite respectively, left their careers and planted vines at Ambriel for a debut harvest in 2010. 23 acres sit on greensand – probably the unsung hero soil of the South East, such is its free-draining and heat-retaining potential. Just down the road from Nyetimber, Ambriel, like many others, followed their lead in planting Chardonnay, Pinot Noir and Meunier across varied, lower-yielding clones for maximum flavour extraction.

The vineyards don't use insecticides or herbicides, and aim to promote biodiversity throughout, so during the winter they are mob-grazed by Ouessant sheep – the world's smallest breed – and hedges are kept in trim by Golden Guernsey goats.

The Multi Vintage Classic Cuvée is a blend of more than two thirds Pinot Noir, with all but 1% of the balance being Chardonnay, aged on lees for four and a half years. I can't believe the calibre and quality of these wines will be in the sub-£30 price bracket for long; it's outstanding value which really is synonymous with the best of English sparkling wine production.

English Reserve is designed to best match 'wedding cake, fruity puddings and our favourite cheese', according to Wendy. Ultimately, it's the

Ambriel vines

same wine as the MV, but with the addition of 32 grams of sugar dosage as opposed to the more conventional Brut style of 8 grams per litre in the former. I'd add spicy Asian stir fry to the food matching list; the sugar uplift is not super sweet, just bright and spice softening.

Ambriel Rosé is from the pick of thirty-seven rows of Pinot Noir vines, from the famed 777 clone. Maceration on skins for thirty-six hours and only the free-run juice is vinified, which sees fifty-nine months on lees. It is super premium production and, although this one just penetrates the over-£30 price point, it's almost the best value of the lot, given the supreme quality and handling.

There's a very limited, 125-magnum release of 'Cloud Ten' from their maiden vintage in 2010, at 70% Chardonnay, with a huge 112 months on lees. Magnum really is the best format for ageing, as the bottle neck is the same size as a regular 750ml bottle, so there's twice as much juice to air, slowing the wine's development.

Another site from the heart of the West Sussex wine country, and one that is every bit as premium as their neighbours.

©Wendy Outhwaite

Ashling Park Estate

@ASHLINGPARK

West Ashling, Chichester, PO18 9DJ
https://www.ashlingpark.co.uk

What: Cellar door sales, tastings and tours, restaurant Thurs–Sun, eco-lodges
Recommended wines: Blanc de Blancs, Meunier Rosé, Classic Cuvée, sparkling rosé

The roughly 50-acre estate at Ashling Park was formerly home to 1st Viscount Portal, Commander-in-Chief of Bomber Command and Commander-in-Chief of Air Staff from October 1940. A long-time aide to Winston Churchill, the Manor was also home to cabinet war rooms that were in use throughout the Second World War.

Barrie and Janet Gardner are the current owners of Ashling Park, an estate that was completely private until the vineyard hosted its first tours in April 2021. Barrie, having read that planting vines was a good way to add value to an estate, acquired an already established vineyard just down the road from where 4 additional hectares of the 'home' vineyard were planted in 2017.

Just a mile from the sea at the foot of the Downs, this is one of those little pockets on the south coast that seems to attract the sun, recording up to 2 degrees more warmth than elsewhere in the locality. The tree-lined vineyard is nicely protected from those coastal breezes blowing in past Chichester harbour, the greensand and flint soil contrasting the satellite site's chalk as a base for the holy trinity of sparkling wine grapes that Ashling have in the ground. In predominantly

Meet you at the tasting barrel

the two Pinots over Chardonnay, sparkling winemaker Dermot Sugrue had never seen such sugar ripeness in British grapes as he did here in 2019. He told Gail Gardner that if she delivered to him clean grapes he would use them to make world-class wine, and it seems that both sides of the bargain are panning out rather nicely.

Where else to start on the wines than with the double-trophy-winning Classic Cuvée; where else to do so than served from one of the re-purposed barrels now full of chilled bottles, strategically positioned at different parts of the vineyard? 60% Chardonnay, 30% Pinot Noir and 10% Meunier, at five years on lees it has all the toasty, creamy richness that sings classic method. Standing up to this body of texture is plenty of baked and stewed apple, all in sync and all class, so much so it could easily be a great Grower Champagne. Which is why I think I like the sparkling rosé so much, because this is truly an expression of land, specifically the green and pleasant. An expression of elegant English fruit, so delicate and pure, but in no way lacking any intensity or ripe red fruit from the predominantly Pinot Noir composition; cider apples, hedgerow and even a touch of rhubarb and herbs.

The two-level tasting room and restaurant is as striking as the vineyard views from either balcony or terrace, currently serving a menu paired to the range of wines, for lunches and early dinners, just a stroll away from five premium eco-lodges.

These all look as good as a glass of the citrus-zest and zingy Blanc de Blancs, or the Meunier-dominant still rosé. There's even some estate gin made from the pressings of Pinot Noir grapes named after Rocco the vineyard dog, 'Pointer's Paw', and a rum named after Bean, the plump beagle. Whether for the dogs, views, stays, food, gins, rums, or just because you now can, whatever the reason you visit Ashling Park, make sure you taste the wine.

Picked a good day for a wander around Ashling Park – a formerly private estate until vineyard tours started in 2021

Vine-side tasting room and restaurant

DILLIONS VINEYARD
@DILLIONS_VINEYARD

Tanyard Lane, Staplefield, Haywards Heath, RH17 6HH
https://www.dillionsvineyard.co.uk

What: Tours, tastings and cellar door tastings by appointment
Recommended wines: Bacchus, rosé

As a child David Trott remembers long road trips around French vineyards and dank cellars in the sixties and seventies, and even less comfortable trips back home, sitting on boxes of wine with his feet by his chin. Ever immersed in wine, sometimes quite literally, and with a passion for horticulture and self-sufficiency in fruit and veg produce, it was a natural progression for David to go into vineyard ownership in 2019. He and wife Lisa see themselves as custodians of this special site during their period in the estate's history, and under them it has been put back into productive use.

Their 25 acres sit in the High Weald area, not far from the River Ouse and well covered in both wildlife and woodland. But the centrepiece here is the stunning fifteenth-century farmstead, so full of character and charm, and now surrounded by vines.

Theirs is an all-encompassing approach to a high-quality wine offering that ultimately starts in the vineyard. Ten acres of Bacchus, Chardonnay, Pinot Noir, Meunier and latterly Cabaret Noir were planted on the south-west-facing, gently sloping bed of silty loam over greensand. From the outset, David and designer-by-trade Lisa looked at their brand from a

Vibrant colours in autumn at Dillions

consumer's point of view, and approached every facet as professionally as they do the vines.

The opportunity for sparkling wine in both site and sales lends itself to plantings of the big three sparkling varieties, but the main focus of Dillion's production will be still, with Bacchus accounting for about 60% of the vineyard, and as of May 2021, 500 Cabaret Noir vines. David's ultimate ambition is to produce a medium- to full-bodied red that his mates are happy drinking in front of the fire while watching the autumn rugby internationals; an admirable philosophy. Cab Noir could well fill this current void – which is so far not particularly feasible due to a lack of sun hours and ripening warmth required for the more robust red grapes. The disease-resistant Swiss crossing of Cabernet Sauvignon and an as yet undisclosed other had its name changed from Cabernet to Cabaret in 2017, and is being explored by several other notable producers.

Both current releases are curated by Defined contract winery in Kent, and both epitomise great English summer drinking. Bacchus is a ripe and an expressive blend of stone-fruit and classic, zesty floral aromatics. The Pinot Noir rosé is equally easy-going, light in colour and very much a strawberries-and-cream style – but easy-going doesn't mean uninteresting. There's a touch of richness with pristine Pinot fruit, lending itself to lots of food-matching potential, as it also does an afternoon in the sun.

Super Sunday sunset at Dillions vineyard near Staplefield

SUGRUE SOUTH DOWNS

@SUGRUE_SOUTH_DOWNS

Storrington, West Sussex
https://www.sugruesouthdowns.com

What: Not open to the public
Recommended wines: Cuvée Boz, #ZODO, Cuvée Dr Brendan O'Regan, The Trouble with
Dreams

The late, great Steven Spurrier called Dermot Sugrue 'England's greatest winemaker'. Dermot, an Irishman, moved to the UK in 1992 aged eighteen and spent a couple of years as an independent financial advisor. Despite this background in sound financial planning, he still embarked on a career in wine, and after two seasons in France with Bordelais powerhouses Château L'Eglise Clinet and Leoville Barton, from 2003 he oversaw Nyetimber's surge onto the sparkling wine world stage.

From the outside looking in, head winemaker at Nyetimber in 2006 was the place to be, but he resigned, leaving behind Nyetimber's 1988-planted vineyards, their market following, tech and seriously well-funded future, for the Goring family's one-year-old Wiston Estate vineyard and portfolio of wines made, then numbering precisely zero. But they did have an old turkey shed in which they planned to put a winery. The mutual vision Dermot, Harry and Pip Goring had clearly aligned spectacularly, and the opportunity to build a winery and premium West Sussex sparkling brand from scratch was obviously too good to turn down. Now Dermot is probably our most talked-about winemaker, the range under his

Abbey picking at Sugrue's Mount Harry vineyard during the '21 vintage

own label probably the most sought after. Both his reputation and that of his label is in no small part thanks to his partner in every sense, Ana Đogić. She has over a decade of international winemaking experience and is now in charge of the vines and the outstanding fruit they produce for the Sugrue label.

Tucked away near Wiston Estate's trio of vineyards are two of Sugrue's own, even including some cuttings from Bollinger's Vieilles Vignes Françaises vines at Storrington, and Mount Harry near Lewes.

The Wiston Estate opportunity also encompasses a contract winemaking role, so he's behind plenty of other sparkling labels too, and they're almost all just as successful. This wide access to fruit gives a first-hand look at the regionality we're developing as a reflection of every individual site and the sense of place in its unique characteristics. The 2015 Chardonnay from Hampshire's Jenkyn Place vineyard was so good, Sugrue bottled some under the Cuvée Boz label, which was dedicated to his brother and released in 2021. Scintillatingly precise and made with longevity in mind, seeing zero oak but long-lees ageing, it's a contrasting expression to Jenkyn's own version, also made by him. Both wines are incredible expressions of great fruit; Cuvée Boz is crisp and fresh but marries white flowers and textural complexity so eloquently, with that hallmark zingy acidity.

Oak is at times incorporated, but always old and at least 500 litres in format, as a method of adding texture and development rather than direct flavour. There's less of a need for malolactic fermentation to soften acidity as a result, though it's sometimes incorporated in the cooler years. Dosage is all about balance, too – normally around 9 grams per litre, but uplifting fruit takes centre stage. #ZODO, standing for Zero Dosage, is made in years ripe enough not to warrant a single balancing gram of sugar. A Sugrue standard blend of 60% Chardonnay to 40% Pinot Noir, half-fermented in steel with malo, half in barrel without. It is super precise and intense; cooking apple fruit, long, and just so well in sync.

The flagship Cuvée 'Dr Brendan O'Regan', again Chardonnay-dominant and blended from barrel-aged reserve wines of the best years. Rich and powerful, it has incredible structure and fruit weight, yet it is so elegant and defined, and remarkably vibrant. The potential longevity is staggering, so tightly wound but offering so much already at the same time.

This is seriously good gear and as detailed and fine-tuned as any range in Britain. You don't have to be on the circuit long before you've probably heard about Dermot and heard a lot about his wines before you're able to taste them. When you finally do, the over-delivering of quality still outweighs immense expectation. With a tiny production volume, that is ever-increasing in demand and notoriety, these early vintages are the collectors' items of the present, let alone the future.

Looking over the Mount Harry vineyard and the rolling South Downs

Wiston Estate

North Farm, Washington, RH20 4BB
https://www.wistonestate.com

What: Tasting, tours, sales and events
Recommended wines: Vintage Cuvée, Vintage Reserve NV, Vintage Rosé

The 6000-acre Wiston Estate has been in the Goring family since 1743. Harry Goring had requests from people to come and see the vineyard almost as soon as it was planted. Having farmed these fields for thirty years, he said not once before did anyone ever ask to come and look at his wheat and barley.

It was Pip Goring who was the brains behind the idea of a vineyard here. Growing up in Cape Town among the vines of the Western Cape, it seemed obvious to her that the estate's slopes of South Downland chalk would make an ideal place to plant. Thirty-four years later Harry agreed, and what they've achieved since 2006 is as impressive as any other producer here or elsewhere.

Vineyard manager James McLean has worked in British vineyards for over a decade – previously at one of the country's best, Harrow & Hope in the Thames Valley Chilterns. Clearly, he saw plenty of potential in West Sussex to tempt him away, and not just among the vines. One 2005 conversation with the Goring family about their vision was enough to tempt winemaker Dermot Sugrue from Nyetimber; he's been here ever since.

Sugrue had already identified the site as a potentially great choice while on the lookout for his own label. The Wiston vineyards are across three sites: Findon Park, North Farm and Broadwoods. The latter is exclusive to Chardonnay and so well-sheltered, which, combined with its lower altitude, gets up to 2 degrees' extra warmth, and ripens Chardonnay as much as two weeks before the two Pinots.

The original 16-acre Findon vineyard, planted on chalk to all three varieties, is the heart of the operation and home to the tasting barn. There's a block within the eastern part of the vineyard that is consistently providing what Dermot and James consider the best Chardonnay, and it's exclusively this parcel that goes into the duo of Blanc de Blancs wines.

In 2006 North Farm was home to a disused turkey shed that has since become the Wiston winery, inside which is a very special Coquard press. It enables gentle pressing of premium fruit and the preservation of pristine juice as a result. The latest addition to the North Farm winery is the Chalk restaurant, sourcing and showcasing as much produce from across the estate as possible.

The composition of the range is as precise as the wines themselves – a non-vintage Brut, rosé and Blanc de Blancs, matched with premium, vintage expressions of each style too, recently joined by a single season Blanc de Noirs. There are square labels for the non-vintages, round for the vintage wines. The comparisons between each are so interesting,

The tasting lodge at Wiston Estate

similar and stark all at the same time. The pair of rosés are the greatest example of this – the non-vintage is Pinot Noir-led – but almost an equal part blend of the three varietals – lots of approachable, delicate red fruit and super freshness is retained from just two years on lees; it's classy crowd-pleasing summer drinking at its best. The vintage, on the other hand, is distinctively concentrated, rich and complex. It's almost three quarters Pinot Noir, and the balance a majority Meunier with just a 10% Chardonnay finish, two-thirds see old Burgundy barrels and the remaining third malo, to further soften acidity and enhance roundness. Five years on lees develops the red fruit into a tangy, slightly honeyed and spicy cinnamon- and orange peel-driven expression of pure food-matching class, crying out to be enjoyed alongside some game or Christmas pudding.

The 2015 Cuvée is easily a top five wine from this trip, such concentrated and intense ripe fruit – complemented by each of the Pinot Noir, Chardonnay and Meunier varietals ageing separately in barrel. They are powerful and of great structure, though not at all lacking Wiston's signature finesse, in turn aided by three years' softening on lees. It's long, intense and concentrated yet so elegant, fresh and vibrant.

There's not a wine that comes close to missing the mark in the Wiston range. Each one is a reflection of the incredible vineyards and fruit they yield, the processes undertaken in showcasing them and their contrasting styles. Looking at the greatest producers around the world, most have decades and decades more experience than Wiston, but you can absolutely mention them in the same bracket. As for where these wines and their experience will take them, I can't wait to find out, because I'll be following the journey from here on in.

Harvest in full swing at Wiston Estate

Wiston Estate's incredible Coquard press

DIGBY FINE ENGLISH

@DIGBYFINEENGLISH

Tasting room: 55–57 High St, Arundel, BN18 9AJ
https://digby-fine-english.com

What: Tasting flights and food matches, cellar door sales
Recommended wines: Vintage Rosé, Vintage Reserve, Blanc de Noirs, Brut NV

Pirate-turned-inventor Sir Kenelm Digby spent much of his life trying to repair the family name after his father was hanged for a part in Guy Fawkes's gunpowder plot. Sir Ken later invented the modern 750ml wine bottle, the volume being equivalent to an average amount of air in one continuous breath, which made the hand-blown manufacturing process more efficient, and therefore more profitable.

With a punt for added strength and utilising coal-fired glass, his bottles were strong enough to withhold the CO_2 pressure of secondary-fermented fizz, and paved the way for Champagne being enjoyed as a sparkling wine.

Founders of Digby Fine English, Trevor and Jason, embarked on a particularly tough gig visiting wine producers in California when researching for their own wine start-up. The advice was unequivocal: get the best fruit by working with established, premium growers and build a brand that is 100% focused on quality at every stage.

Digby are to a certain extent unique in their *négociant* model approach, working with vineyards across the south of England, from Kent to Dorset, sourcing a variety of Pinot Noir, Meunier and Chardonnay that are also

A toast…

242

made under contract by Dermot Sugrue.

The level of attention to detail is staggering – there's even Digby-designed glassware (a merging of the classic flute and more open glass) to best showcase the wines. The labels are a tribute to the curved bottle that Digby invented: peel back the neck foil and there's a flash of purple – a nod to British tailoring and the inside of a jacket. On the back of the neck there's a toast: 'To past and present, to modesty and refinement, to fables and follies, to courage and curiosity, to adventure and abandon, to science and satire, to bishops and brigands, to green and pleasant. To England.' Well, cheers to that.

Securing their first piece of real estate in 2022 with the acquisition of their favourite vineyard site, Digby are also the proud proprietors of Britain's first town-centre cellar door. In an old bank on Arundel's high street you can sit beneath a huge portrait of Sir Ken and taste your way through the range, with Sussex cheese, British pairing plate, or both.

But for all the nods to tradition and charming old England, the wines blend the super modern, as do the stories behind them – each having its own place in the family. The 2014 sparkling rosé is the 'hairy-chested foodie brother': good with Cantonese Duck and maybe the best food pairing in this entire book. Natural acidity in the wine cuts through duck's fatty meat, and all the richness, texture and spice meet the vibrant red fruit and equally robust body and rich texture in the wine, from 20% barrel fermentation and thirty months on yeast lees. Sensational Sunday is that one!

Playing understudy to the vintage release is the 'athletic, Olympian sister' Leander Pink; a non-vintage rosé version, named after the world's oldest rowing club, whose young athlete programme Digby sponsors. Bright in colour and fruit, it's coxed by vibrant Pinot Noir, but there's some slightly ethereal Meunier and rich, aged Chardonnay in the blend. A bankside smasher for sure, but lots of interest and complexity to unpick too.

The 'cheeky baby brother' Non-Vintage Brut is approachable, fruit-first and, while seemingly less serious on initial interaction, is developing superbly. A minimum of two years on lees – but usually more like three – the two-thirds Pinots to third Chardonnay component makes it a pretty tasty early week treat. By Wednesday it's basically time to celebrate the weekend so centre stage is the vintage reserve, a two-thirds Sussex and Hampshire Chardonnay-led, 11% base wine barrel-fermented, sixty-month lees-aged, 'first born brother'. Only produced in years the greensand-based Chardonnay shows power and structure for long ageing, the resulting eight-year-old is still alive with mouth-watering acidity, richness, toasty yeast and lots of pear, green apple and cut hay-like freshness.

Saturday night lights call for the vintage Blanc de Noirs; you won't get much change from sixty quid, but value is always relative to quality as much as it is price. Only 1500 bottles were produced of the 2010 vintage that is a slightly dominant Pinot Noir to Meunier split. Nine years in bottle on lees and with such high-quality Hants and Sussex fruit, it not only hits the hallmark of many a world-class wine in marrying power and elegance in equal measure, but it will still be drinking a long time after the last bottle leaves the cellar door.

Digby Fine English are a tribute to invention and ingenuity of old and present, to site and soil, to modest genius. They are producers of private labels for Harvey Nichols, the House of Commons, pioneers of the *négociant* model and the first town-centre cellar door in this rolling green land that just became even more pleasant.

ALBOURNE ESTATE
@ALBOURNEESTATE

Albourne Farm, Shaves Wood Ln, Albourne, Hassocks, BN6 9DX
https://albourneestate.co.uk

What: Cellar door tastings, sales and tours, charcuterie and cheese platters, Friday supper club, picnics
Recommended wines: Bacchus, Barrel 24 Chardonnay, Sandstone Ridge, Pinot Noir

Alison Nightingale eventually found Albourne Farm following a career in multinational marketing and through a viticulture and winemaking degree at nearby Plumpton Agricultural College. A huge focus of Albourne's is to produce high-quality, site-specific wines with as low a carbon output as possible. Originally planted on the greensand slopes in 2010, a major investment in this direction was 159 winery-roof solar panels that create more than enough energy for their use, so surplus is exported back to the grid.

The 42,000 vines across 30 acres provide the exclusively estate-grown fruit, and not buying in extra means fewer food miles in the production. The winery was put into already existing farm buildings and the cellar door tasting room added on top of it, the mezzanine against the natural gradient of the land. There's even a long-term ambition of moving to non-glass – and thus lighter – packaging.

The thriving cellar door at Albourne also means less volume leaving the estate, encouraging more consumption at source, meaning more reasons for more people to drink more on-site. From Friday supper clubs, pizza nights and dishes served from food trucks, it's a super accessible and inclusive atmosphere which matches what wine is all about. With views across the rolling South Downs, the

Bringing the noise: Albourne Estate American barrel-aged Chardy

spot is a pretty nice place to do your part in helping Albourne hit their environmental targets, too.

A range of vines were put in to allow experimenting and produce contrasting styles depending on what each season decides to send their way. Chardonnay, Pinot Noir, Meunier, Pinot Blanc, Pinot Gris, Bacchus, Ortega and Dornfelder is a nice mix, and many of these can be used for still or sparkling. The focus on still is not solely to reduce the need for thicker glass to contain the pressure in sparkling, but is part of a holistic approach to winemaking that is very much focused on accessibility and growing the wider bracket.

As a result, Albourne's range represents one of the best value offerings in Britain. From the upstairs tasting room you can see down into the winery – a recent release being the American oak-fermented and aged Chardonnay, which is probably the biggest and richest version I've seen yet, a real Chardy for big Chardy lovers, and with just 600 bottles produced.

Leaner in style is Sandstone Ridge, a Chardonnay, Ortega and Pinot Blanc blend that retains a hint of texture from a proportion of second fill oak, but that balances ripe fruit with zingy acidity. The Bacchus is fragrant, floral and expressive, but not overly so. Huge yields in 2018 paved the way for a frizzante version that has made a comeback in 2020 – very lightly tank-fermented without extended lees contact, retaining freshness and showcasing varietal versatility.

As well as a rich and classic four-years-on-lees Blanc de Noirs, there's a classic-method multi-vintage and zero dosage version too, a Blanc de Blancs and Rosé de Noirs, like the stills, all of which are below what you would say is market price for the quality of product. On several fronts, Alison and Albourne's approach is so admirable and focused on great wine, a sound approach, decent value and good times, all just twenty minutes from Brighton. It is very much worth a trip to see for yourself.

Barrel and store room beneath the tasting bar at Albourne

Albourne's cellar door is a great example of our industry's connection between producer and drinker

WOLSTONBURY

@WOLSTONBURY.CO

New Way Ln, Hurstpierpoint, Hassocks, BN6 9BD
https://www.wolstonbury.co

What: Cellar door sales and tastings by appointment
Recommended wines: Orchid Chalk Charmat, Charmat Bacchus, Bacchus

Charlotte and Ivan hand-planted their Wolstonbury vineyard with friends below the steep slope of the famous West Sussex hill in 2015. Plenty of oyster shells came out of the soil when the vines went in – a regular commodity of the Romano period, though not evidence in itself of Roman presence. A vineyard is as good a place as any for a few oysters, after all. The hill's Iron Age settlement and Bronze Age burial site, however, puts human presence here back about 3000 years.

Locals have a unique relationship with the hill, in memories of others who once shared it or people they've been there with. Now the hill has a vineyard and wine with which toasts can be raised and it is a special place that deserves to be celebrated.

Diversity is something that almost all farmers have had to embrace over decades, a skill not at all lost on the Wolstonbury land, from vines to windflowers, fields of hay and a genuine passion for the environment and how it will be passed on. Three thousand Bacchus and Reichensteiner vines were planted over the course of a couple of weekends, late into the night to get the job done. Initially, the couple thought they would make the wine too, and could envisage a winery on-site, but a friend of a friend turned out to be Sam Lintner, a hugely experienced winemaker

Wolstonbury's brace of Charmat sparklings are stunning expressions of naturally aromatic varietals

up the road at Bolney, which was too good an opportunity to turn down in the medium term.

Given the chalk soil beneath the site and the quality of sparkling coming from the local area, 2021 saw the three main sparkling varieties go in (although still wine was the first and major passion, hence the aromatic and efficiently ripening Bacchus and Reichensteiner).

The expression of these varietals in their Charmat, aka 'tank method' style is super refreshing in several ways. Both are so fresh, fruit-forward and approachable, the perfect picnic pair. The 'Orchid Charmat' sparkling Bacchus shows off a bright elderflower and floral style, with a super spritzy zing behind it, but with some air it develops slightly herbaceously; it's fascinatingly interesting and a bit different,

and super easy-going and entertaining in style. Charmat method holds fresh fruit character so well – it has a shorter duration in contact with yeast and there's more juice surface area to yeast – perfect for naturally aromatic varietals like these.

Alongside a full-time job, Ivan realised towards the end of 2020 that as well as drinking it, they probably should try to sell the odd bottle. So they got a temporary events license for an old farm building and swung open the barn-turned-cellar door that December to an amazing local reception.

Sharing wine is so special, especially at source, with likeminded people in an amazing part of the world. With cellar door upgrades completed and visions for a vineyard view restaurant, the sharing here will continue – and the quality is in abundance. I'll see you there.

Charlotte and Ivan at Wolstonbury: fascinating and friendly in equal measure

Kingscote Estate and Vineyard

@KINGSCOTE_ESTATE

· ·

Farm Mill Cl, Vowels Ln, East Grinstead, RH19 4LG
https://kingscoteestate.com

What: Cellar doors sales, tastings and tours
Recommended wines: Silvan Bacchus

Kingscote Estate, situated between Bluebell Railway and Weir Wood Reservoir, just outside East Grinstead, was once part of the Gravetye Estate. The Grade II-listed farmhouse, fifteenth-century tithe barn and winery sit within 150 acres of wider Sussex countryside, originally established by Christen Monge having bought the estate in 1999. Monge first planted in 2010, with further additions in 2011 and 2013. The major growth, however, has come under recent owner Mark Dixon.

The vineyard is part of his MDCV group, which owns vineyards in Provence and is now growing its portfolio in the South East, including Sedlescombe, and the group's biggest project and base at Luddesdown, Kent.

The three traditional sparkling varieties of Chardonnay, Pinot Noir and Pinot Meunier are the focus, but still wines are also made from Bacchus, Regent and Pinot Blanc. Guided wine tours and tastings are held throughout April to October with lunch or afternoon tea also available afterwards. The wine garden backs out onto the vineyard which itself runs alongside the Bluebell railway line, and there's trout fishing available on-site, too.

The Bacchus is along the riper lines: bright, floral and tropical, and it is one of the better versions I've seen. Continuing my growing love of the textured, lees-aged expressions is the Silvan Bacchus. It is worth the extra couple of quid – it's rich and fragrant, and the slightly creamy texture from light oak just softens the often-effervescent Bacchus. Really well-balanced, it is the pick of the still tasting flight of three, although the Chardonnay is a zesty little number for a sunny picnic table.

Textural, lees-aged Bacchus: the pick of the Kingscote range

Kingscote's railway line vineyard

East Sussex

ARTELIUM WINE ESTATE

@KINGSCOTE_ESTATE

....

Artelium Wine Estate, Malthouse Farm, Streat Lane, Streat, Hassocks, BN6 8SA
https://www.artelium.com

What: tours, tastings, cellar door bar, sales and events
Recommended wines: Curators Cuvée, Artefact White Pinot, Artefact Chardonnay,
Meunier Rosé

Not often mentioned in winemaking circles, and lesser still in reference to East Sussex, is the Dalai Lama. For twenty years he held the record for the world's smallest vineyard, having been bequeathed three vines in the mountainous Swiss region of Valais. Until, that is, an English lawyer planted two vines in his garden near Lewes, officially registering the site so that he could sell its produce.

As bars go, the one at Malthouse Farm – also known as Artelium wines – is a pretty good one to prop up. There's a lot to like, from the converted barn cellar door to the wine garden with views over the vines and the sweeping South Downs behind them, and best of all the quality of the offering being served. Initially planting 24,000 vines of the big three sparkling varieties, these were followed by Pinot Gris and the exciting Divico and Cabaret Noir – the latter two perhaps providing the potential to fill the 'fuller-bodied red' gap in the Great British market. Several are experimenting with the latter; Artelium have invested in 20,000 vines of these varieties alone, which is easily the biggest planting of them in Britain. There are a total of 150,000 vines planted across two sites either side of the East and West Sussex border – and in doing so, Artelium fast-forwarded themselves to serious producers, but

Artelium winemakers: Owen Elias and Dermot Sugrue

that's just half of the story. Julie and Mark had an all-English wine wedding in 2013, inspired by their respective origins close to pioneering producers Ridgeview and Chapel Down.

The name Artelium is a blend of the word art and the suffix given for the study of nature. From two sites the vineyard can benefit from the natural differences in location, but Artelium also intend to grow their 'stable' of winemakers, seeing each as an individual artist in their own right, imparting their own characteristics in each wine. This is an invigorating approach to contrasting styles normally referenced in terms of site and production techniques, as different as human fingerprints. But every wine is in some way a reflection of not just place, but the hands from which it was made, leading to a more contrasting, complex range, which is what interesting wine is all about.

Currently, the fizz comes with the fingerprint of the extremely handy Dermot Sugrue, whose characteristic zingy approach to complex yet fresh wines is evident in the Curators Cuvée. Despite sixty months on lees, it's so vibrant and elegant, being predominantly single-site Chardonnay hanging on to all its natural acidity.

Owen Elias made the still range of Pinot Gris, 100% Meunier Rosé and Chardonnay. The trio all share a super aromatic fragrance, with the Gris especially showing all that late-ripening acidity, along with high-grade fruit, both of which will let the wines continue to develop.

It's artistry at every level for the 'Artefact' range – Sarah Emily Porter was awarded the first commission to create new work for the labels – and a month's residency at cellar door. There's just one 500 litre 'Puncheon', of single variety Chardonnay which adds body and complexity, also made by Elias, which is also true to the natural fresh acidity. There were also just 500 bottles of bright and crunchy Barrel-Aged Pinot Noir which saw nine months in new French and American oak, and

a stunningly fragrant 'White Pinot' version too.

So much attention to detail has gone into Artelium's cellar door offering at every stage – it's a year-round venue that's a short wander from the garden, across the stable yard and inside to seats between the bar and a log burner. It's surrounded by art and events and so much care is taken to curate the range of wines – when Julie and Mark met Dermot Sugrue, he had one space left for contract-making; they know a good thing when they see it and I doubt he'll have space anytime soon.

2021 Pinot Noir harvest at Artelium, a challenging one to say the least

BLUEBELL VINEYARD ESTATES
@BLUEBELLVINEYARD

Glenmore Farm, Slider's Lane, Furner's Green, Uckfield, TN22 3RU
https://www.bluebellvineyard.org

What: Cellar door tours, tasting, sales, blending workshops and events
Recommended wines: Hindleap Barrel-Aged Blanc de Blancs, Seyval Blanc, Classic
Cuvée, Ashdown Bacchus, Rosé, Ruby Sparkling

From swine to the vine at Bluebell Vineyard: in 2004 there were 10,000 pigs on-site at Furner's Green, which is a lot of sausages, and now there are 40 hectares of vines producing upwards of 100,000 bottles of wine a year.

The 10-acre home vineyard even includes trial plantings of the late-ripening Riesling and Merlot which are, in theory, equally ill-suited to cool climate grape-growing. Across separate 40- and 50-acre vineyards, Bluebell, named after an adjoining wood, have plantings of the holy trinity of sparkling varietals plus Bacchus, Ortega and even the Swiss grape Chasselas.

After initially planting in 2005, there are now nine different Chardonnay clones; fourteen of Pinot Noir and four of Meunier, all selected and planted according to soil and the blocks within each site. Every wine across the range is an estate-grown blend of these, and they're all vintage wines too, to best express season.

A temporary winery was put into an old, small barn opposite the farmhouse when the first vines went in the ground and, sixteen years later, is still fully operational. There's a new, bigger, modern version at the second site, but the original will remain, for small batch experiments, tours, tank sampling, harvest experience days and blending workshops.

The bumper crop in 2018 provided both the

The home vineyard at Bluebell, experimental plantings of Riesling and Merlot

fruit and the ripeness to be able to release the estate's first commercial collection of still wines, under the Ashdown label. However, 70% of Bluebell's production remains sparkling, labelled Hindleap, which has five different blends. Led by their signature Blanc de Blancs from the estate's premium Chardonnay plot at the Valley View site, on lees for nineteen months, it's rich and toasty but – as a range hallmark – has its focus on a fruit-forward approach. This is a style summed up by the Hindleap Rosé, that sees the most characterful and the brightest selection of Pinot Noir and Meunier, usually around an 80/20 split, resulting in an 'Eton Mess in a glass' style. Seyval too, is fruit at the fore. Classic English orchard and zesty acidity is softened by two and a half years lees time, but it still manages to be naturally light and expressive.

The sparkling Ruby Red marries a love of chilled reds with sparkling. Nine months on lees keeps it bright and fresh; there's such an attractive richness, spice and length. Absolutely great with a hog roast and some open-minded drinkers eager to try something not often seen.

Merlot gets a run in the still, Ashdown Rosé too, in varying degrees – with it providing almost half of the blend in the super-ripe 2018 – which is easy-going but with just a perfect hint of body and texture to keep it nice and interesting. Ashdown Estate white is 100% Chasselas, of delicate fruit and a slightly fleshy character.

Some of the former pig sheds are being turned into a 'Californian style' farm shop – there are vineyard trails and an increasing events calendar, but the real highlight is what's going on in the tasting room – and long may the 'temporary' winery remain as an experimental hub.

I highly recommend migrating in the direction of Bluebell

BREAKY BOTTOM
@BREAKY_BOTTOM

. . . .

Breaky Bottom Vineyard, White Way, Rodmell, Lewes BN7 3EX
https://www.breakybottom.co.uk

What: Visits by appointment
Recommended wines: 2010 Cuvée Reynolds Stone, 2015 Cuvée Jack Pike, 2015 Cuvée David Pearson

Throughout my career I've been so fortunate to enjoy many memorable days and experiences, very few of which will be looked back upon more fondly than the morning with Peter Hall at Breaky Bottom. He was born 'while the bombs were dropping' in 1943 to a French mother, and with four grandparents owing to different heritages. Peter was a country boy at heart and one who wanted to farm, a desire which brought him to this burrowed pocket of Sussex. At the end of a very long, bumpy old farm track, the chalk 'bottom' is revealed, tucked away between the windswept rolling hills above and all around the old flint farm cottage at the heart of the 5-acre vineyard.

When Peter arrived here to look after some livestock on behalf of a local farmer there was no electricity and just a standpipe for water. In 1974, with the help of his great friend Jack Pike, he planted 8500 Seyval and Müller-Thurgau vines, by hand, with a spade, a measuring tape and a long piece of string, and a very special christening ceremony was had for that inaugural vine. After his forty-fifth consecutive vintage he's still here, with his wife Christine, but now they own the old stone farmhouse and his wines have become probably the most sought after in England.

The old farm track

But it didn't get off to the best start: the hot summer of 1976 yielded some great fruit before September rain set in, and Breaky Bottom's first crop was taken off to be processed at another vineyard, and promptly was ruined. The plan was always for the wine to be made on-site, but this initial setback hastened proceedings, and Peter has made the wine here ever since. A reputation built on still, the first bottle-fermented wine was produced in 1995, and since 2000 is a range that is now exclusively sparkling. The 'Millennium Cuvée Maman Mercier', dedicated to his mother, also began the tradition of naming each wine after inspirational people in his life.

Though Müller was replaced with the traditional three Champagne varietals in 2002 and 2004, that first bottle of 1995 Sparkling was from Seyval, a varietal which remains, and here is where you'll find Britain's best.

I love Seyval, how classically English it is, how expressive, fresh and approachable yet elegant and precise it can be. Peter's versions are not so much an example of pristine Seyval Blanc, but the example, and a version

The iconic Breaky Bottom

Peter Hall: forty-five consecutive vintages and counting

that every other expression can be measured against, because his are simply sublime. These are the great wines that those unsure of Seyval's full potential are yet to taste.

The day before I visited, Peter had an Alaskan poet in tears on tasting the 2015 vintage, 'Cuvée Jack Pike', the aroma so reminiscent of his Minnesotan grandmother's apple pie. I can still taste it, and do nothing but smile, thinking of a wine with such incredible length and purity. So straight-lined, so flavoursome and fresh; zingy but rounded.

Reynolds Stone, the world's greatest wood engraver, designed the original label for Breaky Bottom, having also designed £5 and £10 notes and the British passport coat of arms, as well as having cut the memorial stone to Winston Churchill in Westminster Abbey. The 2010 Cuvée that bears his name is Chardonnay-dominant, with a balance of Pinot Noir and Pinot Meunier, as is the general style at Breaky Bottom. The world's most successful wine writer, Hugh Johnson, chose this as one of his ten wines of the world to cheer us all up in 2021, the only wine of British origin to feature. It is two additional years on lees to six in total and a completely different wine to Cuvée Jack Pike, richer and fuller, slightly toastier, but no less subtle and elegant. Slightly lavender-esque, like the best lemon drizzle cake you ever ate, except better, with greater potential longevity than any of us so fortunate to taste it.

The 2015 expression of the same blend is named after Breaky Bottom's first cardboard box supplier, who worked on the vineyard and became known as 'Mr CBBM' – Mr Cardboard Box Man. That name very nearly made it onto the label, too, ultimately making way for 'Cuvée David Pearson.' This is another bullseye wine, almost richer again, creamy and so pure of fruit – tasting it is like looking into the future; it hints

at what it might become, sensational at six years old but has so much left to say. All four varietals are occasionally blended too, and each wine is so unique to site and season and a great expression of both – the very epitome of the greatest wines.

But wine is very little without the people behind it. Peter's forty-five vintages and counting have not come without trial and tribulation; five complete floods, recent frosts and commercialised corporate pheasant shoots sending ever more grape-hungry birds down among the vines, costing thousands of bottles' worth. There are so few vineyards in Britain of this age, fewer still that have remained in one pair of hands. This could only really be England, and Peter, of multicultural heritage, could only really be English – in his 'labelling room', a space as full of character and charm as its owner. He hand-labels his bottles ready for ever more frequent collections of increasingly in-demand wines. Seeing 100 emails a day full of requests to visit, he could charge a lot more for his range and still sell out several times over, but has no care for money or extravagance and is instead so modest, humble and eager to help. Another rolled cigarette, another wonderful tangent to embark on: Peter tells me he is a lover of classical music and fan of the composer Sir Andrew Davis, who became a friend and now also has a wine named after him.

As another harvest approaches, the story of Breaky Bottom gets greater still, as these amazing vines develop further and their produce in bottle do the same. We talk a lot about precision in wine, in such fine detail – almost clinically in some ways – wines that are concise and so full of class. The Breaky Bottom range is the very definition of this. I implore you to get your hands on some and see for yourself what it means; history, people and place as good as it gets, and the most charming range of wines you'll ever taste.

Rathfinny Wine Estate

@RATHFINNYESTATE

· ·

Alfriston, Polegate, East Sussex, BN26 5TU
https://rathfinnyestate.com

What: Cellar door sales, tours, tastings, restaurant and stays
Recommended wines: Blanc de Noirs, Blanc de Blancs, Sparkling Rosé

Established in 2010 on their working farm, just a couple of miles from the coast at Seaford, Mark and Sarah Driver's ultimate aim is for Sussex to be used as a term like Champagne is – synonymous with a region full of world-class sparkling wine producers. Their original 50 acres were planted in 2012, and now sit at 230 acres under vine. All of which is protected in a huge bowl among the rolling hills on either side, just a few miles from the south coast at Seaford.

Chardonnay, Pinot Noir and Pinot Meunier dominate the plantings, but there's a small amount of Pinot Gris and Pinot Blanc in the ground also, both of which could go into a sparkling wine but are currently used for the Cradle Valley still offering.

Since launching their first sparkling wines at Somerset House in 2018, Rathfinny now have a range of four wines, all vintage, and are as classic an offering as the method that makes them. Pinot Noir is the dominant varietal across the blends, and both the Classic Cuvée and rosé are normally around the 60% mark. The original plan for a sparkling offering at Rathfinny was for it to be non-vintage, in the mould of the major Champagne houses, producing a consistent style from a blend of years. This was as much

Staggering set-up and the very embodiment of the shift to professionalism

Tucked away in a bowl by the sea, Rathfinny's 200 acres of vines

inspired by the challenging early vintages of 2012 and 2013 as it was the Champagne model. Ultimately, Mark felt that making wine from 100% estate-grown grapes, rather than facing the occasional supply issues associated with relying on out-sourcing, gives Rathfinny the opportunity to focus on quality through vintage-only releases. Having almost 400,000 vines in the ground helps supply too, and Rathfinny are very much expressors of site and season in their approach, which is what I like most about it.

First released in 2018, the hallmark of Rathfinny's 'Sussex Sparkling' is Pinot Noir and low dosage – it's got structure, richness and purity of fruit. Classic Cuvée is all of these things; almost 60% Pinot Noir and an equal split of Chardonnay and Meunier, showcasing crunchy red fruit and, even at three years on lees, is still drinking fresh

and crisp. The Blanc de Blancs has reverted back to the traditional, exclusively Chardonnay approach since 2017, and again, three years on lees and full malo makes for a creamy, baked richness not at all lacking in depth and power.

The signature of the range, however, is without doubt the Blanc de Noirs, made up of 93% Pinot Noir and 7% Meunier. Just 3 grams dosage and again at thirty-six months on lees adds balance and supporting texture, all of which goes so well with the rich, savoury, slightly nutty and flavoursome style.

The harvest marquee restaurant pops up for two- or three-course lunches, dinners and other events inspired by locally sourced fare. But Rathfinny is well worth a visit outside of harvest time as well, for its Flint Barns dining or, at the very least, the tasting room.

HOLLOW LANE VINEYARD

@HOLLOWLANEVINEYARD

Hollow Lane, Nr Blackboys, East Sussex, TN22 5JB
https://www.hollowlanevineyard.co.uk

What: Tours and tastings by appointment
Recommended wines: Blanc de Noirs, Blanc de Blancs, Pinot Noir Blush

Originally from just outside Barnsley, Chris used to make wine in his airing cupboard from grapes grown in his greenhouse. First 'getting the bug' in 2004, he went down to Plumpton college for a course in viticulture, expecting there to be half a dozen attendees. He was surprised to see almost forty others from all over the world, though he was the only Yorkshireman. Together with wife Jan he's come a long way since then; they've planted almost 6000 vines in the heart of Sussex.

The couple also operate a stud farm on the property, so you might see some of their dressage mares or jumping stallions like Keira, Luna, Pickle and Nugget if you visit, lending a watchful and ever-inquisitive eye on proceedings.

The vineyard takes the name of the road that runs alongside it, and the only place you can buy their wine is right here. Passing on foot, bike or horseback, people often stop here to enquire, and then return to collect bottles from the gate on their way back.

Authenticity is a hallmark, and everything is done on-site; the winery is in an old row of stables that weren't the only thing in need of repair when the couple acquired the site in 2010. They had to remove a jungle of brambles on what is now one of the two adjoining vineyards.

With Pinot Noir, Meunier and Chardonnay

Barnsley boy Chris, now very much at home in the wine heartland of Sussex

in the ground it's bubbles they're about, with Chris having been on an additional Plumpton winemaking course in 2012, a year after planting. There's a relatively tiny 200-kilo press in one stable – that's the kind of kit many producers would love to have the flexibility to experiment with on such a small scale. The advantage, for Chris, is being able to press individual batches of fruit at optimum ripeness and to single out the most desirable characteristics in each parcel.

In the stable next door there's the riddling rack and bottle-neck freezer, and there's enough storage throughout to be in the fortunate position of having a range where the current release is six years old. Not only does this let the wine develop in bottle, it negates the risk of an average season or two of either inferior quality or low yields – or both.

Other than sampling direct from tank or barrel, you're about as close to the action as it gets at one of the tours and tastings. Either in the last stable of the block, or the patio tasting area in front, it's the chef's table equivalent of wineries. Nine wines come out for blind tasting, because this is the most objective way to work out which ones you like the best – which for me is their super fresh, clean and crisp Chardonnay Blanc de Blancs, and slightly off-dry and tangy blush Pinot Noir.

It's a single varietal approach in the wines, with a focus on showcasing and maximising the flavour profile of the individual grapes. Side by side it's a tough gig to pick one as a stand-out, and natural tendencies will probably take over. There is a lot to like about Hollow Lane, from approach to delivery, grape to glass.

Equine to wine: a sensational combo of passions

HENNERS VINEYARD

@HENNERSVINEYARD

Herstmonceux, Hailsham, BN27 1RJ
https://www.hennersvineyard.co.uk

What: Cellar door sales, events, Henners Vine Club and tastings
Recommended wines: Brut NV, Vintage Brut, Sparkling Rosé, Native Grace Barrel
Chardonnay

The story of Henners marries old and new, and the best of British with a distinctly European flair. It's all delivered with a low-key modesty and a local community-centric, super-approachable cellar door experience that is all built around a stunning range of wine.

Originally French, Henners-Dubois fled his home country for England during the French revolution. One of his descendants, former F1 engineer Larry Warr, planted 7 acres of Chardonnay, Pinot Noir and Meunier in 2007, taking the first half of his ancestor's name for the label.

From the first vintage in 2011 Boutinot were signed as distributors for the 15,000 or so annual bottles Larry was producing, which, along with fixing up vintage Jags, was a pretty impressive workload, and led to the former taking ownership in 2017. The group's international winemaking expertise, spanning old and new world, is hugely beneficial to this 'next world' approach, in shaping the modern direction of Henners.

The team and offering at cellar door are as close-knit and approachable as any family-run business. It's all about the local community and engaging, entertaining and educating those who want to be a part of the journey. Behind the scenes there's the

Great booze: Vintage Henners

professionalism and winemaking know-how that is the very epitome of the transformation from the amateur era of winemaking in Britain.

Along with the new cellar door, part of the 2021 investment was in doubling the winery's capacity to 300,000 bottles. As a result, the Brut NV can be made from an increasingly bigger range of reserve wines from different vintages, adding complexity and consistency, and negating the threat of poorer seasons.

Protected by the south-easterly tip of the South Downs, this pocket is one of the driest and warmest parts of the country. Herstmonceux's clay soil provided the material for one of Britain's first brick buildings, the fifteenth-century castle that shares its name. Now its moisture and heat retention – combined with drainage beneath the vines – help build the ripe and rich character that's so evident across the resulting range. Just 5 miles from the sea, the cool coastal breezes aid a slow ripening process that's crucial for delicate and complex flavour profile.

After working at wineries in Sussex, California and South Africa, Collette O'Leary joined the Estate in 2019 to curate this extremely precise range of sparkling. Some Chardonnay comes from the chalk soils next door and fronts up the non-vintage, adding freshness and further structure to the Pinot Noir body and depth, plus some signature Meunier approachability. At three years on lees it's complex, rich and long but super vibrant. It's eighteen months on lees for the Saignée method rosé that's really well placed in the soft, red fruit-driven yet textured and interesting sweet spot of the rosé category. It is seven years in bottle for the vintage – including four on lees, which makes the 70/30 Chardonnay /Pinot Noir blend incredibly rounded, creamy and multi-layered. The richness and weight are evident, as is an impressive freshness and vibrancy.

The super-ripe 2018 vintage brought an inaugural range of stills – including a great barrel-fermented Chardonnay under the 'Native Grace' label. There's also a Bacchus-led still wine, blended with a touch of barrel-fermented Chardonnay for the inaugural 'Gardner Street' Classic.

There is lots of local wildlife attracted in from Pevensey Levels by the array of wildflowers and probably the sweet scent of sensational fruit, and the modern build and visitor offering is complemented by a very traditional approach to a good old warm welcome and, best of all, some seriously classy wines.

…and great people to drink it with: Becca and Collette at Henners

Off the Line Vineyard

@OFFTHELINEVINEYARD

North Street, Hellingly, East Sussex, BN27 4EA
https://www.offthelinevineyard.com

What: Cellar door sales, tasting and tours by appointment
Recommended wines: Dog Rosé, Hip Rosé

Oh, how jugs of Pimm's all got together and laughed at rosé when it first made its way onto the British summertime drinking scene. Rosé used to be largely a warm-weather drink, mostly for the garden. Now it's a year-round category worth the best part of £600 million in retail alone, and, anyway, can you remember your last Pimm's?

The major motivation for most of the producers I've met on this journey has been making the kind of wine they like to drink. None more specific than Kristina and Ann-Marie at Off The Line, who are rosé specialists-in-chief. They had initially, however, fallen in love with the South of France, and looked at one point as though they might be headed that way for good.

But they could see England's potential and, after two years at Plumpton and a vintage working in Bordeaux and the Rhone, they planted almost 8 acres of exclusively red grapes just south of Heathfield, in Tonbridge sandstone and Wealden clay.

From Pinot Noir, Regent, Dornfelder and Rondo, there are currently three still rosés in the range, but as fans of the ancestral method of producing sparkling wine, aka Pet-Nat style, there's some fizz to come in the near future, and I get the distinct impression that it may well be pink in colour.

As for the current three wines, it's well worth the

Kristina and Ann-Marie at Off The Line

Rosé specialists Off The Line

'turn up and taste for a fiver' option at the cellar door tasting room. All three are inspired by the wild roses lining the hedgerows adjoining the vineyard, and all absolutely tick the fresh and approachable box but there's just so much more flavour and texture than your average, almost water-pale Provence style. Dog Rosé is an all but equal split of Pinot, Regent and Rondo. It is lean, but with a nice rich hit of slightly candied fruit, orange peel and chewy redcurrant. Dancing Dog is a happy dog, with the same three varieties but a larger proportion of Regent providing added structure and a brighter still uplift of fruit thanks to the touch of residual sugar. Although still at the genuinely dry end of the scale, the fragrance and mouthfeel are long and luscious. Hip Rosé is vastly Pinot Noir-dominant and, texturally, is well-rounded thanks to some lees stirring, with additional regent which provides added depth and a touch of tannin. It's the lightest in colour of the three but don't judge a book by its cover, or a rosé, for that matter.

Adrian at Westwell sourced some Regent from Off The Line for his own super-on-trend label and was so impressed by the quality it inspired him to plant his own. Next-door-neighbour Georgie has watched the evolution of the vineyard since its time as a draught horse breeding ground, all from her bedroom window since she was eight years old. Now eighteen, she helps out in the winery. One of the many great things that increasing numbers of quality producers provides is opportunities for young people to benefit from vocational experience with local businesses in an industry that marries nature, art and science, learning from role models like Kristina and Ann-Marie. To top it all off, Georgie is now old enough to drink the stuff, too. I just hope she likes rosé.

BEACON DOWN

@BEACONDOWNWINES

··

Browns Ln, Cross in Hand, Heathfield, TN21 0QJ
https://www.beacondown.co.uk

What: vineyard tours, tastings and picnics
Recommended wines: Blanc de Blancs, Blanc de Noirs, Bacchus-Gris

In 2012, Paul Pippard had just finished working on the London Olympics. On a family holiday in Cuba, he and wife Al were wondering what the next forty-odd years had in store. Bored of civil service and wanting to do something a bit more hands-on, and as lovers of wine, the fateful 'what if' words descended on them.

WSET courses led to Plumpton college, which in turn took Paul to Greyfriars in Surrey, working under Mike Wagstaff. Two years after that initial conversation, 18 acres across two paddocks near Heathfeld became available and, though a touch unsure if their decision was down to a gut feeling, or just as a result of a stressful career, or a bit of both, Paul and Al went for it. They sold their Camberwell flat and, with all of their savings, bought the site and set up a tasting barn and storage shed.

The sandstone site drops dramatically down the southern slope, with two plots split by a hedgerow, also acting as a windbreak. Given the county, and the country, it was no surprise to see signature sparkling varietals – Chardonnay and Pinot Noir – go in the ground a year after acquisition. It's a pretty versatile range, though, with Bacchus and Pinot Gris providing both still and further sparkling options.

With 10,000 vines across 18 acres, Paul wanted to experiment with the last 5% of the

One of best tables going

site. Initially, the plan was to plant 50 vines of ten trial varietals including Albariño and Sauvignon Blanc. Al said to Paul, how about you choose one, your favourite, and plant 500 of those instead? I like Paul's maverick approach, but Al's more sensible theory was probably the way to go. In the end they combined the two, Paul opting for 500 Riesling vines, a hugely courageous ploy given the grape's notoriously late ripening and natural high acidity. Adding a 'cloche' to the fruiting wire – in this case a tarpaulin cover – provides an extra 4 degrees of ripening warmth. Fermentation is stopped early leaving natural sugars to balance out that ultra-prominent acidity.

The Bacchus and Pinot Gris blend varies in percentage of each but is usually around three-quarters the former. It's floral-driven but the Gris adds a ripe roundness to the wine and just a touch of spice without losing any of that classic refreshing English elderflower. The still wines are in the safe hands of Gris specialist Simon Woodhead at his Stopham winery.

Simon Roberts at Ridgeview makes the sparkling wines; single varietal and single vintage, and great expressions of the contrasting styles of these classic wines. There's a Blanc de Noirs that is rich and opulent and of such depth and structure that belies its vines' early years. The Blanc de Blancs is all freshness and finesse but also creamy and long. Rosé de Noirs is 100% Pinot Noir, summer red fruit-driven, vibrant and just about the perfect wine to enjoy from one of the best cellar door views in Britain. The picnic tables at the top of the second plot of vines look down the slope onto the South Downs and are about as good a place as any to relax and work your way through the wider range.

Cloched Riesling at Beacon Down

DAVENPORT VINEYARDS

@LIMNEYFARM

. . . .

Limney Farm, Castle Hill, Rotherfield, TN6 3RR
https://www.davenportvineyards.co.uk

What: Cellar door sales by appointment
Recommended wines: Diamond Fields Pinot Noir, Horsmonden, Limney Estate
Sparkling, Limney Estate Sparkling Rosé

Few vineyards in Britain are into their fourth decade, fewer still in the same individuals' hands as they started with. Will Davenport planted 5 acres of vines at Horsmonden in Kent, in 1991. He has single-handedly witnessed a shift to professionalism – and been a pioneer of it – he's now up to 24 acres across five plots, made up of nine grape varieties and a multitude of soil types and climates patterns.

When converting to organic in 2000, in our very marginal – and especially wet – climate that means disease pressure makes this risky at the best of times, Will was ultimately inspired by the potential of great fruit from healthy vines. He believes the resulting wines show a depth of character that he doesn't believe could be achieved with the use of chemicals in the vineyard and winery.

The winery itself is at the East Sussex site in Rotherfield, with a capacity of 70,000 bottles of wine annually, making just over half of this under the Davenport label. It is hugely dependent on specific season.

Following studies at the legendary winemaking college Roseworthy in Adelaide, Will worked in the London wine trade along with having various spells in Alsace, California,

Will Davenport: walking the walk for thirty years

Australia and elsewhere in Britain, before setting up his own winery. Will also looks after the rest of the farm at Rotherfield, which includes a small flock of Wiltshire Horn sheep, some bees and a lot of wildlife and woodland.

Planted in 2000 on sandy clay, Diamond Fields is probably one of England's greatest vineyards. Burgundy clone Pinot Noir, combined with the ripeness of 2018, produced the fruit for one of those still wines that – though sadly long since gone – will be remembered as one of the best reds of the modern era of British winemaking. There are few other sites – or winemakers – who are able to produce red wines with such depth and concentration in Britain. Oak barrel-ageing adds weight and complexity, and this rich and savoury style of Pinot Noir is so sought after; there are few better, if any.

The original 5 acres of Ortega, Bacchus, Faber and Huxelrebe, planted at Lewes Heath, are blended with Siegerrebe for the complex, fragrant, yet light Horsmonden White. Wild yeast fermented in foudre – huge oak vats Will originally saw in Alsace – provides a soft and slightly creamy texture. It's a wine Adrian Pike tasted at lunch one day that inspired him to become a winemaker, working under Will until he set up his Westwell label.

Limney vineyard was planted in 1993, with Pinot Noir and Auxerrois, and, completing the classic sparkling trio in 2007, on sandy silt over sandstone, in went Chardonnay and Meunier, as well as further Bacchus and Otega.

There are wildflower hay meadows and twenty new bird-nesting boxes installed each winter, which are home to a pair of nesting kestrels who've raised fifteen chicks over the last three years. The various sites are also home to some of the most premium vines in all of Britain, and if anyone was in doubt about the potential for organic viticulture, they'd just need to taste some Davenport.

Barrel room at Limney Farm, home to Will Davenport's superb range

Busi Jacobsohn Wine Estate
@BUSIJACOBSOHN

....

Blackdon Farm, Eridge Green, TN3 9HX
https://www.busijacobsohn.com

What: Tastings by appointment, vineyard events
Recommended wines: Cuvée Brut, Rosé Brut, Blanc de Blancs, Blanc de Noirs

Susanna Busi and Douglas Jacobsohn were planning on a retirement in southern France, until they visited the East Sussex countryside on the outskirts of Eridge, and swapped *les bleus* for the green and pleasant.

They quickly became accustomed to the local cuisine, and it was at a local curry night where a chance conversation with a fellow grower inspired Susanna to think of the land beneath their new home in terms of vine potential.

Douglas quite literally put the foundations in place, installing a drainage system beneath the vineyard; it was an obvious thing to do according to him, just like buying insurance.

Letting the rainwater run off and away means the naturally heat-retaining sandstone can focus on ripening Busi Jacobsohn's equal split of predominantly Burgundy clone, Chardonnay and Pinot Noir, with a balance of 20% Meunier.

If wine is a reflection of site, then it also speaks of professional approach and commitment to quality, which is a positive mark of Douglas and Susanna's future-proofing and the range they've curated. There is no still wine offering at present and there's not likely to be one in the future. They're sparkling specialists,

Susanna and Douglas; Busi and Jacobsohn

and there's no desire to risk diluting quality by trying to cover too many bases. In what was a winemaking win-win, Busi opted for Simon Robinson at Ridgeview. Despite being relatively new on the scene, Busi Jacobsohn have set out to be one of the most respected names in English sparkling winemaking. Among those in the know, they're already there.

There are currently four wines in the range, all vintage, to best express single season. The crop was a small one in 2020, but the fruit was concentrated, so Douglas and Susanna opted to bottle in magnum format only, the result of which I absolutely love. Wine does taste better from magnum, and it's not at all to do with show. The 1500ml magnum neck is the same size as a regular 750ml, which means there's half the amount of oxygen for twice the juice. Jeroboam – or double magnums outside of Champagne – 3000ml by volume and larger, all have their own neck sizes. The less oxygen per surface area in a mag means a slower – and in theory more complex – flavour development under cork.

At twenty-four months on lees, the Chardonnay-dominant Cuvée Brut is rich and savoury, but not at all lacking in what becomes a range-hallmark of incredibly precise fruit. The acidity is vibrant and long, suggesting great ageing potential, but it's looking pretty tasty right about now. Just like the rosé, both wines are distinctly fresh English fruit-first, with the body and texture of the classic method, and the rosé especially, benefiting from additional mouth-feel via its 7% base wine barrel-fermenting.

From 5 hectares in total there's not much of either the Blanc de Blanc or Blanc de Noirs to go around, and these two are built to last. Winemaking fingerprint is such an element of wine in glass – even if the

handling is in the minimal intervention bracket. The quality of the handling here is such a tribute to this incredible site, and it is especially evident in the duo of single varietals' expressions. The Blanc de Blancs is fresher still, and super zingy, but full of lots of ripe fruit. There's some tangy red fruit and also a hint of Christmas spices coming through on the classically richer Blanc de Noirs.

Like the entire range, it's tricky to pick my favourite thing about the premium pair. Both are great food wines, getting better with age, and preferably served in magnum.

Scandinavian sleek: the cellar door at Busi Jacobsohn

WILDWOOD VINEYARD

@WILDWOOD_VINEYARD

. . . .

Eridge Road, Rotherfield, Tunbridge Wells, TN3 9EQ
https://www.wildwoodvineyard.co.uk

What: Cellar door sales and tours by appointment
Recommended wines: Blanc de Noirs, Bacchus, Regent

In the mid-2000s, BBC documentary-maker Paul Olding was one of many home winemakers, fermenting juice according to instructions delivered with basic kit. 'Everyone seemed to have a dad who made awful wine in their airing cupboard in the seventies,' he says. But in 2007 he took on an allotment and planted forty vines near his home in Lewisham, growing slightly more regular allotment fare between the vines. In the kitchen-winery the family agreement was that everything was bottled and cleaned up by Christmas, normally yielding an annual production of about 120 bottles. Buoyed by the decidedly not awful results, he wondered if he, akin to the wider industry at the time, could move from the amateur to the professional. He employed a land agent who came to him with three fields split into twelve plots just off the A21 south of Tunbridge Wells. On a decent gradient of south-facing slope, the best draining plot – that includes an ancient woodland – was selected and purchased by Paul, in partnership with his mother and in-laws.

The site isn't readily accessible by road, rather a lay-by and a short wander through a tree-lined trail though the wild wood itself. There are roe deer, badgers, rabbits, buzzards and kites here, and once a large male peacock visited the woods from a nearby estate.

After the team filled in the hedgerows for more

Head on down to the woods today

Bee kind

efficient use as natural windbreaks and corrected the soil with – among other things – 3 metric tonnes of hand-scattered lime, in 2014, the slope was ready to be planted. Almost 2000 vines were put in; an equal split of Bacchus and Regent, and two separate clones of Pinot Noir accounting for half of the entire site. Paul was attracted by the versatility of Pinot and the approachability of Bacchus, and inspired by his prior experience of Regent from the urban vineyard days. This means there's a pretty good range available, and potentially a couple of further styles are to be added.

Wildwood Bacchus is super fresh and floral, but not overpowering in aromatics. As an example of the versatility that Pinot Noir provides, aside from a still red that might come from future warm vintages, the 2019 went through secondary bottle fermentation and was split into two batches as sparkling whites. The first was on lees for nine months and released as a fresh, bright and fruit-forward style. The other half is still in bottle, developing into a richer, toastier classic method.

Regent is soft and supple, more juicy than full, and well worth sticking in the fridge for twenty minutes if the weather materialises in a barbecue-friendly direction.

There's jazz in the vines featuring Paul's band, and you can still buy his first book, charting his journey and best tips for any other budding allotment-based urban winemakers out there.

Defined make the wines near Canterbury, where Nick Lane is head winemaker. A massive advantage of this contract model is that instead of making wine in his kitchen or shed at the vineyard, the Wildwood fruit is made under the stewardship of the former Cloudy Bay winemaker who spent the last five years at Dom Perignon. If that loses a touch of the romanticism, fear not, Paul's lined up some tank space at another winery where he'll be continuing his winemaking journey.

Oastbrook Estate Vineyard
@OASTBROOK

....

Junction Road, Bodiam, Robertsbridge, TN32 5XA
https://oastbrook.com

What: Cellar door tasting, sales and tours, glamping and events
Recommended wines: Pinot Gris, Chardonnay, still Meunier, Sparkling Rosé

The Rother Valley is developing into a little sweet spot within a very attractive part of the country for vine planting. Down here it's generally flatter and clay-based, there is more woodland and there are more natural wind breaks, and it's of course further east, therefore warmer and, crucially, given its clay content, drier.

For wine-loving Lord of the Rings fans, look no further than the Hobbit House at Oastbrook. But make no mistake as to the dedication to quality of wine here – this is one of the most premium sub-regions in Britain, and Oastbrook are at the front end of it.

America Brewer was born on the 4th of July in Brazil, and destined for the States until the early 2000s when she decided to go and stay with a friend in London instead. There she met Nick Brewer, and the rest is history.

Originally, the estate was owned by Guinness and used as hop fields. It regularly hits the same temperatures as Heathrow which, on account of the tarmac, is often recorded as the hottest place in Britain. The shape of the Rother Valley helps hold in the heat, which is accentuated by the mile-and-a-half-long sandstone ridge that the vines

America, Nick and Lora

are planted on, producing some of the ripest fruit in Britain. Being only 15 or so miles from the south coast means a nice sea breeze rolls up and keeps the vines fresh and cool.

Oastbrook are moving in the direction of an almost three-quarters still-heavy portfolio, seeing the ripeness and opportunity in the wider market. When based in Geneva, America and Nick saw first-hand the incredible alpine region wines of Jura and Savoie, and that is so evident in their range today; a reflection of the kind of wine they like to drink.

Both the Gris and the Chardonnay are wonderfully textural and slightly oxidative, but they are not trying too hard to be anything but a great example of the fruit that came from this fine pocket of East Sussex. The Chardonnay is pressed in four batches, the first two to tank, the latter two to oak barrel, which are allowed to hyper-oxidise. Batches one and two go into one-year-old oak; three and four into five-year-old, then are blended together for the final wine, of which only 600 bottles were made in the first vintage of still wines from Oastbrook, 2018. We'll see a lot more in this style, and I for one can't wait.

The still wines are gaining increasing notoriety, but visitors shouldn't discount the sparkling. The rosé blends Pinot Noir and Auxerrois, with depth and freshness and, at thirty-eight months on lees with a slight softening in acidity that is also wonderfully fragrant and in sync.

They even had a visitor from Alsace who tasted the Gris, a noble varietal from that region, who, when looking out over Oastbrook's vines from the tasting room balcony, said he could have been at home. Soon after, a visitor from New Zealand said they preferred Oastbrook's Hobbit House to their native Hobbiton attraction.

The barrel room at Limney Farm, home of Davenport Oast House, Hobbit House and former Guinness-owned hop fields… now producing some of the best still wines in the country

It's so clear just how much fun Nick and America are having. The wines are fun too, but they are seriously well made. Although the duo are both winemakers, Nick says he's all chaos and experiment whereas America is measured and calculated – quite the opposite to their respective approaches to wider life, apparently.

Hoffmann & Rathbone

@HOFFMANNANDRATHBONE

. . . .

New House Winery, Mountfield, East Sussex, TN32 5JP
https://hoffmannandrathbone.co.uk

What: Cellar door sales by appointment
Recommended wines: Blanc de Blancs, rosé, Classic Cuvée, Bacchus, NV Pinot Noir

'We'll go for a quick walk and then we'll sit down and drink.' When a German gives you a suggestion as sound as this, it's worth taking heed. Especially when it's Ulrich and Birgit – Hoffmann and Rathbone – owners of another clear contender for the country's best range of classic-method sparkling wine. This label was on my radar from early on in this trip. Strikingly attractive as the artwork is, it was the minimum eight years on lees – for the core range – that particularly caught my eye.

This extended ageing approach sits within Prestige Cuvée Champagne territory – but at half the price of most of those, and better, too. Long lees time is standard at Hoffmann & Rathbone, a hallmark of the range; the wines are all built on power and structure, longevity and superb food-matching potential, and favour time in 'bricks and mortar', rather than additional sugar-dosage, for balance and finesse.

Now in his third decade of winemaking, Ulrich's career has taken him from Baden to Bordeaux, Navarra to Napa. Following vintages in Surrey, East Sussex and Kent, Ulrich brought his wealth of international experience back to this special little pocket of southern England, and we're exceptionally lucky to have him. The Mountfield Estate is home to both the

Power, structure and elegance: Hoffmann & Rathbone and in this case, their 2012 Blanc de Blancs

winery and the vineyard, planted in 2008, with an additional site in the ground at Headlow Down. In contrast to the South Downs side of East Sussex, the Rother Valley is generally a bit flatter, and has more dense areas of woodland and natural windbreaks. Wealden clay holds the resulting warmth and cracks when dry to allow vine root exploration, and whereas on the Downs there's always a breeze, on a sunny day out here you're often longing for one. The greater potential ripeness is tempered by cooling sea breezes occasionally rolling up the valley, which, combined with England's natural acidity, provides some pretty serious ingredients for all that power, structure and longevity. But that's merely half the battle.

The converted barn winery and barrel room is about as well packed as any I've seen; it's almost like Ulrich and Birgit's heritage suggests some sort of stereotypically efficient engineering ability. Power comes from ripe fruit of ageing potential, but additional complexity is in part derived from its interactions with choice of yeast strain, maturation vessel and, as a result of the greatest commodity of all, time. In three- to five-year-old, 300-, 500- and 600-litre French and German oak, micro-oxygenation through porous staves partially protects but also develops mouthfeel – rather than oak flavour. On yeast lees in bottle over time, serious time, along with layers and texture, acidity continues to soften, and the wine develops an ever-increasing elegance.

At the best part of eight years on lees, the vintage Blanc de Blancs is rich and ripe, full of mouth-filling, baked apple, Chardonnay goodness, but with such a fine streak of elegance.

Ulrich Hoffmann, a world-class winemaker

The well-kitted and fitted Hoffmann & Rathbone winery

I can still taste it. It is still so vibrant, nutty and floral, and, with time in glass, it's developing further, and is just going to get better and better.

The Pinot Noir-driven Classic Cuvée plays its hand a bit sooner, attractively so; it has more approachability and fruit intensity up front as those grippy and rich red fruit flavours lead into a slightly creamy Chardonnay finish. The 30% component of the latter is the same juice that goes into the Blanc de Blancs – there's no reserve wine library programme here, no entry level or flagship end, every release is from the best years and super premium.

The truest expression of that philosophy is perhaps in the rosé – there's not a fresh, fruity and crowd-pleasing non-vintage and a more serious vintage version that's twice the price. Sparkling Rosé is maybe the best food-wine going, and that's exactly how H & R has been made. The 100% Pinot Noir provides the richness, tangy orange peel and hint of spice, which is so good paired with duck and many a game dish.

For so long the view of still wine in England has been that the same money gets you further elsewhere and that Bacchus is our answer to New Zealand Sauvignon Blanc. Don't get me started on the latter, but if you were to choose one wine that smashes both sentiments apart, H & R Bacchus is it. It's all texture, mouthfeel and roundness; it moves away from that English hedgerow-and-nettle style and is more honeyed and riper in stone-fruit than your average, fermented with a nineteenth-century yeast strain called 'sleeping beauty'. The wine is very much alive; it's a great introduction to the brand and 'perfect for a long car journey' according to Ulrich (presumably from the passenger seat). The NV Pinot Noir goes against the grain of otherwise vintage-only wines within the range, but to its credit, a blend of the former three years provides depth, richness and a snapshot of each of those season's variation in characteristics, also known as complexity.

You don't need to be in the barrel room or vineyard with Ulrich to understand how much emphasis is placed upon professionalism and artisanal approach, you just need to taste the wines. He's making probably Britain's best Bacchus and one of the most impressive still Pinots – and the headline is still the quality of the sparkling trio. This is the kind of kit that will all be on allocation in the not-too-distant future, which is the industry way of saying it's all sold before it's released. You don't need to read, talk or think about them, you just need to take their advice and sit down and drink.

The barrel room at Mountfield

281

Sedlescombe Organic

@SEDLESCOMBE_ORGANIC

Hawkhurst Road, Sedlescombe, Robertsbridge, TN32 5SA
https://www.sedlescombeorganic.com

What: Tours, tastings, cellar door sales and lunch
Recommended wines: Pet-Nat, First release white, Premier Brut

Planted in 1979 by Irma and Roy Cook, Sedlescombe is Britain's oldest organic vineyard. Roy inherited 10 acres of land from his grandfather, initially living on-site in a caravan and growing sufficient organic food to provide a basic diet – plus a surplus that could be sold to meet his other needs.

There was a small vine-planting movement developing in the South East at the time, and Roy realised his land was in the perfect spot for it: graced with a south-facing slope and good sun exposure, rather than at the bottom of a valley in the frost or exposed to the high winds at the top.

At a wine course in Germany, which was the go-to region for knowledge and know-how in the late seventies, he met his future wife, Irma. They worked in vineyards in order to be paid in cuttings that they could plant on the newly acquired East Sussex site, where Irma says she 'fell in love with the vineyard and the man was OK'.

They started with 2000 vines over 1.5 of the 10 acres, eventually expanding to a total of 23 acres across thirteen varietals, including most of the old German favourites, led by Müller-Thurgau, Solaris, Reichensteiner, Regent as well as Rondo. Because they had no permanent residence, living in the caravan at the time, the local council tried to evict them, from the land they owned, in 1987.

Biodynamically farmed from the outset

The flat-pack house

As career-long supporters of the 'World Wide Opportunities on Organic Farms' organisation, they managed to arrange help from a group of fellow volunteers and self-build students, and, along with local resources, they effectively built the duo a flat pack eco-house in three weeks. The current vineyard manager lives here today, just behind the winery.

Certified biodynamic in 2011, Sedlescombe had to negotiate at least one concerned customer's query: having been bought their wines as a gift, they worried biodynamic meant they were all made by some sort of naked, cult-worshiping druids. They weren't, of course, as it's an approach where the underlining principle is to best express site and soil via the most natural means and high-quality grapes, while leaving the land in a better place for their presence. The wines here are so fresh and pure –

the Pet-Nat blend especially – of Solaris, Reichensteiner, Johanniter and Müller. There's a slightly more classic Premier Brut, which blends Seyval with Kerner, with Johanniter, as well as a traditional English red blend of Regent and Rondo; light and subtle options.

The on-site winery, tasting room and café building, made from reclaimed material, resembles the inside of a barrel, and is tucked away down the slope off the main road. Mark Dixon and the MDCV group bought Sedlescombe from the Cooks in 2018, which by then also included a further 100 acres under vine at Bodiam Castle. The group have also planted en masse at Luddesdown in Kent, with a total aim of producing between four and five million bottles a year. I hope the history, and more importantly, the practices at Sedlescombe aren't lost along the way.

Charles Palmer Vineyards

@CHARLESPALMERVINEYARDS

Wickham Manor, Wickham Rock Lane, Winchelsea, TN36 4AG
https://www.charlespalmer-vineyards.co.uk

What: Cellar door tours, tasting, sales and events
Recommended wines: Blanc de Blancs, Classic Cuvée, Chardonnay

Charles Palmer, a general under the Duke of Wellington, established the legendary Chateau Palmer in Bordeaux on his way back from the Peninsular War in 1814. Charles Palmer, the Winchelsea farmer, planted his vineyard with a distinct vision for quality sparkling wine in 2006.

The hedgerow-dissecting single tracks that lead up to the farmyard cellar door are worth winding your way around, not least for the view from the top. The marshland below the vineyard actually sits beneath sea level, while opposite them the highest vines climb to around 30 metres above. Only a mile from the ocean, those cold sea breezes threaten the crop, restraining ripening warmth, but, as you can see from one of the country's most attractive tasting tables, the natural bowl-shaped sun trap protects and warms. The airflow that rolls in pushes away spring frosts, for the most part, and being this close to the sea means that if there's a frost here, you know it's bad everywhere else.

The vineyard was once a hop field, but vine roots delve deep enough to hit a bountiful bedrock of Kimmeridgian clay, famous for being the primary soil type of Chablis's Grand and Premier Cru vineyards, though it was named after a village on Dorset's Jurassic coast.

Palmer's still Chardonnay could be described as Chablis-esque – that steely minerality and crisp acidity most will associate with the region and its majority steel tank-fermented and matured wines. However, the best Chablis – and indeed all of the region's wines until steel tanks were implemented in the sixties – see some oak. Instead of trying to emulate others, Palmer are making wine according to site and season. The still Pinot Noir does see some light oak adding a touch of depth to its light core as a result, but Charles Palmer has built its reputation on quality sparkling wine.

From exclusively estate-grown Pinot Noir and Chardonnay, intense, honeyed fruit is softened with each of the range seeing a minimum three years' lees ageing. The Blanc de Blancs especially, at four years on lees and two under cork, still absolutely holds that acidity, which, along with fruit concentration, suggests great longevity.

The Classic Cuvée is a predominantly Pinot blend. It is super rich and complex, with red fruit at the fore and a slightly creamy, Chardonnay citrus finish. Will Davenport was making these wines, and it was his winery that was mirrored in the building of Charles

Palmer's, in a former grain store, completed in time for the 2017 vintage. Now Charles and son Robert are making the wines, under the stewardship of Will Davenport.

The farmhouse was built in 1580, once home to William Penn who went on to found Pennsylvania and, more recently, the building was used in an episode of The Crown. Charles's wife Sally has run a B&B for twenty-one of the last twenty-three years, but 2020 saw the business evolve on a few fronts. The house has now been split into three sections, two of which are available to rent, and the other where Charles and Sally live.

Being inspired by his national heritage from New Zealand, Charles ensures that sheep farming lives on; the cellar door tasting room and shop was used as a lambing barn a year before it opened to the public. There is also a greyhound from the Palmer family crest proudly sitting on the label, and you can usually find one of the current farm dogs wandering around, the Palmer name proudly upheld across the site.

Just a few metres above and away from the sea, the vineyards at Charles Palmer

TILLINGHAM
@TILLINGHAMWINES

Dew Farm, Dew Lane, Peasmarsh, Rye, TN31 6XD
https://tillingham.com

What: Cellar door tasting, sales, restaurant, stays, tours
Recommended wines: Oaked Pinot Noir, Col '19, Field Blend One

Few wine brands have garnered such a following in such a short space of time, as Tillingham. Leading the charge of the natural wine movement in England, from Peasmarsh near Rye, Ben Walgate and his ever-growing portfolio of brilliantly branded booze are in many ways as modern as it gets, but they use methods to make them that are as old as wine itself.

Hailing from a farming family near Grimsby, Ben went on to university in London. Noticing a Majestic Wine warehouse en route, he went in and asked for a Saturday job. Following graduation, his intrigue in the wide world of wine led him to the vineyards of Burgundy.

After a few weeks with large *négociant* Albert Bichot, who was making wine on an industrial scale but with not much to say for the farming practices, a friend of a friend hooked Ben up with a small family Domaine in Volnay. Having seen the state of the soil after years of conventional farming, they, like many others in Burgundy especially, were decidedly moving in a more natural direction. Ben was working hard in the cellar and among the low vines, but instead of ending each day with wheat, barley or pigs, the winemaker was there with wine, cheese and charcuterie – what a life indeed.

Back in Britain Ben worked as an importer

Ben Walgate and one of his first estate releases from 2017-planted vines: the 500ml format 'Field Blend Two'

and distributor, but pretty soon realised he wanted to be back on the producer side of things. English wine was thick in its resurgence, and he moved to Gusbourne as winemaker, overseeing a complete rebrand. However, spending his days smartly dressed with a brand moving in a more conventional and commercial direction was a suit that didn't really fit. Through fortunate timing, a 70-acre, 700-year-old homestead and farm dwelling came up near Rye, and with a little help from his friends, brand Tillingham was born.

The vineyard is complete with traditional Kentish oast house, under which are now buried fourteen Qvevri. Lemon-shaped terracotta vessels like these date back at least 8000 years, to the very beginnings of recorded winemaking in Georgia, Europe. Naturally fermented on wild yeasts within, juice is often left in contact with skins in the making of wines like 'Qvevri Orange' – a blend of Bacchus, Müller-Thurgau, Madeleine and Ortega; a wine that also saw time in foudre vats before being blended in steel.

Farm buildings have been turned into an eleven-bedroom boutique hotel, vine-view restaurant and terrace, and in an old barn lies a pizza oven. It's a fantastic day out; a modern cellar door full of the farm's character and charm, the kind of place you could go for lunch, end up staying for dinner, then the night, and the next day just doing it all over again. Other than the vast Tillingham wine list, the main affair here is the atmosphere. It's exactly what a cellar door should be: fun, accessible and full of interesting wine... and pizza, too.

Planting 40,000 vines in 2017 led to the first estate releases – field blends one and two – in 2021, bottled in 500mls due to the low volumes. A huge focus is on experimenting with varieties and winemaking practices with fruit bought from Essex, Sussex and elsewhere in Kent. Tillingham made twenty-five different wines in 2020, and it's apparently not too tricky trying to reign yourself in, if you have absolutely no desire to do so.

Ben's got some Chardonnay developing in barrel under 'flor', which is a thin film of yeast that develops on top of the juice when a gap is left at the top of the vessel. Interacting with – but largely protecting – the wine underneath, it develops the juice into all kinds of interesting, distinctively tangy, saline and savoury tastiness.

In the winery also are all kinds and sizes of oak, foudre and more Qvevri buried in sand because there's no room left under the oast. In the steel tank Ben's increasingly making wine in a part carbonic co-ferment style, suspending bunches of Pinot Gris grapes, among others, in fermenting juice where the CO_2 present initiates a carbonic maceration until their skins are crushed, releasing the juice to continue fermentation naturally.

Sourcing so many parcels of fruit from almost exclusively natural growers gives Ben so many options to experiment – somewhere he's right at home. Producing such an expansive range, often in small batch releases, means it's tricky to keep up at times. If the wines do make it online, they're often sold out shortly after, which makes the cellar door offering even more attractive, and authentic, and the only place you can see wines at source. A great blend of tradition and ultra-modern – that's Tillingham.

Tillingham's oast, pizza shed, boutique hotel and restaurant

Oxney Organic Estate
@OXNEYORGANICESTATE

Hobbs Lane, Beckley, Rye, East Sussex, TN31 6TU
https://oxneyestate.com

What: Tours, tastings, cellar door sales, stays
Recommended wines: Blanc de Blancs, Meunier sparkling, Sparkling Rosé ZD, Classic Cuvée, still Rosé

Why organic? 'Because why would anyone put chemicals on food or in the soil?' Kristin Syltevik was told countless times that organic grape growing could not be done in Britain, because the land is too wet, with too much disease pressure as a result. Through the range at Oxney she's proving that it is absolutely possible, and doing so across 35 acres under vine, which makes Oxney Britain's largest single-estate organic wine producer.

The reasoning is twofold: a huge passion for wine and food, plus cooking and growing. A love of the environment, which encompasses all those things, has always inspired Kristin to eat organically. So, when she gave up running an international PR firm in 2012 to move into farming, there was only one route in mind. Oxney the wine producer is the centrepiece of a four-farm estate, all of which are organically farmed, but equally it's about growing the highest quality grapes, to deliver in glass the truest expression of site and season, and as a reflection of their vision that the best wines are made in the vineyard. Improved soil health and ever-increasing wildlife and biodiversity is a massive and well-earned bonus.

Planting the first vines in 2012, another 15 acres were added in 2015. The big three sparkling varieties of Chardonnay, Pinot Noir and Meunier were joined by Seyval and looser-bunch clones of the first three. The fungus Downey mildew can develop on grapes following periods of warmth after rain, so loose bunches and increasing the air flow among them – via effective leaf-plucking and wider canopy management – is a key strategy in reducing disease pressure organically.

It is a challenge, especially over this area under vine, but in this way it's possible to establish which particular blocks or rows within a vineyard are consistently producing the best parcels of fruit, and extended observation from time among the vines helps Kristin ascertain which patches seem to be regular trouble spots. In short, it's called ultimate dedication to practising what you believe in, or walking the walk, again and again.

The proof of this approach is in Oxney's entire range – the amazing 100% Meunier Blanc de Noirs, picked from a single block within the vineyard, is about the best expression of this single varietal I've seen. Barrel-fermented with additional lees stirring, this began as an experiment and turned into one of my favourite wines from this entire trip. It's rich, toasty and complex, slightly smoky and marzipan in flavour, but shining through is the fragrant, almost lavender-like pristine and ripe stone-fruit.

Kristin and Freda at Oxney Estate

Right behind it and coming up fast is the Chardonnay Blanc de Blancs; an equal split of base wine barrel and tank fermenting, at thirty-six months on lees it's classic, creamy and delicate, with a nudge of toastiness in there. Long and moreish, it's another stunning wine and a great reflection of single season grapes.

A couple of rosé sparklings are a great side-by-side comparison; enjoy the richer, zero-dosage Pinot Noir 'Vintage Classic' for dinner and discussion after an afternoon in the sun on the uplifting and bright 9-grams-per-litre 'Estate Rosé NV'.

The year 2018 brought the warmth and ripeness to experiment with stills, and Oxney's first still Chardonnay promptly sold out. I would imagine the Pinot Noir that's currently sitting in barrel will have to be moved upon swiftly, and 2020 was the first time the still rosé had an addition of Meunier to its Pinot Noir, and was, in Kristen's view, their best yet.

There are a couple of new shepherd's huts on-site, to go with the brilliant long-barn accommodation, sitting pretty in a part of the country that's not short of premium producers, if you're in the market for a tasty little weekend away.

The vintage range especially is such a tribute to site, season and careful handling. The approach at Oxney should be celebrated for the premium fruit it's producing and the very reflection of it in bottle. Which probably makes for the most exciting part of the story: what happens next. As vines, experience and experiments continually develop side by side, and if the Meunier Blanc de Noirs is a little look into the future, it's very much about getting down there sooner rather than later.

Fox & Fox Mayfield
@FOXANDFOX.WINE

....

Mayfield, East Sussex
https://www.foxandfox.wine

What: Cellar door sales and tours by appointment, events
Recommended wines: Blancs de Gris, Blancs de Noirs, Midnight Rosé

When Jonica and Gerard Fox planted Hobdens vineyard in 2004, their almost 4 acres put them in the top twenty producers by volume in Britain. Fast forward to today and Chapel Down and Nyetimber source fruit from over 1000 acres each.

At an early 2000s event in the city, Gerard was handed a glass of what was almost certainly Ridgeview or Nyetimber. Tasting it was enough for him to have researched viticulture courses at Plumpton, before even suggesting to Jonica that they plant a vineyard.

Jonica was always around wine from a young age, and on family trips to wine regions she was allowed to smell and occasionally taste it. Her mother's famously good palate and love of food meant there was never a barrier to wine, which is an upbringing that came in handy when an ex-boyfriend shared an early product of an English vineyard that was 'full of acidity and absolutely no flavour'. Not entirely sure what part that wine played in the future of the relationship, but a good example to us all that a bad first experience with a grape variety, region or nation's wine is not necessarily a fair reflection of the rest.

The 1.5 hectares of 2004- and 2005-planted Hobdens vineyard are nicely tucked away behind Mayfield Ridge and Crowborough

Frost can threaten fruit at both ends of the season: in 2021 the harvest at Hobdens was completed just before it set in

Hill. Chardonnay, Pinot Noir and Meunier were planted alongside Pinot Blanc and Pinot Gris, inspired by a tasting of a sixteen-year-old version of the latter with Derek Pritchard at Dunkery Vineyard in Minehead.

The additional 11 hectares at the Lakestreet site are just the other side of the 100 metres above sea level mark, but thanks to heat retention in greensand, sandstone and clay soils, the area encourages ripening about a week ahead of Hobdens.

Jonica was enjoying a working break when the vineyard idea was mooted, so she was soon at Plumpton, her year being the first offered the full degree. Even then, all in attendance recognised the opportunity for sparkling wine, among the rolling slopes of the south especially.

Their 2013 'Inspiration' Blanc de Blancs was the first sparkling Pinot Gris produced commercially in Britain, renamed Blanc de Gris for the 2014 release onward. It combines a great intensity of rich and ripe roundness but is super elegant and wonderfully aromatic. There's a dash of Chardy in there too, to add to complexity – a super contemporary wine, as Jonica says; perfect with a few stir-fried prawns, ginger and lemongrass. Like all the best things, in some ways it's a very simple match, yet so effective. I'm not a fan of wine scores, top tens or medals but, if ever a list was being compiled of must-try English wines, Fox & Fox Blanc de Gris should absolutely be on it.

It's great to see exclusively estate-grown, varietal expressions across the range of wines, showcasing the versatility of grapes like Pinot Gris, and Meunier in the case of the Blanc de Noirs, made almost exclusively with this grape so often frowned upon in France. Another hallmark is extended time on lees across the range. Slow ripening allows complex flavour development and, in a cool climate, natural acidity is prominent too, which softens over extended time in bottle and allows greater balance and complexity.

The extremely limited-edition Midnight Rosé, when the quality of vintage dictates, shuns the mass demand for increasingly pale-coloured pinks. This is more of a chilled sparkling red in all honesty; rich, rounded and rewarding – another amazing food wine with all the body and spice to stand up for itself.

The industry in Britain has shifted immeasurably since the Foxes first planted, but their timeless vision of producing site-expressive, approachable, flavoursome and food-friendly wines is just as valid today as it was then.

Autumn colour in Mayfield

Ridgeview Wine Estate

@RIDGEVIEWWINEUK

··

Fragbarrow Lane, Ditchling Common, BN6 8TP
https://www.ridgeview.co.uk

What: Cellar door sales, tours, tastings, bar and restaurant
Recommended wines: Bloomsbury, Cavendish, Blanc de Blancs, Oak Reserve

In 1995 Chris and Mike Roberts set out to establish a winery that was the best showcase of fruit from the Sussex South Downs. Given the marginal climate – the opportunity to ripen grapes bright in flavour yet low in alcohol, with a naturally high acidity – quality sparkling wine was to them the obvious choice.

Taking advice from producers in Epernay, thirteen clones of Chardonnay, Pinot Noir and Pinot Meunier went in. Crucial to their success – and that of the wider industry on the back of their pathfinding – was the capital investment in professionalism that came in this case from the sale of the family IT business. Mike Roberts personally helped many others in the early stages of their own vineyards, and was awarded an MBE for services to English Wine in 2011.

Mike's daughter Tamara, son-in-law Simon and daughter-in-law Mardi front up the Ridgeview team today. Aside from the estate's 17 acres under vine, the vast majority of their fruit is bought in from 'partner growers', most notably Tinwood Estate near Goodwood. Simon has always been attracted by this model, and the potential to blend wines from contrasting parcels of fruit.

With the completion of a new winery, they now have the capacity to double current production to around half a million bottles a year. The focus on non-vintage wines is another hallmark that negates the poorer years by blending wines from several so as to create a 'house style' that is consistent with each release. Ridgeview's is one of freshness and a fruit-forward style, with lesser focus on lees ageing to maintain it.

The wines in the signature range are all named after squares in London: Bloomsbury, Cavendish and Fitzrovia. Bloomsbury is classically fresh, citrus-driven and aperitif style, predominantly Chardonnay with a third equal split of the two Pinots. Beautifully balanced between ripeness, freshness and structure, it's sun and shellfish central.

Reversing that blend and led by Pinot Noir and Pinot Meunier is Cavendish, which is primarily designed for the restaurant scene – and it's easy to see why. Bright summer fruits and richness make it a great charcuterie wine, accompanied by a refreshing zing of Chardonnay at the end. Fitzrovia Rosé completes the 'signature' trio, taking the Chardonnay-driven approach, with Meunier blended back to add colour and complexity; it's a great spice-dish partner, or just as good enjoyed in the garden, with its hallmark freshness.

The vintage range goes up a notch in concentration and fruit intensity, only being made in the best years. A majority Pinot Noir and Meunier blend from the best fruit parcels of each in the Blanc de Noirs provides richness, depth and structure. Single site and season Chardonnay for the Blanc de Blancs, that still drinks zesty and fresh, despite thirty-six months' lees ageing. Those yeasty, creamy flavours are coming through but are all in sync and restrained.

The Oak Reserve represents a special release that's also exclusively Chardonnay, sourced only from the 'home' vineyard that was planted in 1995 at the winery in Ditchling. It's made up of a blend of three vintages; some aged in new oak, some used, some in steel. Blended together, lees ageing adds a touch of complexity, but the focus remains on the fresh-fruit style, with ever attractively developing texture and creaminess imparted from barrel.

Ridgeview are pioneers in their own right, and working with increasingly prolific growers, but if the Oak Reserve is anything to go by, some of the best fruit they produce is right here at home.

True trailblazers: Ridgeview Estate

LONDON

RENEGADE URBAN WINERY

Renegade Urban Winery

@RENEGADEURBANWINERY

. . . .

Arch 12, Gales Gardens, London, E2 0EJ
https://www.renegadelondonwine.com

What: Urban winery, bar and tasting room
Recommended wines: Bacchus Nat Fizz, Barrel Fermented Pinot Noir Rosé,
Chardonnay, Skin-Contact Bacchus

Growing grapes in vineyards and making wine in wineries are connected industries, but jobs that require different skills. Traditionally, wineries were built next to vineyards because the closer the two were, the easier it was to transport grapes from one to the other.

Now every major wine region has producers that buy in fruit, either from elsewhere in the region or further afield, thanks to the invention of cold chain logistics protecting the fruit enroute. This provides regional variation and contributes to potentially more complex wines.

Inspired by a love of wine and the ingenuity, creativeness and explosion of the craft beer scene, Warwick established Renegade Urban Winery in 2016, under a railway arch in Bethnal Green. Most London breweries use hops that aren't even grown in Europe, but from them make beer in London, so it becomes a local 'London' beer. Why not do the same with wine? As Warwick puts it 'You wouldn't walk into Camden Brewery, Beavertown or Meantime and go: "Where's your hops, mate?" Or order a steak at Hawksmoor and ask to see the chef's cattle.'

Originally from Italy, and after gaining winemaking experience here, as well as in France and Australia, plus with Simpsons wine estate

Founder and director: the very entertaining Warwick Smith

296

in Kent, winemaker Andrea Bontempo has the opportunity to make up to around twenty different wines from vastly different grape varieties – from potentially anywhere in Britain or indeed Europe.

There's great variation in style – an honest approach in showcasing the best of Crouch Valley or Felixstowe fruit. By using disease-resistant hybrid varietals, Andrea can make new wine styles for the modern palate, two minutes from the underground. Plans are in place for a new site that'll be four times the size, which could potentially grow annual production to well over 100,000 litres, though the quality-first approach will guard against the pitfalls of scaling up too quickly.

It's very much a low-intervention approach in the winery, and almost every wine is a result of wild yeast ferments. They're fans of the texture and complexity that skin contact or barrel-ageing can add and hardly ever filter, sourcing fruit from Suffolk, Essex, Gloucestershire and Herefordshire, among others. There is such a variety and range of wine on offer, and there are some brilliant expressions of site that happen to be expressing themselves in Bethnal Green.

In what is such a modern and 'renegade' approach to winemaking, there happen to be a lot of artisans here too. Everything is done by hand, including labelling over 100,000 bottles over the last five vintages. There are no signed contracts with growers, just relationships and hand-shake agreements. It's a very personal approach, not least in the labels themselves. Originally inspired to commission local art students to design the artwork each vintage, a backup plan that eventually came to fruition was to put their favourite customers' faces on the labels. All of the labels.

As a result of restrictive former EU label laws, Renegade did so to give each wine an identity. Sara, 68, is a Chardonnay, where 68 reflects the vintage of 2020. When Renegade make a Chardonnay with fruit from the same vineyard in future years, Sara will always be on the label and, as the wine evolves, so will Sara. I like Sara a lot. She's big and rich and powerful but incredibly elegant. She's from the Crouch Valley, almost all whole-bunch-pressed and 100% aged in – mainly older – oak. Complex and slightly buttery but with classic English zing, unfortunately she's a complete sell-out. She's also a teacher from East Sheen.

The cult favourite, 'Bethnal Bubbles', takes Hertfordshire Solaris that's dry hopped after the first fermentation, then secondary fermented in bottle to capture the fizz, with zero dosage. The result is a punchy, aromatic wine/beer hybrid – a range known as Evolution by Renegade – and for these bottles, the people on the labels are replaced with animals. The first vintage sparkling wine made in London came from Pinot Noir and Meunier grown in Suffolk, pressed to Burgundy barrels for fermentation and eventually aged in bottle, in the crypt of Christ Church, Spitalfields. Jamie is a Pet-Nat, branded 'Nat-Fizz', which makes more sense, really. What only makes sense when you taste it is Shilpa, a 'norf Landan gurl' (according to the label) that's also a barrel-fermented Pinot Noir Rosé. With fruit from Essex, it comes with the warning: 'Not a Provence pinky plonk', which I absolutely love. It is whole bunch-pressed to French oak barrel for fermentation, malo and maturation, concentrated, rich, textural and full, yet zingy and, above all, it works incredibly well and is much more interesting than most southern French versions.

This is a hugely exciting, forward-thinking way of making wine with an extremely human element in careful touch and honest delivery. If you're still not convinced, simply try the wine anywhere from under the arch to on your sofa, and I'm sure that wherever you are, you'll be as impressed as I am.

BLACKBOOK WINERY

@BLACKBOOKWINERY

....

Arch 41, London Stone Business Estate, Broughton St, London, SW8 3QR
https://www.blackbookwinery.com

What: Urban winery, cellar door sales, tours and tastings
Recommended wines: 'Nightjar' Pinot Noir, 'Painter of Light' Chardonnay, 'Sea of Love'
Pinot Blanc, 'Trouble Every Day' Pinot Noir

Blackbook was born from a love of three things: cool climate Pinot Noir and Chardonnay; the English wine industry; and the fair old city that Sergio and Lynsey call home, London. The winery is in a railway arch in Battersea. Sourcing fruit from within a couple of hours of London, Blackbook are curating a modern range showcasing the quality of English fruit.

The single, fundamental goal is, in Sergio's words, 'to make bloody good wine, endeavouring to bring the hard work of vineyard owners to the forefront by creating a range that showcases the quality and potential for making world-leading still wine here in England.'

I get the impression Chardy and Pinot will always be at the top of the tree here, but additional varieties are sourced annually to produce experimental releases that keep them on their toes. Sergio is experimenting with Cabaret Noir with a view to providing a fuller-bodied English red option.

Blackbook are clearly very proud to be a London winery and a London business, seeking to reflect the vibrancy, colour, culture and energy in the wines.

Sergio grew up in the US, and is the son of Italian and Hungarian immigrants. He was surrounded by wine lovers who would 'make their own blends in the back garden and drink wine with breakfast'.

Sergio Verrillo, winemaker and owner

A range full of fruit purity, texture, layers and class

His wine career took off at pace when he moved to London and worked as a sommelier at signature London venues Maze, Tamarind, Nopi and Chez Bruce. He quickly realised that although wine was the industry for him, the production side was where his future lay. Graduating from Plumpton in 2014, he spent the next few years as a travelling winemaker, from California to Martinborough and back to England at Greyfriars in Surrey. Which is where he sourced some Chardonnay for 'Pygmalion', which is whole bunch-pressed and barrel-fermented, and it stayed in barrel with regular lees stirring for twenty months. Fans of the big, ripe and rich, Essex is consistently providing the fruit most likely to stand up to most extraction of oak or skins. The Sea of Love Pinot Blanc came from Crouch Valley vineyard, saw seven months in barrel and is textural and structured, with attractive and classic floral aromatics.

There's an evolving and ever-increasing range at Blackbook – small batch experiments that turn into firm fan favourites. The Nightjar Pinot Noir – also Crouch Valley fruit, from Clayhill vineyard – is certainly one of my picks. It's so bright and of such pure blue fruit character that, tasting blind, I'm thinking central Otago, rather than an Essex-by-Battersea mega-mix. Geographically it's about 10,000 miles away, too. Being in Burgundy barrels for nine months supports the ripeness, and is something to marvel over.

With one of London's best steak restaurants – Santa Maria del Sur – just around the corner, you could do a lot worse than take a couple of these along with you. They would absolutely stand up to a proper fillet, and, in comparison to anything on a wine list for anywhere near the same price, Blackbook will absolutely blow them apart.

Forty Hall Vineyard

@FORTYHALLFARM

Gardener's Rest, Forty Hall Farm, Forty Hill, Enfield, EN2 9HA
https://www.fortyhallvineyard.com

What: Community vineyard, tours, sales, farmers' market
Recommended wines: London Brut, Ortega

Forty Hall Vineyard is a multi-award-winning social enterprise and London's only commercial-scale vineyard, the first in the city since the Middle Ages.

Founded by Sarah Vaughan-Roberts in partnership with Capel Manor College, the project was the result of a merging of Sarah's passions for both horticulture and wine, enabling people to experience the social and therapeutic benefits of outdoor activity.

Situated on 10 acres of green space at Forty Hall Farm in Enfield, and maintained by volunteers, the aim is to bring people together in the growing, cooking and eating of local, organic produce. Certified organic and dedicated to demonstrating environmentally sustainable agricultural practices, the wines are made at Will Davenport's organic vineyard and winery in Sussex.

The first acre of vines was planted by 100 volunteers in 2009, and currently they have up to 14,000 vines of Bacchus, Ortega and, with classic-method sparkling in mind, Pinot Noir, Meunier and Chardonnay.

Forty Hall itself is a 170-acre organic, mixed farm and local food hub. The farm has a variety of rare breeds, and is also home to a thriving community orchard, a forest garden and a new market garden. The farm's meat, vegetables and fruit are sold to shops and restaurants across London, and at the monthly farmers' market, normally on the second Sunday of every month.

All profits from the vineyard go back into the project with the aim of delivering health and wellbeing benefits to the local community, including people recovering from or living with mild to moderate mental health issues, particularly those from marginalised groups.

This is in part achieved through Forty Hall's 'ecotherapy' project, which provides volunteering opportunities in the vineyard. The aim is to improve mental and physical health through working outdoors in a green environment, and in being socially connected and engaged with horticultural activity and the production of Forty Hall's own label wines. They celebrated their tenth anniversary in 2019.

Autumn leaves about to drop

Kent

WESTWELL WINE ESTATES

HARBOURNE VINEYARD

. . . .

Wittersham, Tenterden, TN30 7NP
http://www.harbournevineyard.co.uk

What: Cellar door sales
Recommended wines: Ortega, Amber Old Vines

'The Wine Garden of England' is what seven of the counties' producers have branded a little Kent-based wine trail. You can be at Ashford International in forty-five minutes from St Pancras, with a host of great producers in every direction from there. The history of Kent's growing is mainly in hops, but while they're making a resurgence, they are now vastly outnumbered by vines in the region. The hugely attractive traditional hop-drying oast houses remain, however. Here, there's character, characters, British icons, decades of history and Anglo-French alliances. Above all, there's some seriously great booze.

The phrase 'minimum intervention' is used regularly, an on-trend descriptive to suggest a leaning towards natural winemaking. Susan and Laurence Williams have favoured the hands-off approach to let wine express grape, site and season, since 1979. When they planted the 3 acres of Harbourne vineyard, there were 6 acres under vine, down the road at Spots Farm. The latter is now known as Chapel Down, who source fruit from almost 1000 acres. Susan and Laurence still have their three, and are still making minimal intervention wine.

The original vines are still yielding fruit and all are at least thirty years old, they are

Skin-contact time for texture, complexity and balance

worked by hand, and all of the fruit produced is vinified on-site by Laurence. As you would imagine for vines planted in England in the seventies and eighties, the traditional Germanic varietals of Ortega, Bacchus, Müller-Thurgau and Seyval feature, as well as some Meunier too. There was a time when these aromatic grapes became unfashionable, during the rush to plant Champagne varietals exclusively, but now they're seeing a resurgence, especially among natural winemakers, who often champion the fragrant styles of wine they produce, and their versatility in taking skin contact.

The cellar door, a tiny annexe-style shop where the range is on sale, is also the front door to their house. It's worth a call ahead if you're planning on dropping by, just to make sure they're in. The wines are amazing value, with so much history behind them. Just 158 bottles were produced of the 'Amber Orange' in 2014, from Seyval vines that have never been fertilised or sprayed. It has just a week on skins so it's not over-the-top in extraction; with just some added richness, it's slightly honeyed and chewy. The Ortega is brilliantly bright and aromatic, and there's an equally expressive Bacchus – Laurence's favourite – usually a Müller-Seyval blend and both a red and a rosé from Meunier and Blauer Portugieser.

Whole-skin contact and minimal-intervention winemaking have become increasingly popular, led by new-wave producers like Ben Walgate just down the road at Tillingham, but Harbourne have been quietly producing wine this way for more than forty years.

Susan at home at Harbourne cellar door

Chapel Down
@CHAPELDOWN

Small Hythe, Tenterden, Kent, TN30 7NG
https://www.chapeldown.com

What: Cellar door sales, tours, tastings, restaurant
Recommended wines: Brut NV, English Rosé NV, Barrel-Aged Bacchus

The hugely experienced Stephen Skelton planted the first 6 acres of vines at Tenterden in 1977. Then called Spots Farm, it was eventually sold in 1986, and Skelton continued as consultant and winemaker, having considerable success with Seyval especially. The farm changed hands again in 1990, and has regularly seen investment in equipment and visitor experience, but also the odd spell of financial trouble, too. Changing hands twice more – once, to the bank – the site was bought in 1995 by Chapel Down Wines Ltd., who moved in their winemaking operation.

Named after Chapel Farm vineyard on the Isle of Wight, which became their first supplier, the business ultimately introduced the large-scale *négociant* model to the UK. Contracting grape-growing to concentrate on the making and the marketing, they saw sparkling wine as the style most suited to the British climate, and set out to make a more premium version than other large producers.

By 2000 they had the capacity to produce one million bottles annually, split between a contract winemaking offering and their own label, for which they were buying in fruit from almost thirty separate vineyards. Owen Elias had by then been promoted to head winemaker

Almost fifty years with vines for neighbours

and would later go on to establish Balfour Wines at Hush Heath estate, under another Chapel Down investor, Richard Balfour-Lynn.

Commercially, Chapel Down were perhaps a good decade ahead of their time, maybe two. The business became English Wines Group plc. under Frazer Thompson as CEO, where he remained until retiring in 2021. Investment in equipment and tourism continued, with The Swan restaurant and, what's more, the business even returned an annual profit, their first, in 2007.

From humble original plantings at Spots Farm in 1977, approaching five decades later, Chapel Down now source fruit from almost 1000 acres, the majority of which is under long-term lease. Gin works and London bars have come and gone, their Curious Brewery brand went into administration in 2020, but by 2021 they crowdfunded almost £7 million in a share scheme to further invest in winemaking capability and visitor experience.

One of the best investments has been the 95-acre Kit's Coty vineyard, planted predominantly to Chardonnay, just north of Maidstone. There's a still Chardonnay, Blanc de Blancs, and the flagship 'Kit's Coty Coeur de Cuvée', meaning the 'heart' or 'best' of the 'first-pressed juice'. It's fermented in French oak, where the base wine matured for seven months, before secondary fermentation in bottle and thirty-four months on lees. There's a very attractive barrel-fermented and old French oak-matured Bacchus that's great to see from a large-scale producer, which on this occasion is not going down a mainstream route.

Further investment in 2019 put an additional 388 acres in the ground on the adjoining land to Kit's Coty, but winemakers Josh Donaghay-Spire and Jo Arkle continue the smaller batch experiments with the 'discovery series', including England's first Albariño – as far as I know –

sourced from the 2014 vintage in Sandhurst, Kent, and an Essex Pinot Blanc the same year.

As pioneers, and because so many people will have their first experience of English wine with Chapel Down, they're hugely important to the wider industry. Investment and volume continue to increase, as does the visitor offering. The Brut NV will probably always be the most important wine, but there's plenty more to discover and no doubt plenty more to come too, a considerable transition from the initial 6 acres at Spots Farm.

Winemaker Jo's able assistant Fitz

WOODCHURCH VINEYARD
@WOODCHURCHWINE

Susan's Hill, Woodchurch, Ashford, TN26 3RE
https://woodchurchwine.co.uk

What: Cellar door sales, tasting and tours (weekends)
Recommended wines: Classic, Sparkling Rosé, Chardonnay, Natural Bacchus

From the Kentish slopes looking down to the south coast, Graham and Donna planted their 10 acres of vines and almost immediately took the village name for the label. Graham momentarily thought their surname, Barbour, might look quite nice on the label, but Donna countered that the philosophy was to reflect and represent their place, with wine most suited to the grapes they grow. 'So why would we call it anything other than the place where it is?' Good point, thought Graham. 'But what if the place was called Lower Slaughter, or Middle Wallop?' Donna said, 'It isn't, though, is it? It's called Woodchurch.'

Planted in 2010 to Chardonnay, Meunier and Pinot Noir, with some Bacchus in 2016 and additional Pinot Noir two years later, means that a decade in, both vines and wines are now in a pretty good place to do what the couple set out to do.

As a former librarian, Graham said there was a certain attraction to planting in nice straight rows, but apparently varieties in alphabetical order happened purely by chance. His humility and humour are evident on the entertaining vineyard tours, where he freely admits the couple enjoy looking back on early mistakes during their own 'amateur hour with Graham and Donna.' Their ability to take the stewardship

Graham's vineyard tours, some of the country's most entertaining

forward has led to an exceptional site under great management, yielding top-quality fruit and wines as a result. It also makes them both even more relatable to us as wine drinkers and people.

The reflection of place is most true in the Bacchus, fermented exclusively with indigenous yeast that's not at all overpowering, allowing the equally perfumed elderflower and hedgerow flavours to shine, with some barrel aging imparting additional texture and complexity.

The year 2018 produced 33,000 bottles, and the ripeness to add a still Chardonnay and rosé, but it's a sleek range – varied and interesting but not trying to be everything to everyone. The sparkling range is crafted by Dermot Sugrue at his award-winning Wiston Estate, where he's making some of the best sparkling wines in the country. To which you can very much add Woodchurch. 'Classic', is a 60/30/10 blend of Chardy, Pinot Noir and Meunier, and is a citrus-driven and brilliantly approachable vintage offering, with richer red fruit through the middle and a long crisp finish. If you're in Rochester you can swing by Café Nucleus and add a glass of this to your breakfast, safe in the knowledge that the day is shaping up to be a pretty good one.

The Sparkling Rosé is delightfully coral pink in colour and rich with very attractive English summer fruit and a hint of Christmas spices making it my kind of sparkling rosé; a great food wine, complex and flavoursome. The 20% still Pinot Noir added to the blend was so good on its own that it inspired a range addition for future ripe enough vintages.

I can imagine the wines going pretty well with one of the pizzas coming from the cellar door's wood-fired oven. The balcony above is a fine spot to enjoy a few glasses, with a great view down the slopes over the vines.

Mattheiu Elzinga at Litmus is making the still wines – the still rosé is super light in colour; bright and enticing Meunier with a hint of herbaceousness (not that the sparkling version

Good place, good people, good wine… good times

isn't, but this really is the classic summer's garden easy-goer). The still Chardy leans towards the textural and fleshy: it's ripe and slightly oxidative in style from a bit of barrel time.

Woodchurch absolutely encompasses my kind of people, place and wine. The 'audience with Graham'-style vineyard tour was one of my favourites: very entertaining, informative and an honest account of the journey. Maybe it's just that this modest, self-deprecating style appeals to the British sense of humour, or maybe it wouldn't be quite as rewarding if the wines weren't as good as they are.

BIDDENDEN VINEYARDS & WINERY

@BIDDENDENVINEYARD

Gribble Bridge Lane, Biddenden, Ashford, TN27 8DF
https://biddendenvineyards.com

What: Cellar door sales, tours and tastings
Recommended wines: Gamay, Bacchus, Ortega, Schönburger

This is Kent's oldest vineyard, owned and operated by the Barnes family since 1969. This wasn't a hobbyist, 'few vines in the back paddock' job, either. As food production became global with the emergence of supermarkets and making things harder for smaller farms, Joyce Barnes, with a 40-acre apple orchard, went the way of the vine after hearing a feature about English vineyards on Radio 4's Women's Hour.

The initial test plantings of six varietals are now eleven different grapes grown over 23 acres. Pinot Noir went in the ground as early as 1972 and is almost exclusively used for their range of sparkling. The classic-method Pinot Reserve is another example of absolute value for money regarding sparkling wine drinking on offer here in Britain.

Though it's not the region's signature red grape, some Loire Valley Gamay that second-generation Julian Barnes tasted inspired him to plant some for himself in 1985. He enjoys entering this into international competitions, especially in France, if only 'to wind them up', going by the occasionally cursory comments that come back.

The country's leading wine critic, Jancis Robinson, was seriously impressed when she

Legs day... second- and third-generation family members Julian and Tom Barnes

saw it at a trade tasting in London. Julian watched her moving down a line of wines, making a few notes as she went until she tasted his Gamay, and immediately walked over, put her laptop down in front of him and said, 'Tell me about that wine.' I get the impression he quite enjoyed this comment, too.

The Gamay is relatively rich, savoury and structured for a classically light varietal, but Beaujolais Nouveau this is not – it's reminiscent of the best wines coming from its spiritual home, the kind of Gamay that is made in Beaujolais in a more traditional Burgundian style, at a price point long ago forgotten in the Côte de Nuits.

Third-generation sons Tom, Sam and Will are all part of the business; Tom usually in the winery, Sam importing vines and Will most often out working the vineyard. They're knocking out about 100,000 bottles of cider a year too, with that old apple orchard not going to waste.

Half of the vineyard is planted to Biddenden's signature varietal, Ortega. It's great to see an off-dry version. For a nation of spice-driven cuisine lovers, it's worth having a few of these tucked away if dinner's inspiration takes you in that direction. But we also like a good daytime session too; the sugar uplift makes it so approachable and refreshing, but Ortega's signature roundness and riper flavours give it body and interest.

Bone-dry, classically crisp and floral, Bacchus takes the more conventional route, along with the Dornfelder, which is best slightly chilled, and it's another style that is well suited to days with long sunlight hours. For the first time since 1987, 2018 brought the ripeness to produce a late harvest Ortega, that at 122 grams residual sugar retails at a fairly punchy £1 a gram, in a half bottle.

Biddenden is a great example of a genuine family business that are very good at what they do. With five decade's worth of experience, they've developed an understanding of the site and its equally established vines, through which they're producing a range that's reflective of both site and that supreme stewardship. Future generations don't know it yet, but they've got a good thing coming their way.

1984-planted Ortega vines at Biddenden

Simpsons Wine Estate

@SIMPSONSWINE

....

The Barns, Church Lane, Barham, Canterbury, CT4 6PB
https://simpsonswine.com

What: Cellar door tastings, sales and tours by appointment only
Recommended wines: Flint Fields Blanc de Blancs, Derringstone Pinot Meunier, Roman Road Chardonnay, Rabbit Hole Pinot Noir

In 2002, Ruth and Charles Simpson established Domaine Sainte Rose in the Languedoc with its annual 360 days of sunshine. Ten years later they could no longer ignore the potential for English sparkling wine and a repeat venture this side of the channel, in a region not bound by the fear of overproduction and resulting bureaucratic legislation.

Fifteen minutes south of Canterbury in the village of Barham, tucked away down a country lane and well-protected behind a long-established tree line, is a glorious 30 acres of vines planted to Chardonnay, Pinot Noir and Meunier. Taking its name from the old Roman road it runs alongside, now more commonly referred to as 'the A2', there's a better-than-evens chance that the Simpsons weren't the first to plant vines here.

In 2016, a further 60 acres of the same three varietals went in up the hill next to an old railway line, which, at its highest, sees vines hitting 90 metres above sea level. All the way up the gradient, 'Railway Hill' vineyard is full of dips, burrows and sun traps.

Eight different Champagne and Burgundy clones were selected to provide complexity and structure, but the Simpsons promised themselves

they wouldn't attempt making a still wine in England. Trouble was, just two years after the original plantings, a small yet concentrated yield ripened so well they almost didn't have a choice. Winemaker Leigh Sparrow lives almost equidistant between the two properties, and makes wine at both. Tasting what was intended to be a sparkling-base wine, the Chardonnay was too drinkable, too ripe and just too good as a still wine to be re-fermented into sparkling.

This is a warm pocket; the chalk soil beneath the two vineyards is well-versed in its suitability for vine roots, holding acidity and draining well, further aiding ripening. But from the glass-walled tasting room bar above the winery you're looking down on what's playing the biggest role in the shift to producing great wine, from these pockets of well-thought-out vine plantings across Britain: investment in the right kit and the know-how of skilled people using it. When they're up to full production, Simpsons will be producing around 250,000 bottles a year.

Chalklands is a super fresh, zingy Classic Cuvée, which is so approachable. Refreshing sea spray salinity gives way to mouthfeel and some tasty texture, but is best served as an intro to a great afternoon, or a fantastic first

The Roman Road vineyard

impression of the wider range. The sparkling offering is so concise – through Blanc de Blancs, Blanc de Noirs and rosé – there's almost a wine for any occasion, and the variation for a great range, without mention of the stills.

There's a Provençal-style rosé on the face of it, as you would expect given the southern French influences here, but with a very English twist of rose garden fragrance and a touch of lees richness.

The 100% still Meunier 'Derringstone' is so fragrant and flavoursome that I expect we'll see more and more single-varietal expressions of Meunier, and it's because of wines like this. It's pressed off its dark skins that throw just a touch of colour in the process, so that its blush appearance is an attractive facade to the riper, richer stone-fruit core.

The range is now almost an equal split between sparkling and still. There's a block within the Roman Road vineyard that is consistently producing their best Chardonnay, from which comes the still, single varietal named after its origin. Rich and complex, part barrel-fermented and in French oak for up to nine months, part on lees in tank, I couldn't not buy some, and I'll buy some more at each release in magnum format.

Despite how bright and crunchy the Rabbit Hole Pinot Noir opens, there's depth and structure and a hint of richer, smoky French and American oak, but just three months in one- and two-year-old barrels keeps its focus on pristine fruit. It will age well, and would look good chilled, on its own in the wine garden of England. I was at a tasting recently and the host said he hadn't tasted many English Pinots because 'Why would you?' At Simpsons you'll absolutely see why.

GUSBOURNE

@GUSBOURNE_WINE

. . . .

Kenardington Rd, Appledore, Ashford, TN26 2BE
https://www.gusbourne.com

What: Cellar door tasting, sales and tours, pop-up restaurants
Recommended wines: Guinevere Chardonnay, Blanc de Blancs, Brut Reserve, Sparkling Rosé

John de Goosebourne's Appledore estate was first mentioned in 1410. On the 14.10 from St Pancras these days, you're in Ashford before 3pm and only a fifteen-minute taxi from Gusbourne winery. South African orthopaedic surgeon Andrew Weeber moved to the UK with a retirement dream of owning a vineyard, that would become Gusbourne the wine estate, one of the flag bearers of premium English wine since their first release in 2010.

The estate itself was bought in 2003 and planted to the three main sparkling varietals a year later. There are 150 acres under vine at the original Appledore site and winery, plus a further 70 acres in West Sussex near Goodwood.

Every wine is 100% single season and therefore reflective of that very year. There's no interest in blending multiple years to make a consistent 'house style', and no desire to pay anyone else for their fruit. If a bad vintage comes along, which it will, they'll make less and release fewer wines, or feature more prominently the better of the two growing sites. If there's a year when the premium Blanc de Noirs isn't released, fruit destined for that might end up in the Brut Reserve.

In the abundant years they'll yield more,

Ellie and Adam at Gusbourne

and aside from the major quality benefit of long lees ageing in terms of softening acidity and developing flavours, releases can be staggered and hopefully supply can be evened out over time.

The Appledore winery was built at Southview farm in 2012, surrounded by eleven separate plots of vines. With an excess of vines for the original 'Cherry Garden' plantings, an overspill went in at the 'Pond'. The latter is now seen as the premier plot for Pinot Noir. There is also the exclusively Champagne clone Chardonnay in 'Commanders', and consistently the best Burgundian clone version at 'Boot Hill'.

These plots sit at varying altitudes around 40 metres above sea level, on clay and, at their West Sussex site, just shy of 100 metres, on chalk. The 100 tanks and 200 different barrels take juice from multiple clones, of three different grapes, from these different blocks and rows within different vineyards, all with their own unique characteristics. Depending on individual season, around 250 base wines might be made each year. These are all blind tasted by winemaker Charlie and ambassador, Master Sommelier and winemaker Laura, before the final blend for each wine is assembled into a complete range that might number eight or nine in total.

The final Cuvées are seamless, well-made and, best of all, show off both the ripeness and the quality of the fruit Gusbourne are growing. The Brut Reserve is led by Chardonnay, an almost equal parts blend of their three varieties; citrus fresh upfront but thirty-six months on lees gives a nice creamy roundness and a contrast between light and fresh with rich and ripe. The Guinevere Chardonnay is a still Chardy for big Chardy lovers; rich and creamy but, like all wines and Chardonnay in particular, it's only a good wine if every element is in sync and well balanced. The weight of fruit especially stands up to ten months in French oak, whole bunch-pressed, and full malolactic fermentation adds further roundness and integration.

The flagship Blanc de Blancs consistently comes from the same – blind-tasted – Boot Hill Chardonnay block, and despite the ripeness and forty-two months on lees, exemplifies the signature linear style.

Gusbourne is a great day out; a slick operation with a sublime range to show for it. There are Michelin-starred pop-up restaurants and relaxed lunches on the picnic tables among the vines. When exploring I met Ellie and Adam, who had hopped on that train out of London, enjoying a very easy, very tasty day out vine-side.

Gusbourne are big enough to be exporting to more than twenty countries and growing. You'll see the label on a lot of good booze shop shelves. Other than the wines, the thing I like most of all is that the family grower approach is very much a part of the cellar door offering. A wander among the vines and a few wines is still a wander among the vines and a few wines; it's a genuine, friendly and approachable experience, but there's a lot going on and a lot of interest to unpack, much like their extremely well-made wines.

Gusbourne's tasting tent and wildflower meadow

Heppington Vineyard

@HEPPINGTONWINE

. . . .

Lower Heppington, Street End, CT4 7AN
https://heppingtonvineyard.co.uk

What: Cellar door sales by appointment
Recommended wines: Pinot Gris, Chardonnay, rosé, Pinot Noir, Classic Sparkling

In 1806, Gregory Blaxland left his Canterbury farm and emigrated to New South Wales, a journey which took 220 days. He picked up some vines in the Cape of Good Hope and eventually became one of the first to plant for wine production in Australia, a country that has gone on to produce the odd bottle of wine since then – about 1.13 billion in 2020, to be precise.

Blaxland was the first person to export wine from Australia to the UK in 1822 and, prior to that, the first European settler to cross the Great Dividing Range of the Blue Mountains and its 1 million hectares of Eucalypt forest.

Henry Blaxland, together with wife Gill, live on family farmland near Canterbury today. Following in Henry's forebears' footsteps, metaphorically speaking, in 2016 they planted vines in Kentish clay and flint, after 'a rush of blood to the head.'

The 6.25-hectare single-vineyard Heppington site – named after the stable house – slopes gently off to the south; a wildflower meadow at the top end looks sensational in the late afternoon sunlight. Half of the vineyard is dedicated to Chardonnay, almost a third to Pinot Noir and the remaining 20% split between Meunier and Pinot Gris. The Gris was initially intended to be 'a bit of a side show' to the otherwise exclusively sparkling production, but by the time of their first crop in 2018, the reputation of English still wine was rapidly increasing.

2020 yielded 82 tonnes of fruit – and a pandemic, in case you missed it. Up until that point most of Heppington's produce had gone into the trade. The striking abstract packaging and equally eye-catching prices look so good on the shelves of great independent retailers like The Offy in Whitstable, and might hasten the unscrewing of a few bottle caps, but as much as I love a good label, it's all about the juice.

The zingy Pinot Gris looks absolutely fantastic with a few oysters at Little Swift in Margate – that crisp acidity is a good match for some smoked salmon, too, but ripeness and fruit weight absolutely stands up for itself and makes this one just as good on its own.

Quite compact in youth, the Chardonnay has got so much more to say for itself as time progresses. Part oak-aged at Defined Wines, where all of the stills are made, the porous barrels impart oxygen rather than oak flavour, so this is still down the leaner end; slightly fleshy, with a hint of texture and a whole lot of good times ahead.

The use of 100% Pinot Noir means the

rosé is packing some serious class, though from appearance it looks like it will be all strawberries and cream – it's absolutely not: it's fresh and easy-going, but the pristine purity of fruit is proof, if you ever needed it, not to judge a rosé by its colour, whichever end of the colour spectrum it may sit.

It's in some ways ironic that our cool climate lends itself so well to producing reds that are often best served slightly chilled, on smoking hot days. Though on the occasion of the latter taking place, Heppington's Pinot Noir is about as good an option as I've seen for sticking a red in the fridge for thirty minutes prior to drinking.

With the greatest of respect to any blackcurrant fans reading this, the shift of crop to vines is much more attractive. Especially Heppington, a single-site that could be producing wine for the future of Henry and Gill's children's children's children. It's a measure of the quality of the fruit from the current crop, at such an early stage of these young vines' journey, that I really hope it is still going long after the likes of us are having a few wines at the Elysium bar. This is a well-travelled family when it comes to wine, with a long history spanning several trips around the world, that might just stay put for a while.

© *Tom Russell*

Heppington Chardy

Terlingham Vineyard

@TERLINGHAM_VINEYARD

· ·

Terlingham Manor Farm, Terlingham Lane, Hawkinge, Folkestone, CT18 7AE
https://terlinghamvineyard.co.uk

What: Cellar door sales, tours and tastings, vineyard B&B, wellness retreats
Recommended wines: Sparkling Rosé, Sparkling White, Caesar's Camp

When moving to Folkstone from South Africa in 2007, owning a vineyard wasn't particularly part of the plan for the Wilks family. Until that is, they found their future home, which just happened to be on the market with the vineyard thrown in. As lovers of wine drinking, at least, mum Lorna uttered those notorious words: 'How hard can it be?'

Dad Graham, a solicitor by trade, went 'back to school' – specifically Plumpton agricultural college – and initially the vineyard was farmed conventionally, in line with the approach of the previous owners. Seeing and smelling the chemicals going on the vines did not sit well with Lorna especially so they stopped using them, and moved to natural farming. With wildlife returning in abundance, the site continues as one wider, co-existing ecosystem. Some of the earlier ripening Rondo is left on the vines for the badgers to get their fill, and they leave the rest of the vineyard's crop alone as a result.

High above Folkestone, among the rolling farmlands of Kent, with views all the way down to and out over the south coast, the main plot sits in a little sun trap protected by the tree line behind. The prevailing wind comes off the sea, reducing frost and disease pressure. We're far enough east here to get the ripening warmth to counter those cooling sea breezes, too; the biggest problem being that across 5500 vines,

So well placed; Jackie at Terlingham

Take me down to the English Channel

there's not nearly enough fruit to meet demand.

Daughters Jackie, Caroline and Ashleigh now run the business, bringing with them expertise from their own contrasting careers and a mutual dedication to moving forward via the most regenerative means possible. The bottle label firm employed previously had no eco-option, so they got the boot. Now in employment is a printer down the road in Sandgate who said untreated, non-moisture-proof labels would basically do the opposite of what you ideally want from a wine label, but they could do it, and their work has been hand-applied to Terlingham's bottles ever since.

Up the road in the Elham Valley is the Vineyard Garden Centre, owned by The Fifth Trust charity, set up to provide additional funding for their skills centres and to create work opportunities for adult students with learning impairments. The Wilks family helped them transition to natural farming and employ some of their students. The centre's 1500 vines produce more fruit than is needed for the shop, so Terlingham are partnering with them to buy the grapes and make their wine, supporting them financially and using the excess to increase their own range.

The wines are made just south of Canterbury by Defined, producing reds from Rondo and Dornfelder in the riper years, but normally a rosé otherwise. Wild yeasts are used where possible, but pragmatism is utilised too, such as when, in 2020, the Bacchus needed an extra little ferment-nudge with some non-indigenous yeast.

The Sparkling Rosé is probably the perfect summer's-day, vine and ocean-gaze wine, with lots of crunchy, bright, summer fruits and a mouth-filling vivacity. Luxury B&B retreats as well as vineyard walks, meditation sessions and, of course, wine tastings are a great way to drink in the equally attractive views.

SQUERRYES

@SQUERRYES

Beggars Lane, Westerham, Kent, TN16 1QP
https://www.squerryes.co.uk

What: Cellar door tours, tastings, and sales, restaurant, brewery, farm shop
Recommended wines: Vintage Brut, Blanc de Blancs

The Manor house at Squerryes Court has been in the Warde family for 300 years and eight generations. Sir Patience Warde was elected Lord Mayor of London in 1680, and later tried for perjury. When he eventually returned from exile in 1688, he exported wool to France, some of which he swapped for wine.

In 2004, Champagne House Duval-Leroy approached the Warde family about buying and planting on some of their 2500-acre estate, probably inspired by 2003's extreme levels of heat. Talks eventually broke down, and, when handed a monumental free pass, the current custodians John and son Henry Warde decided to go it alone.

Like much of Kent's vineyards, this site used to be a hop field, and the oast house that once dried them still stands, from where it's only a short walk to the bar at Westerham brewery. There's a vibrant hub of produce here; Squerryes's farm shop sits adjacent to the 'Bottle Store' restaurant, tasting room and terrace, all backing out onto 3000 vines that roll gently southwards. The main site is over the road, home to an equal split of 65,000 further Chardonnay, Pinot Noir and Meunier vines across 36 acres. It's no surprise to see those three, on chalk and at 150 metres above sea level, and the focus in style is supported by Squerryes's vintage-only approach.

A clue to the site's former use

Both sites have interspersed rows of varietals, which provides batches of varied characteristics across the total crop in good years, and means in the not-so-good or frost-affected years, signature blends can at least still be made from surviving sections. Squerryes have a pretty unique frost-defence mechanism, too, situated in Europe's biggest car park. Also known as the M25, the traffic occasionally moving along it acts as a vortex, drawing cool air off the vineyards it runs next to.

The wines are made at Henners, with Squerryes tapping into the talents of Collette O'Leary, to focus on the growing and the serving. Tastings take place in the 'cork room', where a flight of three is a nice entrée to lunch either upstairs or outside.

Meunier plays a pivotal role across the range, accounting for a third of the blend in the Vintage Brut which, like the overall offering, is ultimately led by Chardonnay. This is their 'signature' wine. It is fresh and approachable. The backbone of thirty-six months' lees time provides structure and richness.

The rosé goes in the other direction, is 100% red grape-based and, at two-thirds Meunier, sits in the light, summer fruit and easy-going bracket. Which gives the Blanc de Blancs almost free reign to go down the rich, baked-apple and autolytic route; its forty-five months' lees time is thirty more than the rosé, and in a mini-range of three, shows a concise approach to providing contrasting options. There are some late disgorged releases of the Vintage Brut, and there may even be a few bottles left from their first vintage in 2010, aged on lees for a huge 115 months.

There's a lot going on at Squerryes, but to their great credit the vision of the wine range is streamlined and focused. You could quite easily lose a few quid either side at the brewery or farm shop, but it's probably best to save it for an extra bottle of the Blanc de Blancs. The family motto is 'licet esse beatis' which means 'it is permitted to be joyful'. Worth remembering, especially if you're taking the M25 home.

A pocket of sun

Cork room tasting at Squerryes

Balfour Hush Heath Estate and Winery

@BALFOURWINERY

Hush Heath Estate, Five Oak Lane, Staplehurst, Tonbridge, TN12 0HT
https://balfourwinery.com

What: Cellar door sales, tours, tastings, restaurant
Recommended wines: Sparkling Rosé, Les Sixes, This Septered Isle

Richard Balfour-Lynn bought the sixteenth-century Manor House at Hush Heath Estate as a family home in the 1980s. In 2001 the 400 acres of farmland surrounding it came up for sale, and in the following year the first 5 acres of vines were planted, to the familiar three varieties of Chardonnay, Pinot Noir and Pinot Meunier. By then Richard was investing in, and a part-owner of Chapel Down, which is where the first harvest went for processing. Initially the aim was to just produce one wine: a high-quality, classic-method sparkling rosé.

Owen Elias was then head winemaker at Chapel Down, and his son Fergus grew up there, working in the vineyard and winery, developing a 'healthy loathing' of doing so. It was not until he moved home and was studying to re-take his A-levels, that he says he 'got it', and during his second year at university, he was offered a cellar-hand job at Hush Heath by Balfour-Lynn.

Fergus is now head winemaker, and there are more than 50 acres under vine at Hush Heath. The range is into double figures, almost half of which is still.

In such a diverse offering, the house style is very much one of freshness, finesse and purity of fruit, all underpinned by the flagship Sparkling Rosé, which is the golden thread running through it. A blend of just over half Pinot Noir, Chardonnay and Meunier, all from the original plantings, rich red fruit and hallmark crisp acidity make it a great charcuterie wine, and one which I don't envisage ever being lowered from the top of the Balfour flagpole.

The most interesting changes are taking place in the still range, with a slight tweaking of the vision and a range evolving into richer, fuller styles that are all about texture and layers, through increased barrel usage, lees stirring and something that wouldn't have happened five years ago: acidity softening through malolactic fermentation.

The most interesting part of the vineyard comes in three rows of vines – one each Pinot Blanc, Arbane and Petit Meslier. They were the first English producer to plant the latter two; historic grape varieties are permitted but now rarely used in Champagne. Low yielding but highly aromatic, they've been blended with Chardonnay, Pinot Noir, Meunier and Pinot Blanc to create a 2000-bottle release of 'Les Sixes', which sees five years' ageing on lees. There are seven varieties still permitted in Champagne, Pinot Gris being the one left out of that blend, but all seven come together in a still wine, 'This Septered Isle', which is seriously rare and about as far removed from merely producing one sparkling rosé as you could ever imagine.

Balfour now have a distinct path built around a core range and style of sparkling wines, also embracing the future and experimenting with a focus on richer and softer stills. They've also gone down the can route, with their 'Balfour pink fizz' – a blend of seven varieties and a project that was almost, well, canned, when someone drove a forklift into the canning line.

Here is one of the very few English winemaking families that sees the profession passed down a generation, with both styles and approaches complementing each other. The diverse portfolio provides a huge amount of food pairing opportunities for the series of 'Balfour Dining Club' evenings too, which take place in 'The View' tasting room above the winery.

Harvest in progress

Domaine Evremond

@DOMAINEEVREMOND

Selling, Faversham ME13 9SD
https://www.domaineevremond.com

What: First release expected 2024
Recommended wines: Not yet released

'The winery is a green shed, opposite a pretty house with a white picket fence.' Directions that are about as English as they get. Except this is a Champagne Taittinger partnership in Kent, called Domaine Evremond.

The Taittinger family have a long history with winemaking, and recognised the opportunity for great sparkling in regions outside of Champagne, establishing, for instance, Domaine Carneros in the Napa Valley in 1987. But it wasn't until 2014 that conversations first started between Pierre Emmanuel Taittinger and Patrick McGrath, of the hugely respected UK partners Hatch Mansfield, about the potential of planting in the chalk soils of southern England.

From the very beginning it was decided that were they to do so, it would be part of a long-term project, starting from scratch, rather than with buying in fruit to get a wine on the market before their vines come to fruition. The site was found in 2015 with the help of Stephen Skelton, and purchased from local farmer and apple grower Mark Gaskain, who has since become a very handy viticulturist. About sixty holes were dug for soil analysis and eventually, in 2017, 20 hectares were planted across six plots, added to in 2019, 2020 and 2021, increasing the area

In Taittinger gear, Hatch Mansfield MD Patrick McGrath

under vine to a total of 46 acres. The Evremond wines will be from 100% estate-grown fruit, with a focus on Kentish land around the winery.

Emblazoned on the Taittinger logo is the marauding Thibaut, IV Count of Champagne; his thirteenth-century home is now the Champagne Houses' Reims HQ. Legend says it was he who discovered the Chardonnay vine in the modern-day Middle East, and the Taittinger House Style and wider commercial range is both dominated and defined by Chardonnay elegance as a result. Such is their dedication to quality, however, that they will only plant at Evremond according to the specific plots of soil identified, which, for the time being at least, makes them slightly Pinot Noir-dominant. So that's what will make up the blend of the initial releases, the first of which is due in 2024 and will be a non-vintage Cuvée of several seasons, from 2018 onwards.

In the middle of the 150-acre site is where plans are laid for the new winery and visitor centre, with views over the vines and rolling hills down to the village of Chilham. Initially, Taittinger *chef de cave* Alexandre Ponnavoy will oversee winemaking, but the long-term aim is to have a Kent-based winemaker and GM, similar to the Carneros model in California. The visitor centre will be a great spot for tastings, but there are no plans for a huge restaurant taking away business from the local area.

As the vines become more established and the reserve wine stocks grow in number, the range will grow, but a consistent, non-vintage 'house style', will forever lead the way.

Domaine Evremond is a true collaboration; a great partnership between Taittinger and Hatch Mansfield, Pierre-Emmanuel and Patrick, Champagne and Kent. They have pioneered the Wine Garden of England collective and as a measure of a genuinely special relationship, named their domaine after seventeenth-century poet, soldier and notorious lothario, Charles de Saint-Évremond. Exiled from France, he championed the early sparkling wines of Champagne in England, just a couple of decades after English physician Christopher Merrett had first written of the wine that drinks brisk and sparkling. He's buried in Westminster Abbey, and his name will be on the bottles that represent everything we owe to Champagne as a region, from those early trailblazers to three centuries of history and even act as a reflection of the quality they're able to produce here among the rolling green slopes of Kent.

To be released in bottle in 2024; the first vines went in the ground at Evremond in 2015

325

MEREWORTH VINEYARD & WINERY

@MEREWORTHWINES

....

Brewers Hall, Tonbridge Road, Mereworth, Maidstone, ME18 5JD
https://mereworth.co.uk

What: Cellar door sales, tours and tasting room
Recommended wines: White from White, Sparkling Rosé

Brewers Hall at Mereworth has been booze-based for over 500 years. Some of the country's first hops were planted here, and George Orwell was apparently among the hundreds of pickers to have graced the Mereworth oast house.

In 2016 William Boscawen planted the first vines on the family farm in Kent, with a further 2 hectares in 2017 and a first commercial harvest the following year. The Greensand Ridge, which is one of the earliest flowering sites in England, and the quality of fruit these young vines are producing already, has catapulted Mereworth to the pointy end of an already smart region. By the time of that first vintage, winemaker Scott Gebbie was on board, bringing with him worldwide experience following spells in California, Oregon, Marlborough, Canberra and the Languedoc and, through a love of sparkling wine, Champagne. Back in England, his winemaking journey has gone full circle and he is a great example of how English wine can benefit from people honing their own style as a blend of their experience from contrasting counties and regions the world over.

The first vintage was tiny – just a couple of thousand bottles – but Mereworth are now producing in the region of 15,000 bottles across three core wines annually. There's a rosé, plus 'White from White' and 'White from Black'. The invigorating approach to say it how it is on the label is an honest reflection of the quality on-site which makes these wines absolutely English. There's a willingness, therefore, to make a product that's as accessible as possible, rather than using the French terms to denote white wine made exclusively from either white or black grapes.

Will says that the 'joy of sparkling wine is that it's great at 8am, all the way through to midnight and beyond.' This approach to producing great wine is so evident in the resulting range which absolutely come under the above description.

Almost entirely Pinot Noir, with just a 4% Meunier uplift, the rosé is fruit-forward in style, but at two years on lees, hints at a richness akin to Scott's desires in championing texture and wines with food matching in mind. Pale and light this is not, and it's all the more interesting as a result.

The aim is to craft a non-vintage from several years' reserve wines as a core offering, with vintage wines being saved for the very best years. As vines and library stocks both establish themselves, the initial releases are all single season. 'White from White' is super fresh, and drinking vibrantly, but well-rounded and approachable thanks in part to full-malo, softening that naturally vibrant acidity. 'White from Black' offers great depth, structure and such attractive, flavoursome and aromatic orchard fruit, and both are long and seriously classy.

This is small-scale, premium production, but it's a producer to keep an eye out for at the very least. The best place to enjoy the wine is in the awesome Brewers Hall winery and tap room, which has been turned into a bar, too, so you can drop by for a taste or look out for one of the very limited 'tiny table' dining series. There are pink and oak-aged gins, too, plus the wonderfully rich 'Maroude' apéritif, fortified from honey wine.

Will's great uncle landed at Normandy on D-Day and, along with his tank crew, enjoyed plenty of bottles of 'The Widow', Veuve Clicquot, as they were liberating France. Now his great nephew, thanks also to Scott, is producing a range of wines that are the very epitome of this great region's amazing quality.

Top-shelf gear

WESTWELL WINE ESTATES
@WESTWELLWINES

....

The Vyneyarde, Westwell Lane, Charing, TN27 0BW
https://www.westwellwines.com

What: Tours, tastings and cellar door sales by appointment
Recommended wines: Petulant Nature, Ortega Skin Contact, Pelegrim NV

Sun, dirt, yeast. Adrian Pike has literally got the T-shirt. Probably got a few others, too, as co-founder of Moshi Moshi records, the label that launched Bloc Party, Hot Chip and Florence and the Machine. Every year Adrian and his co-founders would drive through France's wine regions on their way to a music industry conference in Cannes (which sounds *terrible*). He was then considering moving to France as a result until one lunch at Arbutus, Soho, he had a glass of Will Davenport's 'Horsmonden Dry'. He liked it so much he called Will and asked to go and work for him.

After a vintage at Davenport, he stayed on in the winery and enrolled on a winemaking course at Plumpton. Some wines are so good we Google them; this one was so good it inspired him to become a winemaker.

Owned by the Taylor family and originally planted in 2008, the vineyard sits on the south-facing slopes of Kent's North Downs near Ashford. Adrian and vineyard manager Marcus came on board in 2017, adding 20 further acres to the original 13, of Chardy, Meunier and Pinot Noir. Being a big fan of Ortega from his Davenport days, Adrian added another 3000 vines of

Sun... Dirt... Yeast... and cellar door and production manager Jeanette

that too, all planted according to one of the site's six different soil classifications.

Ortega itself is so versatile; Westwell make a hugely popular and equally approachable 'Petulant Nature' Pet-Nat. The variety stands up to oak and skin contact in one of their three 500-litre amphorae, but also produces a ripe, fresh, almost tropical fruit-driven, steel-fermented version too. Co-fermented with some Regent that Adrian sourced from Off The Line vineyard, they made a bright, crunchy rosé. It went so well they planted almost 400 Regent vines themselves, that account for 10% of the final blend.

Right above the wildflower meadow is the Pilgrim's Way of the North Downs. Cold air rises so high up over the ridge line that it jumps the vineyard and lands beyond it, keeping this part of Westwell largely frost-free. Nyetimber planted vines immediately to the east, presumably on tasting Westwell's Pelegrim (middle English for Pilgrim), their classic-method sparkling. With thirty-six months on lees and having that very attractive, chalky Chardonnay salinity, it's long and rich but fruit-forward and fresh. The ridge line is depicted on the bottle label, but for some of the other wines' artwork, organic material collected on-site – like fossils or cross sections of an Ortega vine – are photographed under microscope and hand-drawn by Adrian's partner Galia.

'Special Pink' is a tangy orchard, red fruit-driven, Saignée method sparkling rosé that, even after five years on lees, is vibrant and crisp. Summer Field red – a wild yeast-fermented, almost equal split of the Pinots and 5% Chardonnay – is for me exactly the kind of red that looks best after half an hour in the fridge, and it is a great example of the experiments going on in the winery.

Adrian Pike, founder of Westwell

It's a relatively straightforward approach at Westwell: plant well; respect the soil; make great wine. Biodynamic 'teas', rich in iron and nitrogen, are applied to the vines and there's a four-year cycle to, in theory, cut out herbicide use altogether. They're a real sweet-spot producer in size, range, philosophy and style – these are approachable wines but there is so much complexity within. It's not quite minimal intervention but there is not much added. It's just made with sun, dirt and yeast, and the results are some seriously interesting, tasty booze.

YOTES COURT

Stan Lane, West Peckham, Maidstone, ME18 5JT
https://www.yotescourt.co.uk

What: Cellar door sales, tours and tastings
Recommended wines: On the Nod Bacchus, Hands and Heels Pinot Blanc

Racehorse owner Susannah Ricci purchased the land to the west of the Grade I-listed manor house at Yotes Court in 2014. It was originally a soft fruit farm, but Susannah employed the services of Stephen Skelton, who not only suggested it was a perfect site for vines, it was also the best he'd seen during an illustrious career covering almost fifty years. South-facing, it has greensand and Kentish ragstone gently sloping down towards Tunbridge Wells. The vines are well-protected, and fruit from the initial 60 acres of Chardonnay, Pinot Noir and Meunier was grown exclusively for Chapel Down, Yotes Court being one of their contracted grape growers.

But in 2018, an additional 10 acres of Bacchus and Pinot Blanc were planted at 140 metres above sea level, the highest point of the vineyard and sunny former apricot orchard, all for Yotes Court's own label. They were followed in 2019 by Pinot Gris and Swiss import, Divico. The latter was trialled by Halfpenny Green, Bolney and Chapel Down, among others, in the hopes of providing a fuller-bodied red option which, due to climate, has always been a struggle for British producers. Scott at Mereworth, just 2 miles down the

road, and the team at Defined in Canterbury, are making the wines. The first vintage in 2020 yielded a range of four: two expressions of Bacchus, a Pinot Blanc and the Meunier Rosé. The result is 'Best Turned Out', which is another great expression of Meunier in single varietal form. This is a bracket that is still small but one that will only grow in size with wines of stature like this. It is such a classy wine; flavoursome and expressive but without over-the-top brightness, and its fresh and riper red fruits shine through a floral core.

The barrel-fermented 'Hands and Heels' Pinot Blanc just sings texture, creamy, fragrance and the ripe stone-fruit especially; it's very food friendly and reminiscent of the site's apricot orchard past. 'Hands and Heels' refers to a jockey riding without over-manipulating their mount and letting natural ability shine, which is testament to the approach to tending these vines and the quality they're already producing.

Of the two expressions of Bacchus, 'On the Bridle' is 50% whole bunch-pressed and sits on lees for four months; it is rich, ripe and bordering on the tropical. 'On the Nod' is de-stemmed to steel and gleans some tasty texture from three months on lees, and it is the zestier, more floral of the two, also enjoying almost 5 grams-worth of fruit-uplifting residual sugar.

The sparkling wines – including a single varietal Pinot Gris – are due to be released in 2023 and are as striking in packaging as the site itself. You can't really miss a visit for the current offerings, and, if we're to judge the place by what's currently on offer, there'll be a big queue by the time the sparklings are released.

The sleek and attractive range

Autumn vines at Yotes Court

East Anglia

VALLEY FARM

Saffron Grange

@SAFFRONGRANGE

Saffron Grange, Rowley Hill Farm, Little Walden, CB10 1UZ
https://www.saffrongrange.com

What: Tours, tastings, cellar door sales
Recommended wines: Sparkling Seyval, Classic Cuvée

The only way is not necessarily Essex, but given the choice of anywhere to plant their next vineyard, most of those I've met on this journey have said that it's where they would choose. It's as warm and dry here as it is anywhere else in Britain, but much of Suffolk and Norfolk benefit from the same strong ripening potential. East Anglia is the most intensively farmed region in Europe, but the increase in vines is going a bit easier on the soil, reversing the shift to mechanisation, bringing people back to the countryside and, in doing so, making some of the best wine in Britain.

Having lived in Japan, Singapore and China, Essex boy Paul Edwards always saw himself ending up in Hampshire or Sussex, especially when his love of Champagne dictated his future as a producer of quality English sparkling wine. But it's funny how things sometimes go full circle, and he discovered this special, chalk-laden 40-acre site in 2008, just a stone's throw from where he grew up.

Saffron Walden is named after the threaded spice that once grew here. There's next to no topsoil, the white stuff stretches at least 60 metres below, to the depth of the on-site bore hole. About seventy million years ago, this was the seabed – into which deep ocean-dwelling creatures would burrow – leaving holes that filled with sand and were eventually pressurised into flint. This became the tool of choice for Neanderthal man, partly used in probably futile fights with the woolly mammoth, which roamed this site as recently as 12,000 years ago. Flint benefits the grape-ripening process today. The woolly mammoth, however, is confined to Saffron Grange's label.

In 2008 Paul planted classic sparkling varieties Chardonnay, Meunier and thirteen separate clones of Pinot Noir, along with Pinot Gris and 'the insurance', in the reliable ripening Seyval Blanc. Additional plantings will increase production to an eventual goal of 45,000, with the forever focus being outstanding sparkling wine.

Frost is a threat to new season fruit, reduced thanks to a relatively nifty bit of kit from New Zealand called the 'tow and blow'. It works exactly as you might imagine – it's a portable, propeller-bladed, wheel-based super fan. Towed, tilted and with temperature parameters set accordingly, the fan pushes warm air rising from the ground across the vineyard, like the light of a narrow-beamed torch. They're not cheap, and don't exhaustively solve the problem, but they might just save a crop.

Paul's son Nick gave up his corporate life and embarked on a career in viticulture and winemaking, a role he'll take on in the impressive new tasting room and winery at Saffron. His view is that eventually they would like to make a 'Saffron Grange style', blending an ever-growing collection of the reserve wine library they commenced in 2016. The current range is very much a reflection of every season; the sparkling Seyval is as good an example I've seen. Super detailed, delicate and persistent, the crisp acidity is very moreish, as is the elderflower and English garden freshness.

Classic Cuvée won't be the only English sparkling wine that goes by that name, nor will it be the only one that is built around a blend of half Pinot Noir, a third Chardonnay and the blend of Meunier, but it is the only wine in the entire world that comes from this incredibly special parcel of land where Essex, Cambridgeshire and Hertfordshire meet. Minerality and elegance shine through, but at its fore is the riper stone-fruit. That herb-garden character is present, and there's even a hint of developing savoury nuttiness. It's got so much potential to age well, and there are 1000 bottles of this tucked away developing further. I can't wait to meet it again.

Additional frost-prevention measures in place

335

Tuffon Hall

@TUFFONHALLWINE

High Street Green Graves Hall Road, Sible Hedingham, Halstead, CO9 3LL
https://tuffonhall.co.uk

What: Tastings, tours, cellar door sales, weddings
Recommended wines: Bacchus, Charlotte Sparkling Rosé

It may not surprise you to read that I've seen my fair share of sixteenth-century barns on this little wine-driven jaunt around the British countryside. At not quite halfway through my journey I found my favourite, and it's the tasting room at Tuffon Hall Vineyard, near Sible Hedingham. Having seen five centuries of action, glorious buildings of this ilk are at times in need of careful restoration, and I can't imagine there was a finer job than working on this one. The location has since been used as an exceptional wedding venue, which turns out to be a stunning additional use of England's greatest tasting room.

Four generations of the Crowther family have farmed the land here for over 100 years. After travelling the wine regions of Australia and New Zealand, and being a fan of both produce and cellar door cultures, Angus and Pod Crowther sought to replicate both back home. Having worked on the farm for over fifty years, honorary family member Les was long due retirement. Angus and Pod organised a round-the-world trip for him, which he politely declined, preferring to stay and keep farming. So, the retirement present became a Massey Ferguson tractor and a

As tasting rooms go…

new role as head viticulturist. He's still here.

The desire to plant was born out of passion and travel, but bred from the opportunity Angus recognised for quality English wine; if it was not commercially viable then it would not have happened. So, in 2011, almost half of the 11-acre vineyard was planted to Bacchus, with the balance made up of Chardonnay, Pinot Gris, Pinot Meunier and Pinot Noir. The latter was working so well for the popular still rosé that additional plantings to the tune of a further 5000 vines went in the ground, split between 2017 and 2021, as well as some more Pinot Gris.

The wines are so pure. The 'Amelie' Bacchus is expressive and floral but not overly extracted or trying too hard. 'Beatrice' rosé is slightly textural but is first and foremost an approachable, soft red fruit-driven easy drinker. This really is the sweet spot for this style of lighter white and rosé; crowd pleasing but lots to unpick, ever intriguing and second glass-enticing. The sparkling rosé is exclusively Meunier, and at two years on lees, it retains fresh flavoursome fruit, backed up with a hint of richer mouth-feel. More and more single varietal expressions of Meunier are emerging and, on the back of wines as good as this, that will continue.

The family approach is such a strong element to Tuffon Hall, not least in the multi-generational help in the vineyard or in naming the wines after daughters Amelie, Beatrice and Charlotte. 2020's 'Jazz in the Vines' came and went the way most other things did that year, to be replaced in 2021 with 'Summer Sessions': a DJ in the vines on Friday night followed by the hugely popular jazz edition on the Saturday. With the cuisine provided by Mersea Island Food, all you have to grab is a deckchair and a wine – which shouldn't be too tricky – and sit back and enjoy three hours of the finest along with 300 other happy punters.

Tuffon Pinot in tank

Seeing some of the best ripeness in the country, fine Essex fruit

337

Mersea Island Vineyard

@MERSEAVINEYARD

Rewsalls Lane, Colchester, CO5 8SX
https://merseaislandvineyard.co.uk

What: Vineyard, café, wedding venue, cellar door sales and tastings
Recommended wines: Summer 'Mehalah' Ortega, 'Summer Days' Müller-Thurgau

There's so much hype about Essex as a place for premium quality grape growing. So many say they would choose this county to plant vines ahead of anywhere else. One very good reason for that is sites like Mersea Island, specifically due to its unique weather patterns.

The vineyard sits in between the estuaries of the Blackwater and Colne rivers, 9 miles South of Colchester and exactly halfway between one of Britain's sunniest towns, Clacton-on-Sea to the north, and one of the driest to the south, Bradfield-on-Sea. Mark Barber now runs the family business and a visit to the 'Cork 'n' Cap' cellar door shop is worth it solely to catch a few words with one of British wine's most entertaining personalities.

Mark was a lorry driver until joining the family business in 2004, promptly establishing the on-site microbrewery. His parents somewhat stumbled over the vineyard when purchasing it in 1997. Like a lot of builders in Essex and elsewhere in the eighties, Mark's dad, an electrician by trade, refurbished houses the family lived in before moving onto the next project. Mark says his dad's golden rule was 'if it needs decorating, it's time to move on.' His mum worked for the council, and when they were approaching retirement age, the current property came up for sale and they knew straight away it was the right place for them. It just so happens that a decade prior, the former owner had planted a combined 10 acres of Müller-Thurgau, Ortega, Reichensteiner and Solaris.

As well as the shop selling their goods and other local produce, there's a café, wedding venue and microbrewery, with its range of five core beers. The Island Oyster stout is brewed with local saltwater delicacies, though Mark points out that if it's the oyster's aphrodisiac benefit that you're after, they've had it calculated you'll need to drink about 36 pints' worth.

But back to the wine side of things; the quality of fruit they're able to grow here is simply outstanding and extremely modestly priced. So much so that Ben Walgate, one of the most talked about winemakers in Britain, has bought grapes from Mark for some of his super on-trend Tillingham range.

For a third of the price, under Mersea Island's 'Mehalah' label, their Ortega is certainly worth sailing away with – but not on the first ship up the estuary after sunrise. Otherwise, it's said that you'll see the ghost of Mehalah – an early-nineteenth-century Mersea resident – wandering across the salt marshes. The wine's ripeness and fruit-weight are as good as I've seen. It's rich and rounded and the kind of wine on which you could slap a funky label and wax seal and charge a lot more than the current price tag.

When I met Mark, he sat me down and said, 'The problem with wine, right, is that there's too much of this hoity-toity nonsense.' I'd have to agree, not on the presumption of background or the relevance of it, but in the long-winded tasting notes and words that normal people can't relate to, that often appear in wine reviews or columns. It's just confusing, and makes what is a very fun subject a bit less fun. Mark's straight up, play-it-as-you-see approach is as rewarding as it is amusing.

Along with the weddings, Mark says he plans to move into the funeral game, too. Only problem, he says, is that unlike a wedding, you can't book them in a year in advance.

Can't not pick up a few bottles of the Island Oyster Stout from the Cork 'n' Cap

Hazel End Vineyard

@HAZELENDWINE

···

Hazel End Farm, Bishop's Stortford, CM23 1HG
https://www.corylet.com

What: Cellar door sales by appointment
Recommended wines: Three Squirrels sparkling, Hudshill Dry

There's a lot to like about the hamlet of Hazel End, not least its pub and cricket ground, but especially lovely is the vineyard. The planting of it was inspired by the heatwave of 1976; a year that Pinot Noir and Chardonnay would probably have ripened in England, had there been any great quantity in the ground.

The warming climate has played a role in the growth of domestic winemaking. With warmth comes ripeness and the likelihood that, in more vintages than not, a decent crop can be harvested. It was only really with the shift to professionalism, and the investment in technology and know-how on a larger scale, have we seen it come to fruition, but that summer of 1976 was good enough to persuade Charles and Petronella Humphreys that it could be done.

They had acquired Hazel End farm two years before, and given that they were one of very few thinking along the same lines, the infrastructure and advice of how to go about doing it was as scarce as the vines themselves. After twenty years of trial and error, which included moving vineyard site, twice, the first commercial crop was eventually harvested in 1996.

Contrary to current trend, exclusively still wines was the initial plan, to be made

Vines that finally found their home at the third time of asking, in 1994

on-site. Struggles in the vineyard meant they focused their efforts on that side of the operation and outsourced the winemaking to Chapel Down. Towards the late 2000s that operation had grown sufficiency enough to cease operating as contract winemakers on this scale, so Rob Capp at Shawsgate took over and has been making the wines ever since.

For two centuries the farm at Hazel End has been part of the Gosling family estate, whose family bank was on Fleet Street located beneath the 'Sign of Ye Three Squirrels.' In 1660, a goldsmith called Edward Pinkey supposedly took the writer Samuel Pepys 'to the tavern and gave us a pint of wine'. There's now a Barclays where the Gosling bank once was, but outside is a replica of 'Ye Sign' hanging above the door. With fruit just at the point of ripeness and maintaining a high acidity as the perfect base for sparkling wine, it was a sound choice to diversify the wine in that direction, and the resulting bubbles have been sold under the Three Squirrels name ever since.

Across their 3 acres under vine, there's still some original Müller-Thurgau, Huxelrebe and Reichensteiner, all three of which go into the vintage sparkling wines that are finished off at Wiston Estate under Dermot Sugrue. Between three and four years on lees helps soften that natural acidity, together with the natural aromatics of those German varietals making it a good blend of aromatics and richness. Bacchus was added in 2009 to fill out the still offering further in single varietal form – which is very much down the English garden elderflower route and great value at £60 a six-pack. There's an intriguing Hux and Reichensteiner blend and the Hudshill Dry, which is almost half Bacchus and the balance made up of the rest of the fruit from their Müller, Hux and Reichensteiner.

The stellar summer of 1976 convinced Charles to plant

Having moved home a couple of times, these vines are now very well-established

Toppesfield Vineyard

@TOPPESFIELDVINEYARD

Bradfields, Harrow Hill, Toppesfield, Halstead, Essex, CO9 4LX
https://www.toppesfieldvineyard.co.uk

What: Premium stays, cellar door sales, tastings and tours
Recommended wines: Bacchus, Pinot Noir rosé

The land around Jane and Peter Moore's home was, possibly, planted to vines by the Romans. In what is now their vineyard, the remains of cups, a metal wine vase and a blade of a Roman centurion's sword were discovered in the nineteenth century. When the land came up for sale in 2011 they were inspired to take it back to its former use, and employed Duncan McNeill to asses site suitability.

His is a name that keeps cropping up in East Anglia; Duncan is a vastly experienced viticulturist whose knowledge and expertise has been of great benefit to those moving into wine, and specifically vine planting, as a second career. The rolling hills around Toppesfield benefit from the winds blowing down them, combined with signature East Anglian warmth, and the chalk over clay soil make this a site of huge potential. Duncan's advice was 'keep it simple', and he suggests focusing on a couple of varietals that best combine passion and potential to maximise quality.

So, Jane and Peter planted just over 12 acres of Bacchus and Pinot Noir Précoce; there are just two wines from these vines – a white and a rosé – and, much like a good restaurant with a small menu, the short and sleek offering inspires confidence in its precision and quality.

The community in Toppesfield is a strong one, and many come up to the vineyard for harvest and stay

Getting cosy

for a quite a few hours afterwards. In 2018, seventy locals picked 11 tonnes of Bacchus and Précoce in five hours, before enjoying a dinner feast – I get the impression the Romans would have appreciated that. The unofficial village wine committee were on a little research trip to the Loire Valley following Toppesfield's first commercial crop in 2016 and, though instinctively a little biased, Jane became increasingly excited because the more wines she tasted the more she preferred her Bacchus to all of them.

Back in Essex, that inaugural wine was entered into the East Anglian wine show, without any major hopes or intentions of even attending the awards. Until, that was, a couple of days beforehand she took a call from the organisers saying it was probably a really, really good idea if she headed up in time for the prize-giving, specifically the time when the best in show trophy winner was announced.

I mentioned how attractive it is to see such precision in an offering; the wines themselves are the very definition of this, such is the purity of fruit here. But what comes through most of all is the balance of concentration and elegance – they're both fragrant but not at all in an overpowering way, as there's a lot of class and finesse. The rosé especially has that chewy texture to it, but goes down a treat in the garden on a sunny day with the rest of the Toppesfield locals.

To complement the offering next to the vineyard is a two-bedroom luxury retreat, with vine views from kitchen, floor-to-ceiling bedroom windows and a veranda hot tub. It's worth checking out the listing on Airbnb for a look at that nickel-plated bar top, then mirroring their fridge offering with a few bottles of each of the Bacchus and rosé.

Vineyard stays at Toppesfield

Danbury Ridge Wine Estate

@DANBURYRIDGEWINE

· ·

Crouch Valley
https://www.danburyridge.com

What: Nothing but booze
Recommended wines: Pinot Noir, Chardonnay, Octagon Block Pinot Noir, Octagon Block Chardonnay

Sitting in Essex's Crouch Valley – probably the brightest light in the best-lit county for grape growing – is Danbury Ridge, and from the outset, their approach is a model of professionalism. Not least in the winery, kitted out as well as any I have ever seen, and one of Europe's, if not the world's, best set-ups for turning grapes into super premium booze. No tours, no tastings, no weddings, just wine. Just the three grapes in the ground too – Chardonnay, Pinot Noir and Pinot Meunier – and though there will be a sparkling release in 2023, unlike the vast majority of the mega-invested wineries further south, the primary focus here is not classic-method sparkling, but possibly the country's best still wine.

In the future, we'll look back on these wines and wish we bought more of them at the time. Seeing the quality of this wine now, and the approach taken to produce it, is as good an indication as any that Essex is the place to be for the best still Pinot Noir and Chardonnay. We're so often told that clay is not a viable soil for optimum fruit ripening, but here is proof completely to the contrary.

Danbury's three sites are planted on varying degrees of depth in sand and gravel on London clay. They are rich in volcanic minerals particularly beneficial to vines – smectite – which

Not a single beat or opportunity missed to showcase the best Essex fruit

344

were deposited about fifty million years ago at the bottom of the sea bed we now refer to as the Thames basin, a similarity shared with the soil beneath Chateau Petrus in Pomerol. As a result, London clay shrinks and swells according to water content, becoming impermeable during wetter spells and minimising the potential dilution of flavour in fruit during wet autumn periods, while often cracking when dry, allowing the vine roots to delve deeper, which they do through the loose and heat-retaining gravel and sand topsoil. The water retention potential also helps keep moisture away from the roots buried well below, further stressing the vines into producing greater quality fruit.

Winemaker Liam Idzikowski, formerly of Lyme Bay, loved the Crouch Valley fruit he worked with there and he knew this was where his future lay, and what an opportunity he has. Planted in 2014, The Octagon Block vineyard provides the fruit for the inaugural single vineyard premium releases, of both Chardonnay and Pinot Noir from the historic 2018 vintage. The depth of weight, richness and purity of fruit combined with remarkable elegance and length of both is just outstanding – unthinkable, really. They're not cheap and nor should they be, and there's not a load of them available either.

The Chardy is aromatic, ripe and slightly honeyed, with well-integrated wood and a savoury nutty complexity in the 888 bottles produced form the Octagon Block in 2018. The 2020 Chardonnay is attractively reductive in style – barrel-aged and eleven months on lees with regular stirring adds body and richness but also, best of all, supreme fruit is right at the front and just so long in the mouth. Meanwhile, 100% of the Pinot matures in French oak for eighteen months. It's dark and brooding, and mesmerising with air. Ultimately, it's an indication of where the fruit from this site will go, and it's quite extraordinary.

The sparkling options will be released as 'something a bit different' to most of our classic-method wines being made in England and Wales currently. There's a solera Blanc de Blancs currently building up vintages and progressing in character as it does. The idea is for much of the wine's development to be done prior to secondary fermentation and lees ageing, so that when it is eventually released it will continue to develop on cork, but being much closer to its complex and optimum drinking window. There will be a Blanc de Noirs, too, and with fruit this good in a country that is probably the single most exciting place for this style in the world, it would be rude not to. However, the forever focus here is the highest quality still wines possible.

Parallel to the premium duo are two 'entry level', single varietal releases of 'estate' Chardonnay and Pinot Noir; both outstanding wines in their own right, especially as understudies or 'second wines'. Both a blend of three sites' fruit and in the same price bracket as most of our sparkling wine, but price is only deserved of judgement in relative terms as a means of deciphering quality versus value for money. Rather than using these wines as an example of 'how expensive' English wine can be, I would be demonstrating just how good it is.

The amazing sight and smell of an incredible barrel room

New Hall Vineyards

@NEWHALL_VINEYARDS

. . . .

Chelmsford Rd, Purleigh, Chelmsford, CM3 6PN
https://www.newhallwines.com

What: Cellar door sales, tours and tastings
Recommended wines: Pinot Noir, Bacchus Fumé, Chardonnay, Barons Red, Classic Brut

New Hall's history dates back further than most. The original vines at Purleigh were planted in 1120; according to local parish records, only 500 yards from where the current vines are in the ground today. Two barrels of Purleigh wine were ordered by the crown, at a cost of eighteen shillings and sixpence each, which works out at less than one pence per bottle in today's money. These were sent to King John, who commissioned further production, and Purleigh wine was drunk during the sealing of the Magna Carta in 1215.

In 1969 Bill and Sheila Greenwood, who were aware of the area's viticultural past, made a commercial agricultural decision to plant vines once more. There was a small wine movement in the sixties, but it was all about German varietals and producing aromatic light whites that were low in alcohol and generally high in sugar. A trellis system of railway sleepers went in with the first 850 Reichensteiner vines, followed by 2800 Huxelrebe and Müller-Thurgau vines a year later in 1970. Mrs Greenwood made the first New Hall wines in her kitchen following the vintage of 1971, a harvest which yielded 30kg of fruit, resulting in eighteen bottles of wine.

Despite the focus of what was a very sparse industry being on these German varietals and styles,

in 1973 the first Pinot Noir vines were planted, and by 1976 a new 30-tonne capacity winery was being built. Bill and his son Piers planted Bacchus as long ago as 1977, supplying fruit all around the country. Their 2250 vines accounted for a quarter of Britain's total supply of the grape, as true pioneers of what has probably become a hugely popular white varietal.

As serial trendsetters, Piers Greenwood in partnership with Kenneth McAlpine at Lamberhurst vineyard made Britain's first classic-method sparkling wine in 1983, from New Hall Pinot Noir and Chardonnay. This was five years before Stuart and Sandy Moss planted the same varieties with that in mind at Nyetimber, and today, though lessening, approaching 65% of our total production is dedicated to this style.

Piers Greenwood retired in 2015, succeeded by his brother-in-law Chris Trembath and daughter Becki, keeping New Hall in the family. With five decades' experience in the heart of the Crouch Valley, a brand-new winery in 2021 has taken capacity to 250,000 bottles annually. There's been further plantings too, of Pinot Noir, Meunier and, as of 2018, they're now up to nine separate plots of Bacchus. Each one is made separately, producing a range of wines that winemaker Chris blends to achieve maximum complexity between contrasting styles. New Hall are living proof that there's no way you can bracket even one site's worth into a single category, let alone across an entire country. The reserve is vibrant and floral, with great ripeness as you would expect from the Crouch; it's easy-going but interesting.

The Bacchus Fumé release is a particular standout; I love the richer style, the subtle use of oak adding texture and mouth-feel, and it is a great example of vast experience and understanding of the site, while embracing a modern approach.

The limited-edition range is probably where it's at, not least in slightly more modern labelling, but as

a great showcase of supreme value for money in what will become the standout varietals from this part of the country – Chardonnay and Pinot Noir. The Pulari Gold is well worth looking out for too, with whole bunch-pressed fruit from Britain's oldest Bacchus and Schönburger vines, aged in chestnut barrels for fifteen months and bottled at 114 grams residual sugar.

There is so much history at New Hall, but the highlight here is the fact that there's not a single miss in the entire range. It's a real testament to the family stewardship and it's looking most exciting for the future; they're in such a good spot in more ways than one.

1971-planted Pinot Noir at New Hall

347

Gutter & Stars Urban Winery
@GUTTERSTARSWINE

Chesterton Mill, Mill Tower Basement, French's Road, Cambridge, CB4 3NP
https://www.gutterandstars.co.uk

What: Cellar door tastings and sales
Recommended wines: Pinot Noir, Chardonnay, Bacchus

Making wine in an emerging market, not bound by tradition or decades-old legislation, means we can pretty much do what we want, how we want, where we want. The 'where' in this case happens to be in the converted basement of a Grade II-listed former windmill, also known as Gutter & Stars, and Cambridge's first winery. More on the what is to follow, but of potentially equal importance is the who?

Like great song lyrics that are so valuable to us in their relevance, we can relate to many domestic winemakers because they're people like us – not doing it because it's been passed down through the family, but mainly because they like drinking wine, and came to it as a second career as a result. Gutter & Stars founder Chris Wilson came to winemaking from a music, sport and, latterly, wine-writing background.

I've been to 1000-tonne capacity wineries, seventeenth-century barn-converts and wineries in rows of old stables and each one is pretty unique, but few have the character of Gutter & Stars. In Chris's octagonal 23-metre-squared set-up he's got everything he needs to make some great wine. It's 'rough and ready', according to him, but I'd say it's authentic and charming. Chris didn't just buy

Cambridge's first Urban Winery

a few barrels, some grapes and let the rest work it out for itself. He studied winemaking at Plumpton and graduated with a degree in 2013 – from the same class as Ben at Flint in Norfolk, Sergio at Battersea's Blackbook and Liam from Danbury Ridge – going on to make wine in Germany, the Napa Valley and Sussex, before setting up in Cambridge.

Working with Missing Gate vineyard in the Essex Crouch Valley, who provided the fruit for the debut releases in 2020, he sourced a combined total of 2 tonnes of Bacchus, Pinot Noir and Chardonnay.

Setting out to express that quality of fruit under his own label, 'I Wanna Be Adored' Bacchus was a nod to his music industry background, that will resonate with fans of The Stone Roses, especially, but might easily not have come to fruition at all. Having seen several versions of Bacchus that were either too lean or overpoweringly floral, he was seriously impressed with the balance between ripeness and acidity from Missing Gate's debut crop. The juice was fermented in third-fill American oak and aged in a combination of tank and old Burgundy barrels on fine lees, before being blended together at bottling. Adored it was, and the very limited release sold in double-quick time.

The second and third releases from Gutter & Stars sold just as quickly; 'Hope is a Good Swimmer' Pinot Noir retains the Mancunian musical link, a tribute to James's 'Getting Away With It (All Messed Up)'. Chris took an often slightly misquoted lyric – frequently recited as 'hope is a good swimmer' – which seemed appropriate in describing the global situation in 2020.

A super-limited release, this is as hand-made as it gets. Missing Gate grapes came down the steps into the basement with the help of an old scaffolding board, fruit is de-stemmed

with mates, beers, a 'banging soundtrack' and an old wire mesh. There's some serious kit here; quality barrels from Pouilly-Fuissé, an on-trend egg-fermenter and basket press, and it's combined with obvious and integral know-how. Chris has clearly invested his money where he needs to, not wasting it where he doesn't – the hand-made punch-down paddle may even see a second vintage. De-stemming took six people four hours, a job that might have taken a machine about twelve minutes, but I know which option sounds like more fun.

The Pinot also saw both tank and barrel. It is bright and crunchy and will look even better with some time under cork. The Chardonnay is another fantastic showcase of just how good Crouch Valley fruit can be. With remarkable depth and weight from such young vines and is a perfect Christmas wine with a well-timed release. It's two-thirds French and one-third American oak, all fourth use, and provides supporting richness and classic Chardonnay roundness. Working with Ed Mitcham's Oxfordshire vineyard in 2021, a skin-contact Ortega was as added to the range to go with some more Bacchus. Across the board, as debuts go from both vines and winery, the future is very bright and, not for the first time in this book, here's an email release list you need to be on.

If you're collecting from the winery, you might even time it well enough to enjoy a little taste, a few tunes and hear Chris's take on all of the above from the few square metres where the wines are made. He's so much more than getting away with it all, and, thanks to the wider shared knowledge and the quality of fruit from vineyards like Missing Gate – the deep water he entered is just a touch shallower than it once was. Crafting wines of this calibre takes understanding, touch and class, all things this particular underground outfit are full of.

VALLEY FARM VINEYARDS

@VALLEYFARMVINEYARDS

Rumburgh Road, Wissett, Halesworth, IP19 0JJ
https://www.valleyfarmvineyards.co.uk

What: Tours and tastings by appointment, cellar door sales
Recommended wines: Sundancer Sparkling, Madeleine, Pinot Gris

Valley Farm Vineyard was initially planted in 1987, and Adrian Cox became its third custodian in January 2021. Just prior to purchasing the property, Adrian knew that as soon as he first pulled into the vineyard drive, he had just found his new project. A builder by trade and a lover of growing produce, he'd even had one solitary vine planted in his garden – possibly Britain's smallest vineyard – and now he has 3000, across five varieties, in two adjoining paddocks.

It's a great site; the natural burrow acts as a sun trap, especially those at the north-western end of the vineyard. Planted in sandy soil to flint over a bedrock of chalk, these heat-retaining and free-draining foundations also enable deeper delving vine roots, maximising flavour-potential and quality.

The top of the south-east-facing vineyard isn't just a great place for vines: 'The Grape Escape' cabin-in-the-vines accommodation is nestled right among them. With sheep-wool insulation and solar energy power, the log cabin's veranda provides a perfect place to watch the sun set over the vines, while enjoying a few glasses of their produce. With another cabin and wood-fired hot-tub on the way, Adrian has a pretty strong vision for the future of Valley Farm, and it's a future that is absolutely centred around quality of product.

A restoration job heading in a good direction

Vineyard stays at Valley Farm

A blend of Pinots Noir and Meunier with a hint of Pinot Gris, aged on lees for three years, is really an ode to the complexity of layers possible in sparkling wine produced from quality fruit in the classic method. As with the sparkling rosé – at fifteen months on lees – the layered, yeasty brioche and rich toastiness doesn't at all mask the fruit quality shining through. The still wine selection at Valley Farm Vineyards expresses Adrian's desire for his wines to be 'real'; estate-grown single-vineyard, single-varietal wines that are 100% a reflection in bottle of the season and the land from which they came.

The warmth in site and resulting ripening potential is so very evident in the tasting of both the Madeleine and Pinot Gris. The former is slightly lighter, yet lifted and bright, with ripe and tropical fruit – it's summer drinking as good as it gets. The Gris is very much in the Gris – rather than Grigio – in its style; fatter, richer but not at all losing any elegance, it's a more floral number and is slightly honeyed. It's as good a Pinot Gris as I've tasted on my travels, and one worth visiting for alone.

A tasting room, café and bar at the front entrance to the site is the next project within a project. Following that, expect to see an on-site winery in the coming years, to further enhance the wines as a sense of place. There are plans to install a cellar for additional storage of the back vintage catalogue, and maybe some plans to plant Bacchus in the ground, too. Diversification is motivated by the opportunity to provide greater resources back into wine production, Valley Farm Vineyard's primary function. Adrian has taken on that function in a pretty awesome place, and I think its best days are yet to come.

Wyken Vineyard & Leaping Hare Restaurant
@WYKENVINEYARDS

· ·

Wyken House, Wyken Road, Stanton, Bury Saint Edmunds, IP31 2DW
https://wykenvineyards.co.uk

What: Vineyard, restaurant, cellar door sales, tasting tours, café, woodland walk
Recommended wines: Wyken white, Wyken Sonata

Once occupied by Romans and recorded in the Domesday book, the estate at Wyken Hall now encompasses a 1200-acre working farm and fine dining restaurant that's been recommended in the Good Food Guide for the last twenty-six years in a row.

The Elizabethan manor house is the centrepiece to the maze and gardens – lots of gardens, in fact. There's a knot garden, a herb garden, a rose garden and a woodland garden. Basically, there are all of your favourite styles of garden, including the best kind, which lies on a south-facing slope and is planted to 12,000 vines.

A close second in the best kind of garden stakes is the restaurant's kitchen garden which, along with estate-grown and farm-reared produce, provides the ingredients for both the estate's Leaping Hare restaurant and the recently established Moonshine Café. Created mid-pandemic in a renovated farm workshop building, the wood-fired pizza oven proved so popular it's now a permanent fixture, where inside they even put a distinctly Suffolk twist on traditional Neapolitan style pizza bases, using a sourdough starter derived from the yeast on Wyken's own grape skins.

The 7 acres of vines produce on average around 12,000 bottles a year, which are all sold

Harvest in full swing

in either the restaurant, café, or at cellar door – 'The Country Store'. Originally planted in 1988, the vines prosper in the free-draining and heat-retaining sandy loam over chalk soil. So great is the ripening potential that Kernling, a cousin of the notoriously late-ripening Riesling grape, thrives here and is blended with Bacchus and labelled as the 'Wyken White'. It's super fresh and lively but elegantly lean; the minerality throughout marries so well with a hint of elderflower, jasmine and English rose – things that are all growing in those gardens.

Wyken Sonata takes more Bacchus and is this time blended with Madeleine; it is equally delicate and just as floral-driven as the white, but more rounded, with peach and a honeyed roundness. It's such a delight with the Chalk Stream trout served up in The Hare.

From the restaurant you're welcome to wander through 'home meadow', over to the ancient woodland. I generally find it quite easy to spend lots of time in wineries and around vineyards, but Wyken's list of attractive pastimes lingers with me still, which is lucky, because you'll need to walk off lunch before tucking into the Wyken venison sausage pizza…

From restaurant to pizza oven and back again… with a few wines along the way

Shotley Vineyard

· ·

Frogs Alley, Ipswich, IP9 1FB
https://shotleyvineyard.co.uk

What: Tours, tastings, cellar door sales
Recommended wines: Bacchus, Pinot Noir, Charmat Sparkling

Charlotte Davitt-Mills grew up in the village of Shotley, which sits on a spit of south-east Suffolk land, sandwiched between the Stour and Orwell estuaries. It's an awesome spot, not least for the airflow drifting in among the vines and its signature eastern warmth, but also for the far-reaching views from the top of the hill.

Both Charlotte and her husband Craig were working in insurance and based in India. They moved home and saw this site, which was then being sold merely as vacant land. Vines had originally been planted here in the mid-nineties, with additional Chardonnay in 2010, though it had run into complete disrepair and all but been abandoned.

A career change into vineyard management and wine production was not the exclusive aim, but falling for the place and seeing potential for it in 2017, despite its condition, made them look into wine more seriously. Amazing things these vigorous vines can sometimes be, but these being a few years out of nick left the duo a serious job in bringing them back to health.

In doing so, though, they may just have stumbled upon one of the best sites in all of Britain, a great example of success breeding success; there are so many great stories out there,

The queue to buy their fruit gets longer with each release: get your hands on this kit and see why

infrastructure and advice networks supporting the industry today, without which the vineyard might still just be left, growing beyond repair. Owing to their vision – and a three-year restoration project – and having studied at Plumpton, the initial purchase was expanded and now covers 15,000 vines across 16 acres.

There's a mix of eight different varieties, Germanic and French, and all are planted in a fifteen-year window. There are plenty of options for wine styles as a result, but primarily through dedication to land and vines, nothing is being forced too soon. It's exciting to think what might come from Shotley – if the first few releases are anything to go by, it's worth taking note of what they're up to.

3000 Bacchus vines were planted across three plots in 1997, 1998 and 2003, which, along with 4000 Pinot Noir vines planted in 1990, cropped the first fruit of the new era via two single varietal releases. It's a mark of how well established the vines are and how good these wines look as a result that the likes of Tillingham, Blackbook and Renegade have bought Shotley fruit for their own brands. Bacchus is super fresh, approachable and floral but restrained, elegant and long. Equally classy is the Pinot Noir, a great showcase of East Anglian warmth and resulting ripeness, with depth and structure that looks so good alongside the standout, savoury red fruit.

When much of the country focuses on classic-method sparkling wines, Shotley have gone down the Charmat route with a blend of Auxerrois, Chardonnay, Seyval and Reichensteiner. Tank-method freshness suits these aromatic varietals, but there's plenty of complexity to unpick in what is outstanding value. Made at Bolney, and along with Flint Vineyard's Charmat Rosé, East Anglia are leading the way in this bracket.

Charlotte and family at Shotley

Following the 300-bottle, Limited Release Bacchus in 2021, I can see more small-batch, 'wildcard' releases coming from Shotley. From old vines of contrasting styles and versatility, there are almost too many options, but they are in very safe and measured hands. A new tasting building was completed in 2021, with glamping options to follow. Of all the producers to look out for in the coming years, Shotley are up there with the best of them.

FLINT VINEYARD

@FLINTVINEYARD

Middle Road, Earsham, NR35 2AH
https://flintvineyard.com

What: Tours, tastings, cellar door sales
Recommended wines: Charmat Rosé, Pinot Noir Précoce, Silex Blanc

Despite their relative youth, just how far Flint Vineyard and the vines they planted in 2016 have come, in the short time since then, is about as exciting as it gets. How they achieved it, and how far they've yet to go, is more exciting still.

So many of us follow the path we assume we're supposed to; at some stage almost waking up from this daze of social conformity, wondering why we're not doing something we love instead. Not to say that Ben and Hannah weren't passionate about their respective careers in IT and travel, but they were always attracted to wine and the desire to continually discover more. Tastings led to online courses and eventually, Plumpton college. Initially considering taking on an evening class, Ben, ever fascinated by the scientific side, called Hannah and told her he wanted to enrol on the three-year BSc in viticulture and oenology.

If you're going to win any awards at Plumpton it may as well be for 'best winemaker', following which Ben secured his first professional post in Beaujolais, where centuries-old tradition takes precedent and the winemaking rule book is thrown out of the window quicker than your dad discards an Ikea instruction leaflet. Going against a scientific Plumpton-based background

Peter the winery cat

and time spent at super-high-tech Napa Valley wineries, the traditional French approach opened Ben's eyes to a different way of doing things, one steeped in tradition and passed down through generations. The combination of contrasting experiences and freedom in Britain to curate our own path enabled Ben to hone his own style as a winemaker; merging the best parts of everything he witnessed.

Flint is based in the sunny and sheltered Waveney Valley near Bungay, and the work here incorporates both innovation and tradition, and this philosophy is reflected in the Venn diagram adorning the bottle labels. What's inside impressed me as much as any range on this entire trip – I was blown away by the precision, purity and remarkable depth in the wines coming from such young vines.

The Charmat Rosé is possibly Britain's best expression of this tank-method sparkling and exactly the kind of wine that will lead to so many more. Some say that 'Prosecco style' is so associated with 'cheaper' sparkling wines, that people won't make the jump up. They should taste Flint's; though it's the same style, it's worth every single penny of the retail cost and in truth so much more. It's so fresh and bright yet elegant and long – it's usually a blend of Cabernet Cortis, Solaris, Reichensteiner and Rondo; there's texture and just a hint of richness.

From my favourite Charmat, to a top five still white, the Silex is reminiscent of great white Burgundy; those ripe stone-fruit and white flowers fragrantly shining through from the blend of 'Chardonnay family' grapes, including, along with Chardonnay, Pinots Gris, Blanc and skinless Noir. As well as the pure and bright Pinot Noir Précoce – half of which was whole bunch fermented and in neutral oak for six months – there are some small, one-barrel experiments going on at the winery too. You can

only get your hands on these via the Venn Club membership, but the value for money is just ridiculously good, and it's a great way to support a small business in their continued experiments.

Ampersand Brew Co are on-site too – another place where it's quite easy to lose a few quid. More importantly, it's drinking proof of Norfolk's potential, right up there with Essex for ripeness and quality. Olly Smith seems to be a bit of an ambassador of Flint, having championed them from an early stage. He's a great guy, too, and an even better judge of wine.

Shop local, drink well… it's an easy game

WINBIRRI VINEYARD

@WINBIRRI

Bramerton Road, Surlingham, Norwich, NR14 7DE
https://www.winbirri.com

What: Cellar door sales, tours and wine garden tastings
Recommended wines: Dornfelder, Pinot Noir, Vintage Reserve Sparkling

Winbirri received ten years' worth of orders over six hours in 2017, when news broke of their 2015 Bacchus winning 'best in show varietal white' at the 2015 Decanter Awards. Such is the power and coverage of the biggest shows that four years later, demand still outstrips supply for their Bacchus, despite the award-winning 2015 version being long gone.

The Winbirri vineyard started life in 2007, when the Dyer family planted 200 vines of Madeleine, Siegerrebe, Seyval, Rondo and Solaris. By 2012 things were picking up across the wider industry and those on the eastern side of the country were starting to realise its potential for riper fruit and a more commercial approach. So, in 2012 Bacchus, Dornfelder, Pinot Noir, Meunier and Chardonnay went in, and out came Madeleine and Siegerrebe. Further Bacchus and Pinot Noir were added in 2017, not least to grow the production of their award-winning wine, but as the two continue to establish themselves as the country's flagship red and white varietals, and it was a smart choice to tap into the potential of them from East Anglia.

The winery was built in 2012, and from Winbirri's 33 acres, the site has the capacity for 150,000 bottles a year.

Winbirri Rosé Brut Sparkling

Now in the hands of second-generation winemaker Lee Dyer, Winbirri is carving out a reputation for their reds, despite the ongoing popularity of the Bacchus-led whites.

His signature red is 100% Dornfelder, and through it they're striving to fill the understandable void of fuller-bodied English reds. If anyone's going to do it, it's probably going to come from this side of the country. It sees maximum extraction from three weeks on skins; part whole bunch and part carbonic maceration, the juice is eventually racked to American oak for eighteen months, half of which are new barrels. A bold approach, for a bold wine.

The Pinot Noir goes down a more classic English red route – it's super soft and fragrant, but there's some depth too, and even some silky tannins. With a name taken from the Anglo-Saxon for wine (win) and grape (birri), the brand may always be best known for the grape that takes its name from the Roman god of wine, but – along with a classic-method, long-lees-aged sparkling – it's very much worth checking out their reds too.

Chet Valley Vineyard

@CHETVINEYARD

Loddon Rd, Norwich, NR15 1BT
https://chetvineyard.co.uk

What: Cellar door sales, tours and tastings
Recommended wines: Redwing Rosé, Cerberus red

At the southern end of Norfolk sits Chet Valley on a mix of sandy loam, gravel and chalk over clay, where the first 10 acres of vines were planted in 2010. Winemaking owner John Hemmant is carving his own path, not swayed by the volume of on-trend varietals or styles – to which end, from his blend of classic sparkling varietals and Germanic crosses, the latter dominate the sparkling offering.

Both the Skylark and Skylark demi-sec are led by 80% Phoenix and a balance of Seyval, with the latter also seeing 5% Regent. For the first time in 2019, the brut was made in the classic method, and it benefits from added richness as a result. The demi-sec's bright aromatics are underlined by its Charmat persuasion, lifted further by 20 grams of sugar. It's good to see a sparkling red in the range under the 'Redwing' label – and it's an easy choice to continue the bird theme with that one. It's 100% Regent, packed full of summer fruits and super approachable. Sparkling reds are always worth going to left-field with, and it's a refreshing, brilliant barbecue wine – better still if it's about 30 degrees, but worth having a few of these in the wine rack just in case.

The same blend as the Skylark demi, but produced in the classic method as opposed to tank, the fragrant Phoenix and Seyval lend themselves well to this style or rosé; the hint of lees richness adds further complexity and at five years the acidity has rounded out nicely. It may not be what you might expect from a sparkling range consisting of four wines, but it's all the more interesting for the approach.

There are a couple of still wines, too, the Redwing Rosé from 100% Pinot Noir and the ever-intriguing Cerberus red – a non-vintage blend of Regent and Rondo.

We call this one the washing vine

CHET & WAVENEY
VALLEY WINERY

Norfolk's sparkling specialists, Chet Valley

Acknowledgements

For my mum, Judy, who inspired me to drink wine and still does, and my dad, Keith, who first motivated me to pick up a camera. For so much more than this, too. Will Dallers, who I'm forever grateful to be able to call my brother – an inspiration in a way that only a big brother could be, despite being my little brother. Special thanks also to Uncle Colin and Wales's greatest fly fisherman, Uncle Brian. I very much include Claudia and Tom Wright in the family bracket, for always looking after me, and the entire James family, Robert, Elisabeth and Venetia, for broadening my horizons in so many ways, not least when it comes to the beauty of travel. Matilda Florence for her creative and evergreen suggestions, support, advice, willingness to help with research and single best taste in music, and for standing by me, always.

Without the support, guidance, backing and valuable lessons in grammar of Louise and Laura, marketing and typesetting by Daniela, Sarah and Rebecca, and all at Fairlight Books, this project would be nothing on what it has become. Huge thanks also to Christina for the copyediting.

The single best way to learn about wine is among the vines and via open bottles with the people who make it. I owe so much to all of you who have opened your cellar doors for me this year, welcomed me into this great domestic industry and truly given me the opportunity to tell your story. It's been so, so rewarding to meet many like-minded people along the way, and I'm incredibly grateful to you all – especially Tommy, Olly and Fi at Langham; Daniel at Offbeat; Danni and James at Roebuck; Balbina at Bsixtwelve; Graham at Woodchurch; Andy at Velfrey; Jacob and Zoë at Black Chalk; Simon at Laurel; Tori at Wiston; Becca and Tom at Henners; and the esteemed 'Freanovino', Robin at Nutbourne, whom I initially met briefly and who, within a couple of minutes, had invited me for dinner saying he thought I 'seemed like a good lad who loves his wine'. You were at least half right. A very special thanks, too, to Peter Hall at Breaky Bottom, who – among 100 emails a day of requests to come and see him – found time and a few spare bottles for me.

I'm not a fan of wine scores or ratings, but there were several tastings this year that remain at the front of my mind and though it's impossible to choose a 'favourite' – despise often being asked this question – I think it's only fair to say thanks to those responsible for the most memorable of 'meetings': Henry at Harrow & Hope; Emma at Hattingley (also in part responsible for Raimes, Roebuck and Alder Ridge, among others); Ulrich at Hoffmann and Rathbone; Kristin at Oxney; Tim at Charlie Herring; America and Nick at Oastbrook; Dermot at Wiston and Jenkyn Place and of course with Ana under their Sugrue South Downs label; Mark at Black Mountain; Liam at Danbury Ridge; Marie and Simon at Stopham; and of course, once again, all at Langham and the great man, Peter at Breaky Bottom.

I also want to make special mention of all those producers in England and Wales who are championing organic and biodynamic viticulture, who are as passionate about the land on which they farm as they are about the great wine they produce. Not only are these methods usually implemented with quality of fruit front and centre, often these are the wines that are the most fun to drink, too.

A fantastic side note has been driving around the green and pleasant land for a year, having been away for the best part of ten, and appreciating how beautiful it is. Being able to stop in and join the odd family dinner on the way and share some of the wine I had collected was almost the best part. So a huge thanks to Jo, Bob and the Lock family for having me in Tilford; Mel, Ed, Bea and Harry in Nantwich; Andy and Marion in Halesworth; Jane and Peter Plewes in Foxton; and most of all, love always to Martin and Rowena at the now straw-pig-adorned Pighle Cottage.

It is with such gratitude that I thank everyone who pre-ordered a copy of this book, some a good twelve months ahead of publication! The 'Ian Bothams' deserve special mention: a group of people who would probably always support me regardless of the nature of the endeavour. Sam Forman – metal leg and the greatest inspiration of all – and East Leake Luke – one-third of the Northern Beaches' best band – who both doubled up on pre-ordering books, wines and pictures. Gaslight Stu – as good a guy as the album that inspired his nickname – and Rose, too, who refers to me simply as '59', which always makes me smile. Matt Lloyd Davies; Jimmy Starr; Jonty and original Manly Lad, 'The Suit', Plewes; Tom 'The Courgette' Bramah; the best-looking Clydesdale there is, Tom Eckhardt; Power of Scotland himself, Alex Hendy; Jeremy 'Paddy' Ireland; Dooleys ambassador Olé Sidwell; Manly's number one Ben Kilpatrick; the best hockey player I've ever seen, Josh Gunnell; Ginto; and Stannard – there's a special seat at Eddy's bar for you all. To the latter of these great individuals especially – most of my very few 'days off' over the last year were due to previous late nights at Stannard's

house, where great beers and an even better soundtrack are absolutely guaranteed. Andy and Beth; Polish Darren; Geordie Dave Lindo; my friend Jon for always upping the pace; it's good to have you, Withers; Sleepy Joe; Richard Bacon Arkle; Ems and Phil; original beard inspiration and Tassie's best, Stu Warren; and Andy Goode lookalike Rich Westbro. Huge thanks to Joe and Sarah for not only supporting me but insisting I supply them – and their friends – with case after case of Great British booze; there really could be no finer compliment as to the quality than repeat drinking!

Thanks to everyone I've shared a wine and a discussion about it with, from the Majestic days – especially Luce, Soph, Dave and Woodbridge – to Oz – Adrian Sparks and the entire crew at one of the most exceptional places there is, Mount Pleasant winery. Sarah Crowe, Reid Boaward, Clio Collar, Stu Dolby, Alex Anderson, Steve Hutchinson and so many more: I love so much hearing what others think, and your opinions, intelligence and things you've said have stayed with me and shaped my views and approach – and still do.

To my dogs, Cambridge, Ruffle and Cromwell, the epitome of loyalty, and thanks also to all the very loyal wine dogs I've met while writing this book.

For the soundtrack to many a motorway mile, supplied in vast majority by Bruce Springsteen, because you can't start a fire without a spark.

Last but not at all least, a huge thank you to really the most important person of all – you, the wine drinker, for reading this. I hope it has gone some way to bringing even more enjoyment to your wine drinking – without you, we who grow, make, sell and write about wine are absolutely nothing. Keep enjoying wine, stay open-minded, support local and share great booze. Drink well. *Ar hyd y nos*. Cheers.

GLOSSARY

Amphora (plural amphorae) – traditional terracotta vessels used in winemaking

Ancestral method – traditional pre-Champagne method of producing sparkling wine by bottling and sealing a wine during one continuous fermentation, capturing the resulting CO_2 and not usually disgorged; see also *Pet-Nat*

Assemblage – process of blending batches of wine or different grape varieties, common in rosé production, when combining red and white wine

Autolysis/autolytics – chemical reaction between wine and lees, when enzymes break down dead yeast cells, imparting desirable characteristics in the resulting wine

Barrique – oak barrel used for fermentation, maturation or both, usually holding 225 litres if originating in Bordeaux or 228 litres in Burgundy

Base wine – still wine produced prior to undergoing secondary fermentation, during the process of sparkling wine production

Biodynamic – holistic, ecological and ethical approach to farming, employing organic practices and seeing all components of the site as one whole entity and ecosystem, with practices followed according to the biodynamic calendar

Blanc de Blancs – 'white of whites'; usually sparkling white wine made from 100% white-skinned grapes, often Chardonnay in Champagne and elsewhere

Blanc de Noirs – 'white of blacks'; usually sparkling white wine made from 100% black-skinned grapes, where the skins are removed before they can impart any colour, often Pinot Noir and Pinot Meunier in Champagne and elsewhere

Botrytis/noble rot – a type of fungus that shrivels and decays grapes, that can be desirable in concentrating sugars in a grape, prior to the production of sweet wine

Brut – meaning dry; a measure of the level of dosage or added sugar, usually to sparkling wine, usually below 12 grams per litre and often more than 6

Cellar door – place at a winery or vineyard where you can usually buy wine direct from source

Champagne – region in northern France famous for producing sparkling wine in the traditional or classic method; also used to refer to a wine from this region produced according to a defined set of grapes and regulations

Charmat – method of producing sparkling wine where secondary fermentation takes place in a tank, rather than bottle, as in the classic method (see below)

Classic method – process of producing sparkling wine via a secondary fermentation in bottle, similar to Champagne

Col fondo – sixteenth-century traditionally Italian method for producing sparkling wine via a secondary fermentation in bottle, that is not disgorged

Cotes de Nuits – northern region in Burgundy famous for still red wine made from Pinot Noir

Crémant – method of producing sparkling wine where the secondary fermentation takes place in bottle like classic method, but is usually bottled at less pressure

Cuvée – either the specific blend within a wine of several batches, or usually in reference to sparkling wine, the first pressed and generally most desirable juice

Domaine – refers to a territory or area and is usually associated with the wineries of Burgundy

Demi – oak barrel usually holding 600 litres

Demi-sec – a measure of the level of dosage or added sugar, usually to sparkling wine, usually between 32 and 50 grams per litre

Disgorged/disgorgement – process of removing the sediment in a bottle, usually following secondary fermentation as part of the classic method of sparkling wine production

Dosage – 'liqueur d'expedition'; a mix of sugar and wine usually added to a sparkling wine after disgorgement, usually measured in grams per litre (gpl) to either add sweetness, balance acidity, or both

Double magnum – 3-litre bottle of wine from outside of Champagne, Jeroboam in the same format within Champagne

Extra brut – a measure of the level of dosage or added sugar, usually to sparkling wine, usually below 6 grams per litre

Fermentation – natural process in which microorganisms like yeast and bacteria convert carbs like starch and sugar into alcohol or acids; CO_2 is also a by-product retained in the production of sparkling wine

Fine lees – smaller particles from dead yeast cells that form in wine after fermentation, usually settling more slowly into the wine than gross lees

Flor – film of yeast developing on the surface of wine ageing in vessel; can protect the wine from oxygen and impart flavour; common in the process of producing fino sherry

Foudre – large wooden vat, usually holding 2000 litres, but can be up to 30,000 litres

Frizzante – lightly sparkling wines defined as 'semi-sparkling' by law; often bottled at less than half the pressure of traditional-method sparkling wine

Gross lees – general sediment that forms from dead yeast cells in wine after fermentation, naturally falling to the bottom of the winemaking vessel

Gyropalette – piece of mechanical equipment used to gently turn bottles in the process of riddling during the production of classic-method sparkling wine

Hogshead – oak barrel usually holding 300 litres

Hyperoxidation – exposing grape juice to large quantities of oxygen prior to fermentation in order to both clarify and protect the resulting wine from oxidation further down the line

Jeroboam – 3-litre bottle of Champagne, a double magnum in the same format from outside of Champagne

Jura – iconic wine region in Eastern France situated between Burgundy and Switzerland

Lees – usually 'yeast lees', 'lees time', or 'aged on lees' – predominantly dead yeast cells left over from the fermentation process, left in contact with wine for desirable flavour development, richness and texture

Mildew – downy and powdery fungal disease prevalent in damp, humid conditions, attacking multiple parts of a vine, potentially devastating to grape crop and quality

MV – 'multi-vintage'; a wine made from grapes grown in several different years, usually used to indicate several, as a mark of complexity and quality

Natural wine – usually wine made from organic or biodynamically grown grapes, often with natural yeast and no synthetic products and little or no preservatives

Négociant – French for 'merchant'; in terms of Champagne production, short for 'négociant manipulant', meaning a producer who buys in their grapes, rather than growing them: a classic approach employed by the bigger producers to allow them to focus on winemaking and marketing

NV – 'non-vintage'; a wine made from grapes grown in more than one year

Oenology – the study of wines

Organic – production without the use of chemical fertilisers, pesticides or other artificial chemicals

Oxidation – group of chemical reactions that occur when wine comes into contact with air, often developing desirable flavour characteristics

Parcel – a batch of either fruit, juice or bottled wine

Pet-Nat – 'pétillant naturel'; see *Ancestral method*

Phylloxera – native North American vine root-devastating louse, responsible for destroying vineyards across the world since the nineteenth century

Plumpton – agricultural college in Sussex, offering courses in viticulture and winemaking

Pouilly-Fuissé – appellation for white wine in the Mâconnais subregion of Burgundy in central France

Press – winemaking equipment used to separate grape juice from their skins

Prestige Cuvée, or tête de cuvée – term used in Champagne to denote the most premium wine made by any given Champagne house

Prosecco – northern Italian sparkling wine produced in Charmat or tank method

Puncheon – oak barrel usually holding 500 litres

Qvevri – also spelt 'Kvevri'; traditional Greek vessel used for winemaking and maturation, often buried in the ground

Riddling/remuage – gradually shifting a bottle from horizontal to upside-down vertical so sediment falls to the bottle neck, usually prior to removal via disgorgement in classic-method sparkling wine production

Saignée – meaning 'bleeding'/'bled'; a method of making rosé wine that 'bleeds' off a portion of red wine juice after a limited period of contact with skins and seeds

Sec – a measure of the level of dosage or added sugar, usually to sparkling wine, usually between 17 to 32 grams per litre

Skin-contact – winemaking term describing the process of making white wine like red where the juice spends time in contact with grape skins, deriving colour, flavour and texture from them

Solera – system of rational blending over consecutive years where up to a third is drawn off and replaced with current vintage wine; wine within is ever-evolving and will always contain a portion of the original base as a result

Tank method – method of producing sparkling wine where the secondary fermentation takes place in a tank, also called Charmat method

Tirage/'liqueur de tirage' – liquid solution of yeast, wine and sugar that is added to a still base wine in order to create a secondary fermentation

Traditional method/méthode traditionnelle/méthode champenoise – see classic method

Vine – grape-producing plant

Vineyard – a plantation of grape-bearing vines grown for winemaking

Vintage – harvest in a particular given year, also used to refer to a specific year's wine or as an indication that a wine was made from grapes grown in one specific year

Viticulture – science, study and production of grapes

Winery – collection of equipment used to turn grapes into wine, usually a building

WSET – The Wine & Spirit Education Trust; London-based organisation offering internationally recognised education and awards in wine and spirits

Zero dosage – indicates no dosage or added sugar after disgorgement, usually in reference to sparkling wine

Zingy – with attractive and lively acidity

Notes

i 'Boom time for British vineyards', WineGB (5 March 2019). Available at: https://www.winegb.co.uk/2019/03/05/boom-time-for-british-vineyards/

ii Dudley, R. *The Drunken Monkey: Why We Drink and Abuse Alcohol.* Berkeley: University of California Press, 2014.

iii Brown, A. G., et al. 'Roman vineyards in Britain: stratigraphic and palynological data from in the Nene Valley, England', *Antiquity* 75(290) (2015), 745–757. doi:10.1017/S0003598X00089250

iv Smith, J. *The New English Vineyard.* London: Sidgwick & Jackson, 1979.

v Win, T. L. 'Planting more heat-tolerant grapes could stop wine shortages', Global Center on Adaptation/Thomson Reuters Foundation (29 January 2020). Available at: https://www.gca.org/planting-more-heat-tolerant-grapes-could-stop-wine-shortages/

vi Selley, R. *The Winelands of Britain: Past, Present and Prospective.* 2nd edn. Betchworth, Surrey: Petravin, 2008.

vii Spurrier, S. *A Life in Wine.* Ascot, Berkshire: Académie du Vin Library, 2020.

viii Ibid.

ix Selley, R. *The Winelands of Britain.*

x Skelton, S. 'Vineyards in the UK, the Republic of Ireland and the Channel Islands', English Wine (11 November 2020). Available at: http://www.englishwine.com/vineyards.htm